WHAT TO DO ABOUT YOUR TROUBLED CHILD

A PRACTICAL GUIDE FOR ALL PARENTS AT THEIR WITS' END

LAURA J. STEVENS, MSci
RICHARD W. WALKER, JR., MD

The information and advice contained in this book are based upon the research and the personal and professional experiences of the authors. They are not intended as a substitute for consulting with a healthcare professional. The publisher and authors are not responsible for any adverse effects or consequences resulting from the use of any of the suggestions, preparations, or procedures discussed in this book. All matters pertaining to your physical health should be supervised by a healthcare professional. It is a sign of wisdom, not cowardice, to seek a second or third opinion.

Typesetting and cover design: Gary A. Rosenberg

Square One Publishers
115 Herricks Road
Garden City Park, NY 11040
(516) 535-2010 • (877) 900-BOOK
www.squareonepublishers.com

Library of Congress Cataloging-in-Publication Data
Names: Stevens, Laura J., 1945- author.
Title: What to do about your troubled child / Laura J. Stevens, MSci, Richard W. Walker, Jr., MD.
Description: Garden City Park, NY : Square One Publishers, [2022] | Includes bibliographical references and index.
Identifiers: LCCN 2021062483 (print) | LCCN 2021062484 (ebook) | ISBN 9780757005145 (paperback) | ISBN 9780757055140 (epub)
Subjects: LCSH: Child psychology. | Behavior disorders in children. | Behavior therapy.
Classification: LCC BF721 .S777 2022 (print) | LCC BF721 (ebook) | DDC 155.4—dc23/eng/20220111
LC record available at https://lccn.loc.gov/2021062483
LC ebook record available at https://lccn.loc.gov/2021062484

Printed in the United States of America

10 9 8 7 6 5 4 3 2 1

Contents

For parents of troubled children everywhere.

Foreword

I am writing the foreword to this book in order to express my gratitude to Laura Stevens for her enduring efforts to educate the public on the roles that lifestyle, diet, and the environment can play in behavioral problems—especially those in young children. Although I am currently serving as a superior court judge in California, many years ago I was one of the troubled children her work sought to help.

When I was only in elementary school, my mother had already given up hope that I would ever be successful academically. I was constantly in trouble for talking in class, acting out, and not paying attention. I was impulsive and made poor decisions daily. While never diagnosed with any mental health condition, many of the behaviors I exhibited would today be considered symptoms of ADHD. The school nurse and administrators had recommended I see a physician, with the expectation being that I would likely be placed on medication to assist with my behavioral issues.

My mother recognized that my behavior was not always disruptive, and that at times I was calm and well behaved. While my grades were suffering, my mother knew I was intelligent. IQ tests I had taken had indicated I might even be gifted. My mother and my school were perplexed as to why I would have so many problems in school if this were the case. Thankfully, my mother was sure an explanation was out there.

When I was in the fourth grade, my mother began researching alternative reasons for childhood behavioral problems. While at the library one afternoon, she stumbled upon a book called *How to Improve Your Child's Behavior Through Diet* by Laura J. Stevens. It detailed how some children are hypersensitive to artificial colors and flavors in foods, and even to some seemingly healthy foods. My mother decided to eliminate from my diet many of the foods known to trigger behavioral issues in sensitive children. This decision changed my life. Only weeks after removing these foods from my daily meals, the difference in my behavior was so significant that my teacher called my mother to ask if she had put me on medication.

By modifying my diet, I was suddenly able to sit still in class and pay attention. I scored better on tests, and my teachers reported that I was a pleasure to have in their classrooms. I maintained this type of diet throughout the remainder of my childhood and adolescence and continued to thrive. I became a successful member of my high school's speech and debate team and graduated with honors. I went on to attend the University of California at San Diego, where I earned a bachelor's degree in psychology with honors. I then attended law school at the University of San Diego, where I was made a member of the prestigious San Diego Law Review and graduated at the top of my class. I spent the next twenty-three years working as a prosecutor in Southern California, striving to achieve justice for crime victims in some of the most serious cases I could have imagined. In September of 2021, I was appointed by the Governor of California to the Riverside County Superior Court as a judge.

I recently reached out to Ms. Stevens to thank her for the tremendous impact her work has had on my life. I was fortunate enough to be able to contact her and thank her personally. Since then, we have had many wonderful conversations on the subject of troubled children and the roles that diet and environment can have on behavior. Hearing my story actually motivated her to write another book, in the hope that she might reach even more young people who need help.

If you are a parent of a troubled child, please know that there is hope. While medication may be necessary for some children, for others, relatively simple changes in diet and environment can yield remarkable benefits. The following information may not lead every troubled child to experience the same remarkable transformation I did all those years ago, but if it changes even one more child's life for the better, then all the work that has gone into this book will have been worth it.

I am forever indebted to Laura Stevens. Her work improved my childhood immeasurably and has likely played a huge role in my ability to lead a successful life. I can only imagine how differently things would have turned out for me had my mother not found Laura's book when she did. I often see youthful criminals in my courtroom who have led troubled lives, and I wonder if their lives could have benefited from the same changes made for me when I was young. I am so grateful that Laura has chosen to continue writing books that aim to place children with behavioral issues on a positive path in life, as there are so many who could use her help. Thank you, Laura.

The Honorable Sean P. Crandell
Superior Court Judge, Riverside County, California

Acknowledgments

I'd like to thank all those who have helped me to learn how to help children with behavioral problems. I'd first like to thank Dr. William Crook, Dr. John F. O'Brian, and Dorothy Boyce, RN, who gave me my first lessons on food sensitivities. I'd also like to thank Dr. Donald Rudin for introducing me to the value of essential fatty acids. I appreciate Dr. Sidney Baker and Dr. Leo Galland, who taught me so much about all kinds of nutrients and their roles in health. I appreciate and thank Jay Burgess, PhD, my professor at Purdue in the nutrition science department, who taught me well and insisted on excellence. I would also like to thank Dr. Richard Walker, whose addition to our team made this book complete.

Finally, I'd like to thank Rudy Shur of Square One Publishers, who made this book possible, and my editor, Michael Weatherhead, who made me sound great. I also want to thank my sons for all their love and encouragement, and my two cats, Seis and Bentley, who lay on my desk and kept me company as I wrote.

—Laura J. Stevens, MSci

I would like to thank my grandchildren—Jamila ("Milzy"), a world traveler, chef, and entrepreneur; Samantha ("Z"), a junior at the University of Michigan (my alma mater), full of energy and excitement; Jada and Spencer, cousins, tenth-graders, born a day apart; and Leena, an eighth-grader—for being at the core of every book I write and every contribution I make to society. I would also like to thank my best friend and wife, Marvia, who has made everything possible for me.

I would like to recognize every mother and father who has been challenged by the conditions described in this book. In particular, I would like to acknowledge all the Black, Brown, and Native American parents whose children were never given the benefit of being considered as having a behavioral disorder but instead were punished or expelled by their schools, or sent to the criminal justice system.

Thank you, Laura, for being inspired to write this book, and for inviting me to join you in writing it. Finally, I want to thank Rudy Shur for having the wisdom to see the need for this book, and Michael Weatherhead, for his excellence in the editing of this book.

—Richard W. Walker, Jr., MD, MBA

Introduction

At one time or another, most parents will witness their child exhibiting run-of-the-mill problem behavior, which may include talking back, crying, yelling, not listening, or other mild behavioral issues. While these confrontations can be frustrating, they are typically resolved by proper parenting. There may come a time, however, when parents realize that their child's disruptive conduct is definitely not normal, something is wrong, and even good parenting skills aren't working.

As a new parent, the fact that your baby was born safely—with all ten fingers and ten toes—was likely enough to put your mind at ease for a while. You may not have considered the fact that children don't come with individualized instruction manuals that describe how to take care of them and help them to avoid certain problems in the future. Now that your child is a bit older, if he has been consistently displaying behavioral, emotional, or learning problems, you may wish you had such a manual as you look high and low for an explanation for your child's apparent condition. Please consider *What to Do About Your Troubled Child* your better-late-than-never guide. It is designed to identify your child's condition, explain the possible reasons why it is occurring, and provide potential solutions for the problem.

But what exactly do we mean when we say a child is "troubled"? For the purposes of this book, the term "troubled child" refers to a child who has a moderate to severe behavioral disorder. Such children may also exhibit physical symptoms that are commonly associated with their disorders. Different troubled children may be affected by different disorders, but they all share a common denominator: They are all much more difficult to parent than the average child. The information found in this book is meant to make things easier.

This book has been divided into two parts. Part One focuses on the most common behavioral disorders from which children may suffer, including attention-deficit/hyperactivity disorder, oppositional defiant disorder, conduct disorder, obsessive-compulsive disorder, anxiety disorders, and autism spectrum disorder. The chapters feature questionnaires designed to help you to identify the specific characteristics of your child's behavior and the disorder to which they point. For each disorder, we describe traditional treatment, which includes therapy and medication, and complementary approaches, which are discussed in greater detail in Part Two. Often a combination of behavioral therapy, medication, and complementary treatment is the most effective approach to helping a troubled child.

Part One goes on to discuss the psychological and physical problems commonly associated with the major disorders described in the book, such as aches and pains, depression, poor gut health, obesity, and learning difficulties. It then explains how to find the right healthcare provider for your child, which is an important step on the path to a better life for your child. This healthcare provider might be your child's regular doctor or a specialist of some kind. No matter the type of doctor, she should always be patient and attentive to your concerns and questions. A doctor who immediately pulls out a prescription pad and offers no other treatment options should be avoided.

In Part Two, you will find further information on the complementary approaches you can take to the treatment of the conditions described in Part One. It outlines four general areas of complementary treatment: lifestyle, nutrition, environment, and helpful programs and devices.

Whether you address your child's sleep patterns, exercise level, diet, or sensitivity and exposure to toxic elements in his environment, these medication-free treatment methods are backed by medical science and can make a big difference in your child's behavioral disorder. Moreover, allowing your child to take part in the right summer camp or even play the right video game can lead to noticeable positive changes in his behavior.

You may have noticed that this book uses male gender pronouns to describe children with behavioral disorders. This choice was made partly for convenience but also because boys are more likely than girls to be affected by these conditions (although girls are certainly no strangers to these problems). In an attempt at gender equality, this book uses female pronouns when referring to healthcare professionals and educators, including doctors, psychologists, therapists, and teachers.

Finally, as the authors of *What to Do About Your Troubled Child,* we are deeply aware of the inequities in healthcare overall, and of the implicit bias that children and families of certain racial backgrounds—particularly African American, Hispanic, and Native American children and families—and underserved communities face in relation to the topics discussed in this book. Unfortunately, the methods used to diagnose behavioral disorders often do not take into account cultural or racial disparities, which may be current or historical, and frequently see things from a Eurocentric perspective. In other words, we must question the system's ability to make accurate diagnoses in particular populations.

This bias is perhaps most apparent in the overly diagnosed condition of conduct disorder and the underdiagnosed condition of attention-deficit/hyperactivity disorder in children of specific racial backgrounds. Children from these communities are overly diagnosed with conduct disorder and more often considered "bad," and less likely to be assessed as having a behavioral issue such as attention-deficit/hyperactivity disorder, which is not as stigmatized. Furthermore, they are much less likely to have had a proper behavioral evaluation, or to have access to healthcare professionals who understand their communities.

If we are truly concerned about the welfare of all children in this country, then we must not forget to take the social and economic differences between their communities into account when we make decisions regarding their wellbeing. Doing otherwise will continue to lead to tragic outcomes for kids in those communities that frequently face bias in the healthcare system, including high rates of school expulsions, incarceration, and drug and alcohol abuse, as well as lost academic and athletic opportunities.

As a parent of a child with a possible behavioral disorder, you practically need to become a detective in order to track down the reasons for your child's problem. Once you've solved the case, however, you may not be in a position to try all the therapies suggested by this book. If so, simply choose the therapies that make sense for you, your child, and your family—taking time, availability, and cost into consideration.

We understand that you have picked up this book most likely because you feel that something is not right about your child's behavior. You may even get so angry at your child's disruptions at times that you lose your temper and even consider the use of physical punishment. Nevertheless, research has shown that physical punishment is not helpful and can actually make your child's behavior worse. Ignoring it and hoping it will go away on its own, however, won't solve your child's problem either. The key to changing your child's behavior—and his life—for the better is to recognize the nature of his behavior and take appropriate steps to deal with it. We think the information provided by this book can put you and your child on this journey. If it seems overwhelming, try to remember that you need only take a single step to start.

PART ONE

Identifying the Problem

1.

Attention-Deficit/ Hyperactivity Disorder

Attention-deficit/hyperactivity disorder, or *ADHD,* is the most common behavioral disorder that affects the brain. Children with ADHD may be inattentive, impulsive, hyperactive, or any combination of these traits. This disorder is usually diagnosed in early childhood, but a diagnosis of ADHD may also be seen during the teen years or adulthood. ADHD affects twice as many males as it does females. According to a 2016 study, the number of children in the United States between the ages of two and seventeen that have been diagnosed with ADHD is estimated to be over 6 million, or approximately 9 percent of this age group. To top it off, about 20 to 30 percent of children with ADHD have parents or siblings with ADHD. The questionnaires on pages 8 and 9 can help you to determine the likelihood of your child having ADHD.

TYPES

A diagnosis of ADHD is categorized as one of three types. The first type is *attention-deficit/hyperactivity disorder, predominantly inattentive,* or *ADHD-PI,* in which inattentiveness is a major problem but impulsivity and hyperactivity are not. The second type is *attention-deficit/hyperactivity disorder, predominantly hyperactive-impulsive,* or *ADHD-PH,* in which impulsivity and hyperactivity are major problems but inattentiveness is not. Finally, *attention-deficit/hyperactivity disorder, combined,* or *ADHD-C,* refers to the presentation of both inattentiveness and hyperactive-impulse behaviors in an individual who is affected by ADHD.

QUESTIONNAIRES

Please complete the following questionnaires. The symptoms you are evaluating should have been present for at least six months in a child usually older than four years of age. They should also be present in more than one setting—at home, at school, with relatives or friends, etc.

Table 1.1. Inattentiveness Questionnaire

Symptom	Frequency			
Inattentiveness	**Never**	**Occasionally**	**Somewhat Often**	**All the Time**
How often does your child make careless mistakes in schoolwork, at work, or in other activities, or fail to pay attention to details?	0	1	2	3
How often does your child have trouble holding his attention on tasks?	0	1	2	3
How often does your child seem not to listen when directly spoken to?	0	1	2	3
How often does your child fail to complete schoolwork, chores, or other duties (i.e., lose focus or get side-tracked)?	0	1	2	3
How often does your child have trouble organizing tasks or activities?	0	1	2	3
How often does your child avoid or show reluctance toward doing tasks that require mental effort over a long period of time (e.g., schoolwork)?	0	1	2	3
How often does your child lose things necessary for tasks or activities (e.g., keys, pencils, books, tools, paperwork, etc.)?	0	1	2	3
How often does your child get easily distracted?	0	1	2	3
How often is your child forgetful in daily activities?	0	1	2	3

Table 1.2. Hyperactivity and Impulsivity Questionnaire

Symptoms	Frequency			
Hyperactivity and Impulsivity	**Never**	**Occasionally**	**Somewhat Often**	**All the Time**
How often does your child fidget with or tap his hands or feet, or squirm in his seat?	0	1	2	3
How often does your child leave his seat in situations in which remaining seated is expected?	0	1	2	3
How often does your child run around or climb in situations in which doing so is not appropriate?	0	1	2	3
How often is your child unable to take part in leisure activities quietly?	0	1	2	3
How often is your child "on the go," acting as if driven by a motor?	0	1	2	3
How often does your child talk excessively?	0	1	2	3
How often does your child blurt out an answer before a question has been completed?	0	1	2	3
How often does your child have trouble waiting his turn?	0	1	2	3
How often does your child interrupt or intrude on others?	0	1	2	3

EVALUATING YOUR RESPONSES

If at least six of your answers landed in the "somewhat often" or "all the time" category on the inattentiveness questionnaire, then your child may have difficulties with attention. If, in addition, you answered "never" or "occasionally" to most questions on the hyperactivity and impulsivity questionnaire, then your child may have attention-deficit/hyperactivity disorder, predominantly inattentive, or ADHD-PI.

If the majority of your answers on the inattentiveness questionnaire landed in the "never" or "occasionally" category, then your child probably does not have significant attention problems. If, however, you also answered "somewhat often" or "all the time" to at least six questions on the hyperactivity and impulsivity questionnaire, then your child may have attention-deficit/hyperactivity disorder, predominantly hyperactive-impulsive, or ADHD-PH.

If, of course, you answered "somewhat often" or "all the time" to at least six questions on both questionnaires, then your child may have attention-deficit/hyperactivity disorder, combined, or ADHD-C.

SYMPTOMS

The term "ADHD" is thrown around so easily these days that it may seem difficult to know exactly what it actually means to experience symptoms of ADHD. The following four symptoms characterize the types of behavior an ADHD child will exhibit on a regular basis.

Fidgeting

Fidgeting is a form of *stimming,* which refers to a self-stimulating behavior characterized by repetitive movements or noises. Children may fidget, often with their hands, in order to calm themselves, self-soothe, or manage their emotions. The act of fidgeting actually produces changes in the brain's chemistry that calm the child. This symptom is also common in children with autism spectrum disorder. (See Chapter 6 on page 119 for more information on autism spectrum disorder.)

Hyperactivity

Hyperactivity refers to being unusually or abnormally active compared with peers in the same situation. A child with hyperactivity may seem always on the go or in constant motion.

Impulsivity

Impulsivity is the tendency to act without thinking or considering whether the action is appropriate, logical, or dangerous. Impulsive behavior does not consider the consequences of speaking or acting.

At school, an impulsive child may raise his hand to answer a question without thinking exactly what is being asked and then blurt out the first thing that comes to mind when called upon. An impulsive child may dart into a street without checking for cars, or may leap to the ground from a dangerously high place.

Inattentiveness

Inattentiveness refers to a lack of focus on a given event or situation. For example, an inattentive child may have difficulty concentrating on parental instructions, details of homework, class lessons, or long conversations. Children with inattentiveness have trouble organizing their homework, school bags, and desks at school. In addition, they often fail to finish projects and activities. If they do complete their homework on time, they may neglect to bring it to school and turn it in. This symptom may also be seen in children who have dyslexia or another form of learning disability, as these kids are prone to get bored and become inattentive due to their learning problems.

OBSERVING YOUR CHILD'S BEHAVIOR

Children with ADHD often frustrate their parents and siblings at home and during family outings with the chaos, turmoil, and disorder they create. Likewise, in school, teachers are forced to take time away from their lesson plans to manage children with ADHD, who cannot stay still, do not listen, and are difficult to teach. The point is that there are a number of environments in which we can observe a child's behavior.

Family Life

Your child may completely disrupt family activities. Parents who have to deal with their child's ADHD every day have reported that their child:

- behaves unpredictably (e.g., suddenly runs off, jumps from high places, plays with dangerous items, etc.).
- cannot get to sleep or stay asleep.
- cannot sit still for any extended period of time, moving around at the dinner table, on the couch, or in the car.

- is unable to stand still, seeming to have an urge to be in motion.
- does not pay attention to what is being said by a parent, friend, or sibling.
- is unorganized and fails to set up his room, school papers, or school bag in a way that would help him to find things.
- is unable to focus on a specific activity, such as doing homework, watching television, or playing games.
- wiggles or squirms in a quiet setting, such as a place of worship.

No matter how frustrating these circumstances may be, before you blame your child for his off-the-wall actions and tell him that he could do better if he'd only try harder, keep in mind that his brain is slightly different from the brain of a child without ADHD. This fact should not be used as an excuse for problematic behavior, of course, but should be kept in mind.

It is not uncommon for the behavior of a child with ADHD to put stress on the child's entire family and impact the child's relationships with all family members. It may feel as though you are grasping at straws simply to have a "normal" family life, and you would not be alone in that feeling. Moreover, the constant fighting between couples that so often happens when they are trying to determine how to deal with their troubled child can quickly lead to separation or divorce. Finding common ground on how to manage this issue is crucial.

As a parent of an ADHD child, your stress level is likely elevated due to your worry about his difficulties out in the world and your struggle to maintain discipline at home. Unfortunately, in a school setting, the troubles of an ADHD child land on a teacher's shoulders.

School

In a more rigid setting, such as school, children with ADHD have a hard time following the rules set by those in charge. These kids usually perform poorly in school due to several behavioral issues, including:

- being unable to sit still in a seat.
- constantly chattering or wandering around the classroom and bumping into desks and other students.

- difficulty paying attention, listening to the teacher, or following instructions.
- constantly fidgeting and having trouble sitting still.
- pushing in front of other children in line to go to recess, the bathroom, or the cafeteria.
- shouting out wrong answers without really considering the question.
- trouble absorbing and processing school lessons.

Due to these behaviors, children with ADHD tend to have trouble keeping up academically with their peers. They may also have specific learning disabilities in reading, math, or handwriting. Language and speech problems may complicate their attempts to communicate with teachers and peers because they speak too quickly. In addition, at recess or in gym class, they may be clumsy and display poor motor coordination. Keep in mind that these issues do not mean your child is not intelligent, only that his intelligence cannot be demonstrated due to these difficulties.

Currently, teachers might have an average of three children with ADHD in a classroom of thirty students. Needless to say, teachers may be frustrated and exhausted, and may tell parents, "I can't deal with your child. He takes up more of my time than all the children together. Please see your child's doctor for medication. I'll send the doctor a report." Despite a teacher's good intentions, however, keep in mind that only you and your child's doctor will decide whether to put your child on medication, and that any label a teacher might apply to your child is not an official diagnosis, which should come from a clinician and be supported by approved testing. Nevertheless, the suggestion to see his doctor may be a good one.

Some children with ADHD are so disruptive in the classroom that they may be placed in special classes or special schools, or even expelled if they also have severe conduct problems. About one-third of them repeat a grade. Approximately 30 to 40 percent require some type of special education class. Almost one-third of children with ADHD drop out of high school or delay completion of high school. As they get older, because of their impulsivity, they may perform illegal acts and become involved in the juvenile justice system. Roughly half of all children in the juvenile justice system have a history of ADHD. These days, thankfully, some schools offer programs that can help children with ADHD to get on the right track and avoid landing in the wrong half of that statistic.

You may find yourself wondering, "Why does my child act like this? Where did I go wrong? Why is my child so different from others I see?" To answer these questions, we must discuss the risk factors for ADHD.

RISK FACTORS

The risk factors for ADHD have been extensively studied but no common single cause has been identified in all cases of ADHD. Nevertheless, a number of major risk factors have been recognized at this point. You may be relieved to know that poor parenting is not thought to be a cause of ADHD. Of course, this is not to say that how you parent a

Special Education

Special education refers to the designing of a school program and learning plan that works for a child with special needs, such as ADHD. There exists a law called the Individuals with Disabilities Education Act (IDEA), which mandates that public education must provide appropriate services to children who cannot learn in a regular classroom. If your child doesn't meet this standard, you may try Section 504 of the 1973 Rehabilitation Act, which requires that students with disabilities be provided "free appropriate public education."

If testing reveals that your child has significant behavioral or learning problems, a special program called an Individualized Education Plan (IEP) should be developed for him. The parents of a child that qualifies for an IEP will meet with school personnel, including his teacher, a special education teacher, a guidance counselor, the school's principal, and perhaps a speech teacher, provided the child has communication problems. The IEP will outline the goals for the child as well as the educational, developmental, and behavioral support and services the school will provide.

The following instructions are some of the ways the classroom of an ADHD child may be made more appropriate.

- Allow the child to take tests or work on assignments in a quiet area.

child with ADHD isn't extremely important. Let us begin to investigate the possible reasons behind ADHD by looking at brain abnormalities.

Brain Abnormalities

The brains of children who have ADHD display structural abnormalities. These abnormalities may cause these children to seem unintelligent when, in fact, they are highly intelligent. Extensive research has been done on children with ADHD, including brain scans. Researchers have found that the brains of children with ADHD contain five areas that are smaller or less active than those same areas in the brains of non-ADHD children.

Additionally, studies have shown notable differences in the brain chemistry of children who have ADHD compared with those who do not, specifically related to neurotransmitters. *Neurotransmitters* are

- Give the child assignments one at a time and break down large assignments into smaller parts.
- Give the child extra time in which to take tests.
- Place the child in special education classes, which have fewer students so the teacher can give more attention to each student. (This placement could be full-time or part-time, allowing the student to participate in regular classrooms.)
- Reduce the child's workload, including both classroom and home assignments.
- Seat the child away from distractions of doors and windows and closer to the teaching area.
- Set up a system of communication between the parent of the ADHD child and the teacher (e.g., a notebook, daily emails, or phone calls).

For more information on special education services available in schools, please visit www.verywellmind.com and the CDC webpage www.cdc.gov/ncbddd/adhd/school-success.html. Children with ADHD can learn and behave more appropriately. They simply need to get the necessary help.

chemicals in the brain that help *neurons* (nerve cells) communicate with each other. In a child with ADHD, two neurotransmitters are low in supply: *dopamine* and *norepinephrine.* Dopamine affects mood, attention, motivation, and movement. Norepinephrine also helps people to pay attention and focus.

The electricity in an ADHD child's brain may also be different. The human brain contains over 100 billion neurons. Each neuron produces a tiny amount of electricity. Using electricity and neurotransmitters, the brain's neurons send and receive messages from other neurons. In children with ADHD, you might assume brain activity to be too fast, but it is actually slower than that of children without ADHD.

Blood flow may also play a role. Active regions of the brain require more blood flow. Blood carries oxygen and nutrients to the billions of brain cells and removes carbon dioxide and waste. In children with ADHD, however, some portions of the brain affecting inhibition and attention have less blood flow.

A child may have ADHD because of abnormal brain development during pregnancy. Pregnancy should be a time of excellent healthcare and good nutrition. It should also be as free from harmful substances as possible. Both nicotine and alcohol are two harmful substances that may cause brain abnormalities in a fetus. Maternal smoking nearly triples the risk of the child having ADHD, and the greater the number of cigarettes smoked each day, the more severe the ADHD. Similarly, children from alcoholic mothers are more likely to have structural brain problems. These children are hyperactive, disruptive, and impulsive, and are at risk for a variety of other psychiatric disorders.

Children who are born prematurely are five to nine times more likely to develop ADHD. Very low birth weight is associated with ADHD. Additionally, children born to women exposed to viruses or bacteria during pregnancy may also exhibit slight brain damage.

After birth, children who experience brain infections or brain tumors may later develop ADHD. Children who have experienced head trauma from an auto accident, a severe blow to the head by a hard ball or rock, or a hard fall in which brain cells are damaged may also develop ADHD.

Brain abnormalities contribute to the symptoms you see in a child with ADHD. When an ADHD child isn't paying attention or acts impulsively, it may not be that he does not want to do the things being asked of him (although that may be part of his reluctance); it may be that his slightly abnormal brain keeps him from acting normally. These brain differences, however, do not necessarily mean the problems associated with ADHD cannot be overcome through behavioral modification, medication, or other interventions.

Diet

Malnutrition affects millions of children worldwide, including children in the United States, where both children and adults are often undernourished even if they are overfed. In other words, children and adults tend to eat too much nutritionally inferior food and not enough healthy food. Many experts agree that behavioral disorders such as ADHD may be caused, in part, by malnutrition. One piece of evidence for this idea is that children with ADHD have higher weights in relation to their heights. This ratio is known as the Body Mass Index (BMI), and children with ADHD tend to have higher BMIs than healthy children, meaning there are more overweight or obese children in the ADHD population than there are among the non-ADHD population.

Diets high in saturated fat, partially hydrogenated oils, sugar, and corn syrup contribute to malnutrition. The consumption of too few vegetables, whole grains, fruits, poultry, fish, dairy, nuts, seeds, and legumes can lead to nutritional deficiencies that affect all cells, especially those in the brain. Children with ADHD display lower levels of several critical nutrients, including B vitamins, iron, magnesium, and zinc. A child with low levels of these substances cannot be expected to behave properly or learn well.

Environmental Toxins

Everyday chemicals that your child inhales, consumes through food, or ingests through drink can cause behavioral disorders, including ADHD, autism, and learning disabilities. Exposure starts during pregnancy when the mother takes in toxic chemicals, which are then delivered to the fetus through the umbilical cord. After birth, exposure to toxins continues to affect the growing child. Infants and young children are especially vulnerable to these chemicals, as they affect and damage the maturing brain. These chemicals include products we use every day, ranging from carpeting and flooring, cleaning and lawn products, pesticides, and personal care products.

The toxic substances found in our environment, such as lead, mercury, and cadmium, are also harmful. Analyses of baby foods have revealed that even well-known baby food brands have been shown to have contaminants, including arsenic, lead, and cadmium. Lead is also found in old paint and vaporized during removal and remodeling of older homes and apartments, both inside and outside. This lead dust poisons young children who inhale it or ingest it when they lick their contaminated fingers because lead tastes sweet. Additionally, old water lines running into homes through lead pipes can contaminate the drinking water.

No amount of lead in the body is safe. Lead causes behavioral and learning problems. Part Two of this book contains further information on environmental pollutants. (See page 211.)

Genetics

One explanation for the abnormal structures, neurotransmitters, and other abnormalities found in the brains of children with ADHD is altered genes. Scientists have found that multiple genes are responsible for ADHD. What's clear is that ADHD runs in families. Studies of identical twins report that if one twin has ADHD, the risk of the second twin having it is high—approximately 90 percent. Nevertheless, just because certain genes may play a role in ADHD does not mean that ADHD is unavoidable if these genes are present.

Sleep Problems

Children with ADHD have more sleep problems than do children without ADHD. Of course, stimulant medication for ADHD can cause sleep problems, but even without medication, children with ADHD have more sleep problems than do healthy children. If your child does not get enough sleep each night, his brain will not function well the next day. These sleep problems contribute to the causes of ADHD.

During sleep, your brain performs "clean-up" tasks, removing waste products and debris that have accumulated over the course of the day. It is critical for a child's brain to get enough good-quality sleep if it is to be ready for the next day. If your child is up and down all night, his sleep will not have been deep and restful. If his nose is congested from allergies, he will not sleep well. If he has enlarged tonsils and adenoids or perhaps a specific sleep disorder, he will not get refreshing sleep. Part Two discusses ways to promote restful sleep. (See page 167.)

Thyroid Problems

Your child's *thyroid gland* may be making too much or too little *thyroid hormone*. This issue can cause behavioral problems for a few children who have ADHD. The thyroid gland is a butterfly-shaped organ in the neck that produces thyroid hormone, which affects nearly every cell in the body. If too much thyroid hormone is produced (*hyperthyroidism*), the body's functions speed up. If too little thyroid is produced (*hypothyroidism*), the body's functions slow down. Both too little thyroid hormone and too much thyroid hormone can affect a small group of children with ADHD. These problems impact the brain and, not surprisingly, behavior and learning.

A few children with ADHD may produce too much thyroid hormone and show emotional outbursts, irritability, shaky hands, or an inability to concentrate. On the other hand, a child with ADHD may produce too little thyroid and be forgetful, tired, and inattentive. Thankfully, a child's doctor can easily test thyroid function with a simple blood test.

ASSOCIATED DISORDERS

Many of the behavioral conditions discussed in Part One may exist alongside ADHD. Technically speaking, associated conditions are called *comorbid disorders*. Six in ten children with ADHD have at least one other mental, emotional, or behavioral disorder. According to research:

- approximately 25 to 75 percent of children with ADHD also have oppositional defiant disorder, or ODD. Anger, irritability, defiance, and vindictiveness are behaviors associated with ODD. (See Chapter 2 on page 31.)
- approximately one-third of children with ADHD also have conduct disorder, or CD. Children with CD lie, cheat, and steal. They are aggressive and violent toward others and may destroy property or set fires. (See Chapter 3 on page 49.)
- approximately 6 to 30 percent of children with ADHD also have childhood depression. These children show severe, persistent sadness

that can interfere with schoolwork, family life, play with friends, and special interests and hobbies. (See Chapter 7 on page 141.)

- approximately three in ten children with ADHD have an anxiety disorder. Children with anxiety disorder are persistently anxious and irrational, with overwhelming worry, fear, and anxiety. (See Chapter 5 on page 101.)

Is It Laziness or ADHD?

Attention-deficit/hyperactivity disorder, predominantly inattentive (sometimes referred to as attention-deficit disorder, or ADD) is extremely common, affecting 23 percent of preschoolers, 45 percent of elementary school children, and 75 percent of adolescents. In other words, it is a major problem for many children.

In some ways, a child with ADHD-PI is different from a child with ADHD-C. Research has shown that the type of inattentiveness associated with ADHD-PI differs from the type associated with ADHD-C. Furthermore, children with ADHD-PI are often hypoactive, meaning they are slow to respond to a stimulus. They display a limited attention span, are distractible and forgetful, and often procrastinate. They are frequently accused of being lazy. They may daydream. They have trouble focusing their attention on the task at hand. They lose things and are unable to find them. Their minds wander when doing homework or reading. They are disorganized, make careless mistakes, and are sloppy. They get bored easily, have trouble completing projects, and find it difficult to complete all their homework correctly and turn it in on time.

Children with ADHD-PI may be introverted and have few friends. Anxiety, depression, and reading and language deficits are more common in children with ADHD-PI than in children with ADHD-C. Teachers and parents are often frustrated by the inaction, sluggishness, and inattentiveness of children with ADHD-PI, and may think of them as "dumb" or "lazy," when actually they may be quite intelligent but lack motivation and self-esteem because they have an imbalance of brain chemicals. You may not be able to tell the difference between laziness and ADHD-PI, but a professional will.

Unlike children with ADHD-C, children with ADHD-PI do not usually act out in class. They don't get into the trouble that a child with ADHD-C

You can imagine how having one or more of the above problems in addition to ADHD would be overwhelming for a child, his parents, and his teachers. (See Chapter 7 on page 141 for more information on the physical or mental disorders that may accompany ADHD.) Although you have completed the questionnaires and learned whether your child may have ADHD, you still don't have an official diagnosis by a

might. Instead, in a class of thirty children, they may be lost and overlooked because they are quiet. Therefore, they are seldom evaluated and treated for their serious problems. While some children with ADHD-C improve as they age, children with ADHD-PI usually do not, and their inattentiveness may forever influence their lives at work and at home.

One underlying reason for ADHD-PI is genetic. More children with ADHD-PI have a particular sequence in a certain gene than do children with ADHD-C. In the brain, children with ADHD-PI seem to have problems in the prefrontal cortex, while children with ADHD have problems in other areas.

Responses to medication vary. Some children with ADHD-PI do not respond to methylphenidate (Ritalin). Some are helped more by amphetamines (Adderall).

Endeavor-Rx is an exciting new computer game that may be quite helpful. It's a prescription game that improves attention. It's proven so successful in improving attention that it has been approved by the FDA. You must get a prescription for it from your child's doctor. Unfortunately, there have been few studies on the role of nutrition, diet, or biochemistry in ADHD-PI. Perhaps this is because children with ADHD-PI don't cause chaos in class or at home, nor do they become juvenile delinquents, so the "squeaky wheels" (difficult children) get the "grease" (research dollars). Certainly, feeding your child a healthy diet makes sense in terms of its important micronutrients. Lifestyle changes, including your child getting enough high-quality sleep and regular exercise, may also help.

The inset titled "Tips for Parents from the CDC" (see page 24) is a helpful guide to getting your child organized. In addition, *ADDitude* magazine has many articles, suggestions, and even webinars for parents of children with ADHD-PI.

doctor. In order to determine an official diagnosis, you should make an appointment to visit your child's doctor.

DIAGNOSIS

While the questionnaires at the beginning of this chapter may provide you with a clearer idea of what your child may be experiencing, they will not provide a definitive diagnosis. Trained professionals, such as pediatricians, child psychiatrists, and child counselors, have the expertise to diagnose and treat ADHD. Diagnosis requires questionnaires like the ones in this chapter to be completed by parents (or caregivers) and teachers, and includes interviews with the child and the child's parents. The doctor should rule out other disorders that may cause similar symptoms, including anxiety, depression, behavioral problems, learning and language disorders, autism, tics, and sleep disorders. If one of these issues is present, the child may be referred to another specialist for treatment.

Computer Assessment Tests

A doctor or psychologist may give your child a twenty-minute computer test to measure his attention and impulsivity. It's like a very boring computer game. For this test, the child sits in front of a computer screen on which various letters appear one at a time as he watches for a specific letter. When he sees the letter, he responds by pressing a key as fast as he can. The computer keeps track of the time it takes for him to see the letter and respond. If he presses the key when the wrong letter is in front of him, however, the computer program counts the error, thus keeping track of his attention and impulsivity.

One such test is the *Tests of Variables of Attention*, or *T.O.V.A.*, and another is the *Conners' Continuous Performance Test*, or *CPT*. One of the benefits of a computer assessment is that it is objective and not swayed by someone's opinion or experience. These tests can be used for diagnosis and to evaluate treatment results, but a computer test should never be used alone to make a diagnosis without a careful history, parent and teacher questionnaires, and interviews. The test is just one diagnostic tool.

So, how are symptoms of ADHD managed? Let's first discuss traditional treatment, which may include therapy or different prescription medications that can be used to treat a child with ADHD. In Part Two of this book, we describe complementary therapies that have helped many children.

TRADITIONAL TREATMENT

As you have just learned, there are two types of traditional treatments for ADHD: therapy and medication. Many doctors write a prescription on the first visit. Other doctors start with therapy and then turn to medication if a child is still having significant problems in school, which is the method recommended by pediatric experts. Medication may be used almost immediately, however, in an attempt to rescue a family from severe disruption due to a child's behavior. As ADHD can vary in severity from child to child, it is crucial for a child's doctor to listen to his entire story when deciding which form of treatment to employ. If medication is required, it will be most effective when used along with therapy and the llifestyle and nutritional approaches suggested in Part Two of this book. (See pages 167 and 185.)

If your child is younger than six years old, the American Academy of Pediatrics recommends parent training in behavioral management as the first line of treatment before medication is tried. According to the CDC, both medication and behavioral management can be helpful for an older child. They also suggest that schools be part of the treatment plan. The CDC recommends behavioral management or organizational training.

Therapy

Your pediatrician may refer your child to a psychologist, social worker, or counselor for therapy, which can be a very effective treatment for children with ADHD under the age of twelve. For children younger than six years old, training parents in behavioral management may be used.

In therapy, parents attend eight to sixteen sessions with a therapist, who teaches them strategies to parent their child effectively. The therapist should be someone who focuses on training parents and has had extra education and experience in using these methods. Your child's doctor can recommend someone she respects and has worked with previously.

Tips from the CDC for Parents

You may have tried spanking or some other form of corporal punishment to punish your child. Parenting a child with ADHD can be exasperating, and some parents resort to threatening or spanking their children when they have misbehaved. (For more information on this type of punishment, see the inset titled "Corporal Punishment" on page 27.) There are better ways to improve your child's behavior.

The Centers for Disease Control has come up with the following suggestions to assist you in helping your child get organized and relieving your child's stress and yours.

- **Embrace routine.** Try to follow the same schedule every day, from wake-up time to bedtime.
- **Get organized.** Encourage your child to put school bags, clothing, and toys in the same place every day, minimizing the chance of losing them.
- **Manage distractions.** Turn off the TV, quiet noise, and provide a clean workspace when your child is doing homework. Some children with ADHD learn well if they are moving or listening to background music. Watch your child and see what works.
- **Limit choices.** To help your child not feel overwhelmed or overstimulated, offer choices with only a few options. For example, have them choose between this outfit or that one, this meal or that one, or this toy or another one.
- **Be clear and specific when you talk with your child.** Let your child know you are listening by describing what you heard him say. Use clear, brief directions when your child needs to do something.
- **Help your child to plan.** Break down complicated tasks into simpler, shorter steps. For long tasks, starting early and taking breaks may reduce stress.
- **Use goals and praise or other rewards.** Use a chart to list goals and track positive behavior, and then let your child know he has done well or reward his efforts in other ways. Be sure the goals are realistic—small steps are important.

- **Discipline effectively.** Instead of scolding, yelling, or spanking, use effective directions, time-outs, or removal of privileges as consequences of inappropriate behavior.
- **Foster positive opportunities.** Children with ADHD may find certain situations stressful. Finding out and encouraging what your child does well—whether it is school, sports, art, music, or play—can foster positive experiences.
- **Provide a healthy lifestyle.** Nutritious food, physical activity, and sufficient sleep are important. They may keep ADHD symptoms from getting worse.

These tips can help you and your child work on his organizational skills while you provide him with positive reinforcement.

Therapy may occur in groups or with just the child's parents. An advantage of a working with a group is that it may be helpful to hear that other parents are experiencing similar problems to your own (or even worse problems than yours), making you feel less alone. You can also encourage and learn from other parents. The cost of group training should be less than that for just the child's parents or caregivers.

In class, parents learn skills and strategies that employ positive reinforcement, structure, and consistent discipline to manage their child's behavior. Parents are taught positive ways to interact and communicate with their child. The therapist may assign activities for parents to practice with their child before the next session. As you now understand, bad parenting does not cause ADHD, but improving your parenting skills can be very helpful in improving matters.

If your child has not improved significantly with therapy, his doctor may choose medication.

Medication

There are several different types of medication used to treat children with ADHD. If one doesn't help, your doctor has lots of other medications to try. Keep in mind that these medications are powerful chemicals that affect your child's brain. When you pick up the prescription at the pharmacy, be sure to read the package insert, and watch your child carefully for possible side effects when he starts taking the new medication. Many children can take these drugs without experiencing any side effects, but it's important to know of the possibilities. If you are concerned by any side effects, be sure to call your doctor and talk to her about the matter. Don't worry; you won't be bothering her. It is her job to help you. If you get the sense that your doctor feels you are disturbing her, it may be time to find a different doctor.

Stimulant Medications

Stimulant medications are the most common and effective medications for ADHD. They work by changing the amounts of neurotransmitters in the brain, which can improve your child's ability to pay attention, focus, and control behavioral problems. There are two types of this medication: *methylphenidate* (Ritalin, Concerta) and *amphetamine* (Adderall, Vyvanse). Some children respond better to one than they do the other.

Ritalin. One of the most commonly prescribed drugs for ADHD is Ritalin. It is a short-acting stimulant that lasts about three to four hours. Another form of this drug is called Focalin. This stimulant starts to work about thirty to forty-five minutes after taking it. If your child has trouble swallowing pills, the medication may be crushed and put into applesauce or other food. There are also liquid and chewable forms. One problem with Ritalin is that it lasts only three to four hours, requiring a noon dose at school. Many children dislike this fact because it makes them look different from their peers. Different forms of this stimulant, however, including Ritalin-LA and Metadate CD, last about six to eight hours. Concerta is a similar medication, but it lasts for eight to twelve hours.

Side Effects of Stimulants

Loss of appetite is the most common side effect of stimulant medications. This side effect tends to last about as long as the effects of the medication. Then the child is ravenous. Take the opportunity to make sure that the food your child eats is nutritious. Don't fall into the trap of letting him choose nutritionally poor foods. Make the most of this opportunity to feed him healthy foods.

Besides loss of appetite, there may be other side effects. One is trouble falling asleep. Children with ADHD may have trouble sleeping to

Corporal Punishment

If you are like most parents, you have probably tried all kinds of punishments in response to your child's behavioral problems but none has helped your child to behave normally. You may have even tried physical punishment, such as spanking or slapping. When it comes to corporal punishment, however, it's important to understand how easy it is to lose control. If one strike doesn't bring a response, then you may be tempted to hit your child again but harder. It can get out of hand and serious injuries may occur. Make no mistake: Corporal punishment is a form of abuse. As such, it must be reported to the authorities by medical professionals and social workers.

Furthermore, physical punishment has been studied by experts, who report that it actually makes existing problems worse. It teaches a child that violence is the answer to problems, leading him to inflict the violence he has experienced on others. In the case of conduct disorder, abusive treatment by adults in the home is actually a risk factor for this disorder in the first place. There are better ways to help a child behave, which are discussed throughout this book.

begin with, so this issue may be worsened by stimulants. Adjustment of the dosage and the timing of the day's last dose by your child's doctor may help. Slower growth has also been a concern associated with stimulants. Some research, however, has reported that stimulants have little or no impact on growth. Some parents complain of behavioral changes as the medication wears off—this occurrence is called *rebound.* Rebound could be due to hunger, so, as recently recommended, make sure your child eats healthy snacks. About 10 percent of children with ADHD have motor tics—with or without medication. Medication does not seem to be the cause of these tics.

Non-Stimulants and Other Medications for ADHD

If stimulants don't work or the side effects associated with them are intolerable, your child's doctor may choose to treat his ADHD with non-stimulants, blood pressure medication, or antidepressants. All three treatments are non-stimulants, so if a child reacts adversely to a stimulant medication, he may do better with one of these choices.

Atomoxetine (Strattera). *Atomoxetine* (Strattera) was the first non-stimulant drug used for ADHD. It is thought to increase neurotransmitter levels. The response seems to work for about half of children with ADHD. Side effects include loss of appetite, nausea, indigestion, fatigue, dizziness, and mood swings.

Clonidine (Catapres). *Clonidine* (Catapres) is a medication that was first used to treat high blood pressure, as it relaxes blood vessels to increase blood flow. It is also used to treat ADHD. It may take several weeks for maximum effect and is not considered as effective as stimulants or antidepressants. Clonidine is available as a tablet or skin patch. The patch only needs to be changed once a week. Side effects of clonidine include anxiety, dry skin, constipation, dry mouth, headaches, and sleepiness.

Antidepressants

Another class of medication sometimes used to treat ADHD is antidepressants, of which there are a number of different types. For example, one class is a *tricyclic antidepressant,* which includes Pamelor, Tofranil, and Norpramin. Your doctor will know which one to try. *Viloxazine* (Quelbree) is the latest antidepressant approved by the FDA for children ages six to seventeen with ADHD. It comes as an extended-release capsule.

Side Effects of Antidepressants

Side effects of antidepressants can range from mild to severe. They can cause increased appetite and weight gain in some and loss of appetite in others. They can cause fatigue, drowsiness, and insomnia. Problems in the digestive tract may also occur, including dry mouth, indigestion, nausea, diarrhea, and constipation. Sudden changes in mood, behavior, thoughts, or feelings should be reported immediately to the prescribing doctor. If your child develops suicidal thoughts or actions, they should be immediately reported to the prescribing doctor.

Before using any drug to treat your child's ADHD, always make sure to read the list of side effects that comes with the medication. While some of these side effects can be serious, most are rare. As your child's primary caretaker, however, you need to be aware of any physical or mental changes that may be due to the medication. If you see any negative side effect that concerns you, call your child's doctor immediately.

If you stop giving your child the medication, then ask your doctor whether there might be any withdrawal side effects of which you should be aware.

Now you know that there are many medications from which a doctor may choose to treat ADHD. Some doctors will use a combination of medications. Your child's doctor needs to follow your child closely to adjust dosages and monitor side effects.

Treatment of ADHD with medication alone is not recommended. Rather, it should include therapy. Even with therapy and medication, however, a large number of children with ADHD continue to have problems with behavior and learning. A very careful, well-designed study of the use of medication and therapy to treat ADHD showed that 56 percent of children experienced excellent results from this approach to treatment. In other words, many children responded very well. The other 44 percent, unfortunately, did not respond as well, thus other forms of treatment are still needed.

COMPLEMENTARY TREATMENT

In addition to traditional therapy or medication, there are a number of other avenues of treatment to consider. These complementary methods can be extremely helpful. Part Two of this book describes various natural, medication-free ways to help your child and discusses them in depth. These options include:

- **addressing environmental factors.** Some children with ADHD are sensitive to things they breathe in or are exposed to, including natural substances such as pollens, molds, or animal dander; chemicals in their environments, such as tobacco smoke, cleaning supplies, perfumes, scents, gas fumes, or wet paint; and toxic substances, such as heavy metals, pesticides, or plastics.

- **the use of helpful programs or devices.** These programs and activities may bring dramatic improvement in behavior and learning. They include neurofeedback (using a special brain wave test, the child learns to manipulate the rhythm of his brain and produce calm waves), a videogame for inattentiveness that is fun to play and shown in medical research to improve attention span, and regular summer camp or a special camp for children with ADHD.

- **changing your child's lifestyle.** Lifestyle changes can greatly improve your child's behavior and school work. Regular exercise improves problems with attention, grades in school, aggression, depression, and sleep. Getting good quality sleep improves behavior and school performance.

- **focusing on nutrition.** The human brain needs fifty or more nutrients to perform its work optimally. There are also non-nutritious foods that can adversely affect the brain. Excessive sugar, corn syrup, salt, refined foods, food additives, may be causing poor behavioral reactions. Micronutrient supplements of vitamins, minerals, and fatty acids have shown to improve behavior and learning in children with ADHD and other disorders.

Some treatments are easier and cheaper to try than others, including addressing environmental factors, using supplements, enforcing good sleep practices, and encouraging exercise. Some may seem impossible to accomplish in a large family, including dietary management. Some are more expensive than others—for example, videogame therapy, neurofeedback, or summer camp. You'll have to figure out which ones are appropriate for you, your child, your family, and your wallet. Thankfully, there are scientific studies to support the effectiveness of each ADHD treatment mentioned.

CONCLUSION

Once your child has been diagnosed with ADHD, one question will inevitably arise: How will this impact my child's life now and in the future? The fact that you now understand the nature of the problem may lead you to a number of ways to deal with this condition. You can help to alleviate it or, in some cases, even eliminate it. The most important thing you can do initially is to accept it. Then you can move forward.

Over time, some people outgrow ADHD. Nevertheless, many successful people have ADHD, including Richard Branson, Michael Phelps, Bill Gates, and Justin Timberlake. They managed to take their overactive energies and direct them to become the people they are today. Just know that your child's future may be a lot brighter than you suspect.

2.

Oppositional Defiant Disorder

Oppositional defiant disorder, or *ODD*, is a common disruptive behavioral disorder in children and teenagers. Children with ODD are uncooperative, defiant, and hostile to parents, teachers, and other authority figures. They are irritable, argumentative, and hold grudges. They are not bothered by their actions even though they frustrate everyone around them. Diagnosis is based on signs and symptoms, using behavioral questionnaires such as the ones found in this chapter.

In the United States, about 10 percent of children suffer from ODD, which affects boys more often than it does girls. Although symptoms of ODD may occur in even younger children, the average age of a child when diagnosed is eight, although a diagnosis may come as late as age twelve. Children with ODD frequently have associated behavioral disorders such as ADHD, conduct disorder, anxiety, or childhood depression. Diagnosis of these disorders is extremely important, as it ensures that the "whole" child will be treated. Treating a child with these disorders with appropriate medication can result in his overall improvement, which is especially helpful in light of the fact that there is no specific medication for ODD.

Parent management training is perhaps the most effective treatment for ODD. This form of therapy works best when it is specially tailored to the affected child's family. During treatment, a therapist teaches parents effective ways to improve the parent-child relationship, as well as how to respond to their child's behavior.

Early diagnosis and treatment of ODD and any associated behavioral disorder is crucial in preventing oppositional defiant disorder from progressing to conduct disorder. The progression to conduct disorder occurs in roughly 30 percent of children with ODD. Mild ODD may get better with time. Thankfully, the outlook for children with ODD who undergo treatment is good.

QUESTIONNAIRES

Please complete the following questionnaires, which, when analyzed together, can help you to determine whether your child might have ODD. When you evaluate the symptoms listed, consider their presence over the last six months.

Table 2.1. Anger/Irritability Questionnaire

Symptoms	Frequency			
Anger/Irritability	**Never**	**Occasionally**	**Somewhat Often**	**All the Time**
How often does your child lose his temper?	0	1	2	3
How often is your child touchy or easily annoyed?	0	1	2	3
How often is your child angry or resentful?	0	1	2	3

Table 2.2. Argumentativeness/Defiance Questionnaire

Symptoms	Frequency			
Argumentativeness/Defiance	**Never**	**Occasionally**	**Somewhat Often**	**All the Time**
How often does your child argue with authority figures, children, adolescents, or adults?	0	1	2	3
How often does your child actively defy requests from authority figures or refuse to comply with rules?	0	1	2	3
How often does your child deliberately annoy others?	0	1	2	3
How often does your child blame others for his mistakes or misbehavior?	0	1	2	3

Table 2.3. Vindictiveness Questionnaire				
Symptom	**Frequency**			
Vindictiveness	**Never**	**Occasionally**	**Somewhat Often**	**All the Time**
How often has your child been vindictive within the past six months?	0	1	2	3

EVALUATING YOUR RESPONSES

If you answered "somewhat often" or "all the time" to at least four questions across all three questionnaires (anger/irritability, argumentativeness/defiance, and vindictiveness), and those answers were associated with interactions between your child and at least one individual who is not your child's sibling, then your child may have ODD and should be evaluated by a professional. If you answered "never" or "occasionally" to most of the questions across all three questionnaires, then your child probably does not have ODD. (Of course, you may still want to mention your concerns regarding your child's behavior to his doctor at his next check-up.)

It may be helpful to know how severe your child's scores are. If symptoms are confined to only one setting—at home, at school, or with peers, then his ODD should be considered *mild.* His ODD should be considered *moderate* if some symptoms are present in at least two settings. Finally, his ODD should be considered *severe* if some symptoms are present in three or more settings.

SYMPTOMS

There are a number of terms used to describe the symptoms of ODD. In learning more about each of them, you may better understand ODD and what having this condition means.

Conduct Disorder (CD)

Conduct disorder, or CD, is a disruptive behavioral disorder that shares similar symptoms with ODD, including temper tantrums, aggression, and defiance. CD, however, can be more serious than ODD, and, at its extreme, may cause teenagers to become involved in unlawful acts. In general, children with CD are physically abusive, while children with ODD are verbally abusive.

Defiance

A defiant child is one who challenges, resists, or fights others verbally. For example, a child who refuses to pick up his toys, clean his room, or do his homework after frequent requests is acting defiantly. He may be verbally abusive to others. He may respond to situations with abusive or offensive language.

Disruptive Behavior Disorders (DBD)

Disruptive behavior disorders, or *DBD,* is a term used to categorize both ODD and CD, as each condition has similar symptoms, including uncooperative behavior, defiance of authority figures (talking back to adults, refusing to comply with parent or teacher requests, etc.), frequent outbursts and temper tantrums, and any other behavior intended to annoy or upset others. Needless to say, these disorders disrupt the normal activities of an affected child and everyone around him.

Opposition

A child who is oppositional shows a pattern of angry or cranky moods, as well as defiant or combative behavior. Such a child seems always to respond to a situation by being antagonistic. If the weather is too cold, he might say it's too hot; if you say he should do his homework, he might refuse to do it; if he is scolded for teasing his sibling, he might accuse that sibling of looking at him in a way he did not like.

Temper Tantrums

Temper tantrums, sometimes called "meltdowns" or "hissy fits," may be defined as emotional outbursts that occur in response to events that seem overwhelming. Temper tantrums are common in preschoolers and even in older children. They consist of crying, aggression, defiance, and perhaps screaming while lying on the floor and refusing to get up.

Vindictiveness

Simply put, vindictive children are those who hold a grudge. When vindictive children feel they have been harmed in some way, whether verbally or physically, they will devise and execute plans to get even with those who, in their opinions, have harmed them.

OBSERVING YOUR CHILD'S BEHAVIOR

Keep in mind that all children will have moments in which they refuse to do things, have temper tantrums, or blame others for their misdeeds. Many children go through a phase in which "no" is their favorite response, but in children with ODD, this phase persists. What sets apart a child with ODD from a "normal" child is the frequency and severity of such behavior. Children with ODD often frustrate and embarrass their parents and siblings, whether at home or during family outings, due to the chaos, turmoil, and disorder they create. Likewise, in school, teachers are often forced to take time away from their lesson plans to manage children with ODD, who may also have other behavioral or learning disorders. As you can see, when attempting to determine whether a child has ODD, it is important to observe the child in both familial situations and at school.

Family Life

A child with ODD may completely disrupt family activities, much to the dismay of his parents and siblings. Parents who deal with their child's ODD on a daily basis have reported that their child:

- delights in bothering and teasing his siblings.
- has explosive temper tantrums.
- refuses to do his homework.
- refuses to follow family rules and may enjoy breaking them.
- refuses to go to bed and is thus sleep deprived.
- uses foul or offensive language at home and in public places.

As is the case with the other disorders discussed in this book, parents of children with ODD can become extremely frustrated. Children with ODD tend to grate on their parents' nerves. Parents are tempted to use foul language in response to their children's outrageous language—or even to strike them in anger. (See the inset titled "Corporal Punishment" on page 27.) It is not uncommon for the behavior of a child with ODD to put stress on his entire family and impact his relationships with all family members, even grandparents, who may be shocked by his foul language. His family may feel restricted in where they can go, worrying about what might happen at friends' houses, their place of worship, or restaurants. Parents may feel as though everyone is judging them behind their backs and wondering why they can't control their child who is loudly swearing. As a parent of a child with ODD, you may wonder, "How did my child get so out of control?"

Unfortunately, in a school setting, the troubles of a child with ODD, who probably has other behavioral disorders or learning disabilities, become the source of a teacher's frustration.

School

In a more rigid setting such as school, children with ODD can be angry or abusive. They may use foul language, talk back to their teachers, or refuse to follow classroom or school rules. These kids are so uncooperative and combative in school that their behavior interferes with their ability to learn and interact well with classmates and teachers. Of course, their behavior also interferes with their classmates' ability to learn. The following examples reflect how a child with ODD might act in school.

- Once he has learned how to pick on a child, he may target this person at recess or lunch.
- He may argue with his teacher just to be argumentative or disrespectful.
- He may declare the course material "stupid."
- He may dispute obvious facts that his teacher presents.
- He may refuse to open his book or do his work and then have a temper tantrum.
- He may taunt other children.

- He may show poor school performance, exhibit antisocial behavior, or be unable to control his impulses.

Due to these behaviors, a child with ODD typically has trouble keeping up academically with his classmates. If he also has ADHD or CD, then he will be a challenge for even the best, most experienced teacher. Like children with ADHD, children with ODD may have specific learning disabilities.

Children with ODD do not qualify for special education classes unless they can prove they have another problem such as anxiety, depression, or a learning disability. (See the inset titled "Special Education" on page 14.)

If you happen to be a teacher, the following examples describe the ways in which you can make the classroom more appropriate for a child with ODD and hopefully alleviate some of the struggles you may be facing as a result of an ODD child.

- Avoid power struggles.
- Be consistent. Keep rules simple but always enforce them.
- Give the ODD child choices so he feels he has some control but doesn't take over.
- Have a "chill-out" space where the ODD child can calm down and rethink his choices.
- Identify triggers ahead of time. Activities with a lot of stimulation may set ODD children off. Let the little things slide.
- Incorporate the interests of the ODD child in particular lessons.
- Keep the classroom calm. The teacher must be relaxed and calm.
- Seat the ODD child away from the distractions of doors and windows and closer to the teaching area.
- Set up a system of communication between the parents of the ODD child and his teacher (e.g., a notebook, daily emails, or phone calls).
- Try to build a connection with the ODD child, which may help you to get to the root of his behavior.

- When the ODD child does something right, reward him with an activity he enjoys.

Children with ODD and other behavioral disorders can behave more appropriately and learn. They simply need to get the necessary help. If an ODD child also has a learning disability, then he may qualify for a special education class, which has fewer students and allows the teacher to give more attention to each student. An ODD student could be placed in full-time special education or part-time special education, the latter of which would see the student participating in regular classrooms for a portion of his school day.

You may find yourself wondering, "Why does my child act in this way? Where did I go wrong? Why is my child so different from others I see?" To answer these questions, we must discuss the risk factors for ODD.

RISK FACTORS

The risk factors for ODD have been extensively studied, but no single cause has been identified in all cases of ODD. Nevertheless, researchers report that a child's environment, genetics, parenting, and biological abnormalities may each play a role. The good news is that we can address many of these factors and, in doing so, improve or even eliminate a child's ODD behavior.

Brain Abnormalities

A child with ODD often has abnormalities in the brain that set him apart from other children. First, there may be structural differences in several parts of the brain, including the *amygdala* and the left *precuneus*. These medical terms might not mean much to you, but they refer to the parts of the brain that are involved with emotional processing, error monitoring, problem solving, and self-control.

There is an amygdala on each side of the brain, and they form part of the *limbic system*, which controls emotions and memory. The precuneus is a region of the brain that lies between both sides of the brain. It is involved in certain aspects of memory, vision, mental imagery, and self-awareness.

Brain scientists also believe that the *prefrontal cortex* may be underdeveloped in children with ODD. This region is located at the most forward part of the brain and is associated with executive tasks such as decision-making, planning, and orchestration.

Neurotransmitters may also be affected in ODD. As you learned in Chapter 1, these brain chemicals allow communication between brain cells. When neurotransmitters don't function properly, messages may not be sent correctly, leading to symptoms of ODD. For example, *serotonin* is one of a combination of neurotransmitters that inhibit aggression toward oneself or others. When it acts abnormally in the brain, this inhibition is reduced.

The next time your child is acting out, remember that his brain may be slightly different from those of the children who are not acting out. Of course, this fact does not excuse his behavior, nor does it mean that better parenting skills, medication, or natural therapies will not be effective.

Diet

Whether or not children with ODD have nutritional deficiencies of important brain nutrients is a subject that has not been studied thoroughly enough to be answered yet. It is worth noting, however, that children with ODD are associated with a greater incidence of overweight or obesity than that of children who do not have ODD. This weight problem suggests the ODD child's diet may be made up of nutritionally poor foods.

In one study, children with ADHD and poor emotional control, which may also be found in children with ODD, were given a special micronutrient supplement that contained more than thirty different vitamins, minerals, and amino acids for approximately ten weeks and then reevaluated. Upon reevaluation, which included input from doctors, parents, and teachers, both symptoms of ADHD and emotional control appeared to have improved. These positive results suggest a possible link between behavioral disorders and deficiencies of one or more nutrients. (See Chapter 10 on page 185 for more information on nutrients and behavioral disorders.)

In addition to the possibility of a poor overall diet leading to ODD, specific foods may trigger a child's ODD behavior. An "elimination diet" is a diet in which common foods from your child's diet are removed and then reintroduced one at a time, allowing you to see which foods trigger changes in his behavior.

Environmental Toxins

Toxicity to various chemicals in the environment may also play a role in the development of ODD in a child. In children, exposure to environmental chemicals such as secondhand smoke, gas fumes, perfumes, and many others can trigger neurological and psychological symptoms and behavioral symptoms. Children born to mothers who smoked, drank alcohol during pregnancy, or had high levels of the lead in their blood find themselves at an increased risk of developing ODD. In children with ODD, research has shown that even very low lead levels are associated with ODD behavior, which suggests there is no safe level of lead, not even that which is considered in the "normal" range.

Familial and Social Factors

A child's familial relationships and social life are important to consider when searching for the cause of his ODD. Poor relationships with parents or caregivers may play a role in ODD, as may the absence of a parent, the neglect of basic needs, and a lack of healthy relationships. These psychological factors can contribute to ODD. Low socioeconomic status and abusive relationships may also contribute to ODD. Of course, all these problems can lead to a vicious circle. A child who has poor self-control and is highly emotional in his responses to everyday annoyances can frustrate his parents, who will likely have no idea how to parent their out-of-control child. They may resort to abusive practices, which actually increase the child's problems, and thus a vicious circle is created. Keep in mind, too, that parents who have symptoms of anger, aggression, and defiance themselves may influence their children to act similarly. (See page 44 for information on effective parenting solutions.)

Genetics

ODD may be inherited. Susceptibility to ODD is increased in those who have a family history (e.g., an affected parent, sibling, or other close family member) of attention-deficit/hyperactivity disorder, oppositional defiant disorder, conduct disorder, mood disorders, alcoholism, or substance abuse. Some researchers have concluded that the association among ODD, CD, and ADHD is explained by shared genetic influences, but each disorder has distinct genetic differences, too. Researching these disorders is not easy, as there are a large number of genes involved.

Sleep Problems

Getting enough high-quality sleep is important for every child, but it is especially so for children with behavioral disorders. If your child displays daytime sleepiness, has trouble getting up in the morning, or seems tired all the time, his behavioral issues could be due to lack of sleep. Even if your child gets sufficient sleep, the quality of sleep may be poor. If you think your child's behavioral problems may be connected to sleep, discuss the matter with his therapist and ask about ways to get him to bed at the right time, and how you might help him to achieve good "sleep hygiene."

Of course, children may have ODD because they have an actual sleep disorder. ODD has been reported in children with *restless legs syndrome*, or *RLS*, and *obstructive sleep apnea*, or *OSA*. Thankfully, both have relatively simple solutions. If your child has RLS, his legs may jerk and move before and during sleep, causing disturbed sleep. Measuring iron levels in children with RLS and treating them with iron supplements if low levels are present can make a difference in both sleep quality and daytime behavior.

Children with obstructive sleep apnea actually stop breathing very briefly during sleep, which lowers oxygen in the brain. This affects daytime behavior. This condition may be due to enlarged tonsils and adenoids, which can be removed to improve breathing, sleeping, and behavior. (For more on good sleep hygiene, RLS, and obstructive sleep apnea, see Chapter 9 on page 167.)

Thyroid Problems

Thyroid problems may play a role in a child's ODD, especially if that child also has ADHD. (For more information about the thyroid gland, see page 19 in Chapter 1.) *Thyroid-stimulating hormone*, or *TSH*, measurements may be used to determine whether a person's thyroid is functioning properly. Levels of TSH are often low in children with

ODD. In fact, it would appear that the lower they drop, the worse an ODD child's behavioral symptoms become. As a result, researchers have concluded that the thyroid may play an important role in the development of ODD.

A doctor can easily test your child's thyroid function by ordering three thyroid blood tests: T3, T4, and TSH. If the doctor finds abnormalities, they may be remedied through the use of thyroid hormone treatment.

ASSOCIATED DISORDERS

Many of the behavioral disorders discussed in Part One may exist alongside ODD. According to research:

- approximately 40 percent of children with ODD also have ADHD. ADHD is characterized by inattentiveness, impulsivity, and hyperactivity. (See Chapter 1 on page 7.)
- approximately 10 to 30 percent of children who have ODD will go on to have conduct disorder. Children with conduct disorder often lie, cheat, and steal. They are aggressive and violent toward others and may destroy property or set fires. (See Chapter 3 on page 49.)
- approximately 14 percent of children with ODD also have an anxiety disorder. Children with an anxiety disorder are persistently anxious and irrational, with overwhelming worry, fear, and anxiety. (See Chapter 5 on page 101.)
- approximately 9 percent of children with ODD also have childhood depression. (See Chapter 7 on page 141.) Children with childhood depression show severe, persistent sadness that can interfere with schoolwork, family life, play with friends, special interests, and hobbies.

Suffice it to say that it is not uncommon for a child with ODD to be affected by at least one other disorder. Diagnosing associated behavioral or mental disorders is extremely important because treating these other disorders may also improve symptoms of ODD. (See Chapter 7 on page 141 for more information on the physical or mental disorders that may accompany ODD.)

A child with ODD and other behavioral disorders is truly difficult to parent. Although you may have completed the questionnaires at the beginning of this chapter and suspect your child has ODD, you will still need an official diagnosis, which may be determined by your child's doctor or a specialist referred to you by your child's doctor.

DIAGNOSIS

As is the case with almost all the behavioral disorders discussed in Part One, there is no lab test that may be used to diagnose ODD. Nevertheless, after your doctor has interviewed you, your partner, and your child, and has reviewed questionnaires you will have completed, imaging or blood tests may be ordered if a medical reason for your child's behavior is suspected.

Be sure to tell your child's doctor about any sleep or eating problems he may be experiencing. Ask your doctor to examine your child's tonsils and adenoids. If they are enlarged, you may be referred to an ear, nose, and throat doctor. If your child has restless legs before or during sleep, his iron levels should be tested.

Your child's doctor may treat him personally or refer you to another trained professional such as a child psychiatrist, child psychologist, or counselor for a diagnosis. One of these experts should rule out other disorders that may cause similar symptoms, including anxiety, depression, behavioral problems, learning or language disorders, autism, tics, and sleep disorders.

In order to understand how doctors typically manage children with ODD, let's first discuss traditional treatment, which may involve therapy or prescription medication.

TRADITIONAL TREATMENT

Experts recommend that a child with ODD be treated initially with therapy, which can be quite effective. Medication should be the second choice if therapy does not prove effective and problems at home and school persist. For younger children, parent training is recommended. For older children for whom therapy was not helpful, and in whom other behavioral disorders are present, such as ADHD or depression, prescription medication may be chosen to alleviate these symptoms.

Tips for Parents

If your child has both ODD and ADHD, you will want to follow the tips below for managing ODD as well as those for managing ADHD. (See page 24.) If you are planning on seeing a therapist but have not yet done so, the following approaches to managing your child's ODD may be beneficial in the meantime.

- Acknowledge that you understand why your child is upset.
- Assign your child family chores he can successfully complete.
- Be specific about behavior that won't be tolerated.
- Explain the consequences of misbehavior to your child and be consistent in following up with these consequences.
- If tantrums are more common when he's tired, work on increasing his sleep time.
- If your child throws a fit or temper tantrum, walk away and ignore him.
- If your child's behavior is worse before meals, give him a high protein snack.
- Make sure your instructions are clear and appropriate for your child's age.
- Reward your child when he does things without complaint, either with verbal praise or tokens he can accumulate to receive a prize.
- Set clear rules.
- Spend time together doing things you both enjoy.
- Stay calm when you ask your child to do a task.
- Use quiet time or a time-out to calm your child.
- When possible avoid stressful, frustrating activities.

Changing how you respond to your child is not easy but it is important. He may get worse before he gets better. Keep a record of the changes you make, and note which ones work and which ones don't. Share this information with your child's therapist.

In addition, addressing nutritional and lifestyle issues, as suggested in Part Two, may be very helpful.

Therapy

Therapy can be very helpful in reducing or eliminating your child's meltdowns, improving his angry reactions to everyday incidents, and getting him to accept rules at home and school.

Therapy for ODD may include psychotherapy, family therapy, or parent management training. How your child is treated depends on many things, including age, severity of symptoms, and how much your child will cooperate.

Family Therapy

Family therapy teaches an ODD child's family members how to cope with his behavior and communicate effectively with him. A central tenet in family therapy is consistency, in that all family members should respond in a similar way to the ODD child. Everyone should remain calm and collected in the face of ODD behavior.

Parent Management Training

Parent management training teaches parents methods to alter their actions with their ODD child in a positive manner. It suggests better ways to respond to their child—ways that do not include anger or threats. A therapist shows parents how to reward good behavior and what the appropriate consequences or punishments might be for negative behavior. This therapy may be conducted in a group of parents whose children all have ODD symptoms. This scenario allows parents to role play as their children and learn how to respond effectively from other members. What works with one child may also work for another. Just being around other parents who are experiencing similar problems can help a parent of a child with ODD to feel less isolated and alone.

Psychotherapy

Psychotherapy, or *talk therapy,* is a form of therapy in which problem behaviors, feelings, and thoughts are discussed and changed through conversations with a therapist. A psychotherapist can help a child to develop better coping, social, and problem-solving skills, and teach the child how to express and control anger. She may use play therapy, in which your child will act out everyday scenarios with the therapist, to help him cope better with these situations.

Medication

There is no specific medication approved by the FDA for ODD, and doctors do not consider medication the first line of action, which remains therapy. Nevertheless, a majority of children with ODD respond to low doses of drugs that have been approved in children with other behavioral disorders, including ADHD, conduct disorder, depression, and anxiety. It is crucial, of course, to find a doctor who is familiar and experienced in using these drugs to treat ODD.

Antidepressants

If your child suffers from depression and ODD, antidepressant medication may help to treat both conditions. Studies show that the antidepressant fluoxetine (Prozac) and other antidepressants can improve associated ODD.

Antipsychotics

Risperidone is an antipsychotic drug, which is a medication used to treat individuals who experience breaks with reality, or psychosis. This drug is typically used to manage schizophrenia but seems to improve symptoms of ODD as well. Although ODD is not linked to psychotic behavior, studies show that risperidone alleviates behavioral symptoms in children with ODD—both with and without ADHD. The doctor who prescribes this medication will want to monitor your child's weight, blood pressure, glucose, lipid profile, and A1C, so regular doctor visits will be required. Many doctors recommend only short-term use of these medications.

Stimulants

As you know, ADHD is a disorder that commonly occurs alongside ODD. Stimulants are the most widely studied medications for ADHD, and they are generally regarded as most effective in ODD children in the treatment of core ADHD symptoms. Methylphenidate and dextroamphetamine are the most commonly used stimulants for ODD. Stimulants can lower aggression and improve attention, which can help children to focus more successfully on therapy. (See page 25 in Chapter 1 for more information on simulants and other medications for ADHD.)

COMPLEMENTARY TREATMENT

There is no reason you cannot complement traditional therapy or medication with other methods of treatment. Several types of alternative therapies have proven capable of improving the symptoms of children with behavioral disorders. Part Two of this book describes these medication-free ways to treat ODD in greater detail. These options include:

- **addressing environmental factors.** In some children, ADHD and ODD may be linked to a sensitivity to things they breathe in from the air, or to which they are exposed in their environments, including natural substances such as pollen, mold, and animal dander; chemicals such as those present in tobacco smoke, cleaning supplies, perfumes and other scented items, gas fumes, and wet paint; and toxic substances such as heavy metals, pesticides, and plastics.

- **helpful programs and devices.** If your child likes to play video games, there are video games approved to treat inattentiveness and impulsivity. (See page 228.) You will have to ask your doctor about them, though, as they may require a prescription. The question is whether or not your child would cooperate in learning how to play these games.

- **lifestyle changes.** A child's behavior and school work can benefit greatly from lifestyle changes. Regular exercise improves problems with attention, grades in school, aggression, depression, and sleep. Getting high-quality sleep improves behavior and school performance. Cooperation on the part of the child is necessary, of course.

- **nutrition.** Micronutrient supplements of vitamins, minerals, and fatty acids have shown to improve behavior and learning in children with ADHD and ODD.

Addressing environmental factors, using supplements, enforcing good sleep practices, and encouraging exercise are all ways that parents can help their children to manage their ODD symptoms—and there are scientific studies to support the effectiveness of each treatment mentioned. Keep in mind, however, that dietary interventions will work best if the whole family embraces the recommended changes. Moreover, as video game therapy can be relatively expensive, you should try to determine if your child will actually use a particular game before you purchase it.

CONCLUSION

Parenting a child with ODD is a challenge for even the best, most well-intentioned parent, but coping with a child's defiance and opposition on a daily basis can be exhausting. As you have learned, ODD is associated with different risk factors, including abnormal brain structure, problems with body chemistry, nutritional deficiencies, harmful environmental exposures, and genetics. Fortunately, therapy, the most effective way to help your child, can make you a better parent and help your child to control his feelings and actions. If therapy isn't enough, there are medications that may help. Of course, don't forget to investigate complementary therapies, such as lifestyle changes and helpful programs, which are discussed further in Part Two.

ODD is very treatable, and the good news is that mild ODD often gets better as the affected child gets older. Follow-up studies have shown that the symptoms of ODD usually improve within three years in approximately two-thirds of children diagnosed with ODD. Unfortunately, about 30 percent of children become worse and eventually develop conduct disorder, which is discussed in the next chapter.

3.

Conduct Disorder

Conduct disorder, or *CD,* is one of the more serious behavioral disorders. It should not be confused with the conduct "problems" a child might have, such as not doing what he is told or his being unable to sit still. According to the diagnostic criteria of the American Psychiatric Association, children and teens with conduct disorder may show repetitive and persistent aggression to people and animals, or engage in destruction of property, deceitfulness, or stealing. Symptoms of CD may be mild, moderate, or severe.

Like ADHD, CD is much more common in males than it is in females. The rate in the general population ranges from 6 percent to 16 percent in boys, and from 2 percent to 9 percent in girls. Children and teens with CD are often diagnosed with ADHD and ODD, too, and may also suffer from severe depression, anxiety, or substance abuse. In addition, as mentioned in this book's introduction, conduct disorder is often diagnosed in African Americans, Native Americans, and Hispanic Americans without these children having received proper behavioral assessments.

There are two main types of CD, which are categorized according to when symptoms begin. *Childhood-onset CD* usually begins around the age of five or six but before the age of ten. *Adolescent conduct disorder* may start as childhood-onset CD and continue into the teen years, or it may begin in adolescence.

According to experts, in about 40 percent of cases of childhood-onset CD, the child develops into a troubled teen and then an adult with an antisocial personality. On the bright side, about 60 percent of cases have more promising futures. With the proper help, your child may grow up to be a well-adjusted adult, hold down a good job, have a family, and contribute to his community.

To see if your child meets the criteria for conduct disorder, please complete the following questionnaire, which is based on information from the CDC and American Psychiatric Association.

QUESTIONNAIRE

As you complete the following questionnaire, evaluate the symptoms that have been present for at least six months. In addition, the symptoms should be present in more than one setting (e.g., home, school, with relatives or friends, etc.)

Table 3.1. Conduct Disorder Questionnaire

Symptom	Frequency			
Conduct Disorder	**Never**	**Occasionally**	**Somewhat Often**	**All the Time**
How often does your child bully, threaten, or intimidate others?	0	1	2	3
How often does your child delight in bullying?	0	1	2	3
How often does your child start physical fights?	0	1	2	3
How often has your child used a weapon that could cause serious physical harm to others, such as a bat, rock, hammer, or brick?	0	1	2	3
How often is your child physically cruel to people or animals?	0	1	2	3
How often has your child stolen from a victim while hurting them?	0	1	2	3
How often has your child forced someone into sexual activity?	0	1	2	3
How often does your child show no genuine remorse after an aggressive episode?	0	1	2	3
How often does your child deliberately engage in setting fires with the intention of causing damage?	0	1	2	3

Conduct Disorder	Never	Occasionally	Somewhat Often	All the Time
How often does your child deliberately destroy other people's property?	0	1	2	3
How often has your child broken into someone else's building, house, or car?	0	1	2	3
How often has your child lied to obtain goods or favors to avoid obligations?	0	1	2	3
How often has your child stolen items without breaking and entering or confronting the victim? (For example, shoplifting.)	0	1	2	3
How often does your child stay out at night despite parental objections?	0	1	2	3
How often has your child run away from home?	0	1	2	3
How often does your child stay away from home?	0	1	2	3

EVALUATING YOUR RESPONSES

If most of your answers fall into the "never" or "occasionally" category, then your child probably does not have conduct disorder. If you answered "somewhat often" or "all the time" to three questions in the past twelve months, with at least one of these answers occurring in the past six months, then your child may have conduct disorder.

You probably noticed that some of the questions are aimed at older children and teens while other questions explore the behavior of both older and younger children. Keep in mind, most children will show instances of poor judgment and bad behavior occasionally. Children with CD, however, break rules repeatedly, are always aggressive, and show no regard for others.

TYPES

As stated earlier, there are two types of CD, which are defined by the age symptoms arise. Childhood-onset CD can start as young as two years of age, but it usually begins around the age of five or six, and before age ten. After the age of ten, the condition is known as adolescent conduct disorder, which is the focus of this chapter.

There are two subgroups of young children with childhood-onset CD. The first is characterized as *limited,* as it gradually improves and may disappear by age ten. The other is called *persistent,* as it starts around age five but persists into the teenage years or even into adulthood. Experts often have difficulty predicting which group a child may be in and what his future may hold. Therefore, all these children should be diagnosed, evaluated, and treated with some form of therapy as soon as possible.

There are also two similar subgroups associated with adolescent conduct disorder. In the first group, adolescent conduct disorder may be *limited* to the teen years and improve with age and maturation. In the second group, some teens with adolescent CD continue to have *persistent* symptoms of antisocial behavior into adulthood.

Those with adolescent CD are as aggressive to people and animals, destructive of property, and prone to lying and stealing as children with childhood CD are, but these teenagers may also have other serious symptoms, which may include substance abuse, the commission of minor to serious crimes, gang participation, and dropping out of school. Even if their CD improves, they are often left with the problems of a criminal record and a lack of education.

Some adolescent CD cases persist past the teenage years and into adulthood, becoming what is termed "antisocial behavior." This term refers to actions that harm or a lack of consideration for the wellbeing of others. Antisocial behavior includes a wide range of behaviors, including starting fights, bullying others, acting recklessly toward others, and even the commission of serious crimes. A person with antisocial behavior displays actions that are similar to those of a child with CD. The important difference between the two is that the person with antisocial behavior is larger, stronger, and more determined to do a lot of damage to property and people.

Next, we will discuss definitions of terms used in describing the behavior of children with CD. Understanding these symptoms will help you identify which behaviors are present in your child and help you to communicate with teachers, psychologists, and doctors.

SYMPTOMS

According to the experts who compiled the *Diagnostic and Statistical Manual of Mental Disorders*, there are three levels of severity of CD symptoms. In mild cases, few if any conduct problems are present beyond those required to make a diagnosis. The conduct problems cause relatively minor harm to others. These problems might include symptoms such as lying, staying out too late, or breaking other rules.

In moderate cases, many more conduct problems are present beyond those needed for a diagnosis. These issues are intermediate in severity, between mild with little harm to others and severe with considerable harm to others. Examples include the hitting of another child or the abuse of an animal without leaving marks or bruises.

In severe cases, many of these conduct problems are obviously present. The worst of these symptoms are repeated time and again, in spite of warning the child to stop. Understanding these criteria will help you know where your child may appear on the spectrum of CD symptoms.

Many times dealing with a child's bad behavior blinds parents to the individual actions that their child exhibits. All they see is a child acting badly. It is critical, however, to recognize the individual symptoms of CD as early as possible. These behaviors show themselves in several different ways. When you discuss your child's symptoms with a teacher or doctor, it is important to understand what each of these signs means.

Abuse

Abuse may be described as the intentionally and persistently cruel or violent treatment of a person or animal. When a child is physically abusive, he may hit, bite, or throw things at others with the intention of hurting them. He may kick or strike another person with a hard object.

As for animal abuse, he may enjoy teasing an animal, which becomes more and more intense until he actually physically harms the family pet, a neighbor's dog, or even a wild animal he has captured. After he has harmed it, he may deliberately kill it. All these examples of abuse are followed by no remorse or recognition that he has done a bad, cruel act. In fact, he may be delighted by his actions. This type of behavior should set off an alarm that something is terribly wrong.

Aggression

Aggression refers to hostile or violent behavior. It may be seen when a child hits other children or physically strikes out at playmates, siblings, parents, caregivers, or teachers. A child may throw things at family members or classmates. He may deliberately break something that is valuable to others. The child may also act aggressively toward a pet, resulting in harm to—or even the death of—the animal. Neighbors may complain of his aggressive and destructive behavior outside the home. He may become more aggressive after viewing a violent movie or TV show, or after playing a violent video game.

Bullying

Bullying refers to the act of harming, coercing, or intimidating others. A child may bully his siblings, neighborhood children, or children at school. Bullying may take the form of physical abuse, name-calling, or the use of social media to harass another child. A bully seems to enjoy intimidating other children.

Deceitfulness

Deceitfulness is the act of not telling the truth either to avoid blame or to blame others for a misdeed. A child may break an object at home or school and then lie that it was someone else who did it, intending to get that person in trouble. A child may lie about where he is spending his free time or the fact that he has been skipping school.

Destruction of Property

Destruction of property describes the deliberate act of causing damage to an item for no apparent reason. A child may break his toys or those of his siblings. He may punch or kick holes in the wall. He may knock over lamps or other breakable objects. When playing with matches, he may deliberately set a fire.

Lack of Empathy

Lack of empathy refers to the inability to demonstrate compassion in a situation that merits a reaction of concern. In other words, a child could seriously hurt another child but show no remorse. His sister's pet might die, but he would show no sympathy toward her.

Stealing

Stealing is the taking of that which belongs to someone else without that person's permission. A child who steals may take money from a parent's wallet without permission, shoplift at the store, or slip someone else's electronic device into his own pocket.

Violation of Rules

A violation of rules refers to when a child knows the rules at home and school but chooses not to follow them. He may know he must be home by a certain hour but arrives hours late, not concerned about how worried his parents or caregivers may be. In school, he knows what time classes start but is deliberately late. He knows hitting is against the rules but hits family members and classmates anyway. He knows he should do his homework before he plays, but instead he plays a video game or turns the TV on to a show he's not supposed to watch. While this type of behavior is not uncommon in many non-CD children, when it is seen with a number of the other traits recently listed, it should set off alarms.

These traits may be hard to observe in preschoolers. However, as a child begins his schooling, a pattern of these behaviors may become all too evident. If the child also has ADHD or ODD, his actions can be overwhelming. By identifying these traits early in your child, there are a number of things you can do to help.

OBSERVING YOUR CHILD'S BEHAVIOR

No one knows your child better than you do. Observations you have made since he was an infant can help you to identify early problem behavior and the situations in which they occur. These observations can help you to recognize triggers that make him angry, destructive, or hostile to you and other members of your family. These triggers could

Conduct Disorder in Preschoolers?

The symptoms of childhood-onset CD usually start at age five or six, but they may begin earlier in a few children. Some children with CD are out of control as early as daycare and preschool. In fact, some parents may have been told that their child was no longer welcome at preschool—"expelled" at age three or four for hitting or hurting other children.

Approximately 3 to 7 percent of preschool children meet the criteria for CD. In a study of preschool-aged children, parents completed questionnaires about their child's behavior at age three and again three years later. Doctors studied 160 preschoolers, both boys and girls, who showed symptoms of CD at age three and then again three years later. They discovered that in many children the early symptoms persisted as the child grew older, with the child now meeting the criteria for CD. This finding suggests that a preschool child can show early signs of CD.

Some forms of bad behavior were observed in all the children studied. These behaviors included breaking things, telling lies, stealing, and loss of temper. The children who appeared to have early CD, however, had more severe forms of these behaviors. Some bullied and threatened their classmates, started fights, damaged property, or stole items and then lied about having done so. These actions seemed to be precursors of conduct disorder once they were older.

If these behaviors describe your young child, report them to his doctor and ask to be referred to an expert who has successfully diagnosed and treated young children with CD. While medication may not be appropriate for a three-year-old, behavioral therapy and some of the interventions found in Part Two could be quite helpful.

be interactions with a particular family member, a food he has eaten, or a chemical he was exposed to right before he acted out. Buy a notebook and record all your memories and observations of his negative behavior.

Equally important is what happens in school. Your teacher has a completely different view of your child in a school setting, which includes many other children. Let us first look at what information you can gather at home, and then at which behaviors may be observed in a school environment.

Family Life

What you witness at home is important, but it must be noted that your child's problematic behavior may also be due to a number of reasons other than CD. Try to step back from your home scene and observe your child, family, and surroundings as objectively as you can. Consider your child's family history. Do you or your partner have any relatives who suffer from behavioral or psychological problems? Do any of your relatives have CD? Is there excessive drinking taking place at home? Is there the use of illegal drugs? Are there historical issues in your family of racial, cultural, or socioeconomic trauma, which may have resulted in your or an immediate family member's physical or emotional trauma negatively influencing your child? Are there any episodes early in your child's life of separation or abandonment? So many different factors can affect a child.

Think about and record your child's health history. Has he ever had a severe head injury from a blow or a fall? Has he ever had a brain infection? Damage to the brain can cause later changes in behavior. If you answered yes to either of these questions, ask the doctors who treated your child to send his records to the doctor who will be diagnosing your child for his behavioral problems.

Of your family members, are there any particular ones who trigger your child's bad behavior? Could there be mental, physical, or sexual abuse in the home? Note particular situations in which he acts out more than in other environments. Also write down if there are times of day when he acts out more than others, such as before meals, after meals, or after snacks. Answering all these questions will help you understand what may be going on at home. If the problems persist, you might contact a healthcare professional to have your child evaluated, which we will discuss later in this chapter. Remember to bring your notes.

School

Now let's consider what goes on in your child's classroom, where he spends about one-third of his day. His teacher's observations will be extremely important, as teachers have a vastly different setting in which to view how a child interacts with other children. Classroom rules will be different from those at home. A different adult is in charge for the purpose of learning. It's important to know how your child copes with these factors. Your child's actions in school are also important to record in your notebook, starting with what you remember about his introduction to a classroom in nursery school or kindergarten, and so on until the present.

Different schools have different ways to consult with parents. Your first contact with your child's school might have been through parent-teacher conferences. Your child's teacher may have called you to set up a meeting with her and the principal if a serious event has taken place. If the school has a school counselor, this counselor may also attend the meeting. Bring your notes about your child's behavior at home to the meeting. Then listen carefully to what you are told in the meeting about your child's behavior and learning ability. Keep in mind that over the years, these professionals have worked with dozens of children like yours. As they describe your child's issues, you may think to yourself that your child has very similar problems at home.

You may also want to discuss your child's yearly test scores on standardized tests and how he compares with other children his age. Ask about his grades and whether he is doing poorly or even failing. If his teacher reports that he doesn't listen to instructions, turn in his papers on time, complete his assigned homework, or sit still at his desk, he may also have ADHD, a learning disorder, such as dyslexia, or a vision or hearing problem. Each of these issues should be assessed by a medical professional. It might also be a good idea to ask if the school counselor (or the school district's psychologist) could meet with you and your child and test him for learning disabilities, ADHD, and CD.

Ask the teacher if your child's behavior differs during the day. Is it worse in the morning, just before lunch, or after lunch? Perhaps he did not eat enough breakfast and his brain is starving. Does he yawn a lot? Does he appear sleepy and tired, indicating he has not had enough sleep? These are pieces of information you need to know so you can make changes at home.

If there is appreciable improvement in your child during the times of day when he is outside the building, it could mean he is being exposed to a toxin inside the building, such as mold, cleaning products, or pesticides, which is affecting him.

Ask what their plans are to control his behavior and help him learn. Are there other classes with fewer children per teacher that might be more appropriate for him? If they think he has learning disabilities, ask that he be tested and possibly placed in a special education classroom, where teachers have the training to teach children who have learning or behavioral problems.

If it is recommended that your child see his doctor to start him on medication, then schedule an appointment. It is an excellent idea to get a doctor's medical assessment and receive a definitive diagnosis, and then to find out if behavioral therapy or medication might be beneficial.

Ask your child's teacher what your child enjoys doing at school. Are there any areas of learning in which he excels? For example, perhaps he's talented at math but struggles with all his other subjects. Does he like computer activities? Are there more lessons that can be taught by computer for him, such as math, reading, or science exercises? Does he have artistic or musical talent? Does he do well in sports? All these factors might be important to know.

Be sure to thank everyone in the meeting for their observations and time. These are people with whom you want to have good, positive relationships. Nevertheless, try not to lose sight of the fact that you are your child's best advocate. If for any reason you get a nagging feeling that you need to do more to explore the situation for your child, follow this instinct. Do not ignore it. Listening to your inner voice is of critical importance, especially for parents from underserved communities.

Hopefully, your child has a caring, outstanding, and observant teacher and a counselor who will go the extra mile to help. When you get home, write down in your notebook all you learned from the meeting.

Is Your Child Eligible for Special Education?

Surprisingly, a diagnosis of CD alone does not entitle your child to special education. However, if he were to have ADHD, ODD, depression, anxiety, or learning disabilities along with CD, then he would become eligible. Very few children have CD without other behavioral disorders, though, so most are eligible. If he doesn't qualify under IDEA (see page 14), in which an Individualized Education Plan, or IEP, is drawn up for him, he may qualify under section 504 of the Rehabilitation Act for educational services designed to meet his individual needs.

Assist school personnel in making sure your child receives the opportunities to learn in a classroom best suited to his needs. Show your concern and desire to help both them and your child.

Now that you have recorded your observations and those of your child's teacher, you may realize that similar symptoms you see at home are also evident at school. It may be time to get professional help.

At a certain point, because of his behavior, you may also find yourself frustrated and angry enough to strike out physically at your child, but remember that corporal punishment can actually cause more harm than good. (See the inset titled "Corporal Punishment" on page 27.)

RISK FACTORS

So, what could be causing your child's behavior? Why doesn't he act like his brothers and sisters or other children in the neighborhood or at school? While there are no exact causes of CD known at this time, there are several known risk factors.

Brain Abnormalities

Some children with conduct disorder have brain abnormalities not seen in healthy children, which may contribute to their behavior. If your child also has ADHD, he may have other, different brain abnormalities associated with that disorder. (See page 15.)

Not surprisingly, a brain injury caused by a blow to the head or serious fall may also cause behavioral problems years later due to permanent brain damage. This type of injury can lead to headaches, dizziness, fatigue, depression, irritability, and memory problems. If areas of the brain that regulate emotions, impulses, and anger (the limbic system) are affected, these may have significant effects on impulsive behavior and even violence. If your child has ever experienced a severe blow to the head or had a brain infection, it is important to inform his doctor of this history and see that she gets records of the event from the treating doctor and hospital.

Brain scans have found other abnormalities in the brains of children with CD that are not present in healthy children. The brain contains areas that are referred to as *grey matter* and *white matter.* Grey matter is made up of numerous brain cells. It makes up about 40 percent of the volume of the brain, is slightly grey in color, and processes information that controls movement, memory, and emotions. Imaging studies have discovered a lower volume of grey matter in children with CD.

Brain scans of some youths with CD have also shown abnormalities in white matter, especially in the largest white matter area called the *corpus callosum.* This area interconnects the right and left halves of the brain. Unlike grey matter, white matter contains relatively few brain cells and is composed mainly of white myelinated (insulated) fibers called *axons,* which connect brain cells to other brain cells. White matter is found deeper in the brain than grey matter and links the brain's emotional centers together. Researchers report that these differences may be responsible for callous behavior, including a lack of empathy and a disregard for the feelings of others.

Neurotransmitters are chemicals that help brain cells communicate with each other. They may also be affected in the brains of children with CD. For example, serotonin is one of the chemicals neurons produce to send signals between nerve cells. In some children with CD, serotonin brain levels are lower than those of healthy children. This fact is important because serotonin is a brain neurotransmitter that affects mood and social behavior, appetite and digestion, sleep, memory, and sexual desire.

Your child's brain may have one or more abnormalities that contribute to his behavioral problems, but other factors may play a role as well.

Diet

A poor diet can lead to all sorts of behavioral and health problems. First, poor nutrition in utero and during infancy and the early years of life is an important risk factor for CD later in life. There is also a strong link between diet quality and other mental health disorders in children and adolescents.

The brain requires several important nutrients to make and maintain its billions of nerve cells and fibers, and to manufacture brain chemicals. These nutrients include multiple vitamins and minerals; glucose, which is the sugar your body uses for energy; particular fats; and amino acids, which are the building blocks of proteins. Many modern ailments, including brain disorders, are caused by poor eating habits.

Familial and Social Factors

Familial and social factors are among the strongest and most consistent elements that influence CD. The parents of a child with CD may have separated or divorced, or the father may have deserted the family or even be in jail. Alcohol and drug use may be routinely used by one or both parents or another household member. There may be physical or verbal abuse in the family, as well as a lack of support and consistent discipline. One parent may be suffering from a mental disorder. Instead of helping a child, poor parenting practices also contribute to CD symptoms, and can even make them worse.

Abusive behavior in the home is also a risk factor for CD. Abusive behavior could include *spousal abuse,* which involves parents or caregivers and their relationships with each other. It may include *physical abuse,* resulting in bodily injury of the child or others. It may involve *sexual abuse,* which refers to unwanted, nonconsensual sexual contact. Finally, it may include *verbal abuse* of the child, which involves yelling, swearing, and repeated verbal harassment. Even silence may be used as an abusive tool against a child. Neglect of a child in providing appropriate food, clothing, or shelter is also child abuse. While any of these factors may be all too common in low-income neighborhoods, dysfunctional family behavior can be found on any economic level and in any neighborhood.

In some circumstances, a child may be cared for by relatives or foster parents who move him around from place to place, which can mean a new school and the loss of friendships and relationships, the difficulties of which may be associated with CD. The effects of a chaotic home, a violent neighborhood, or poor parenting on such children are not clear. After all, there are many poor, abused, or neglected children who do not develop CD, while some children from healthy, functional homes do.

Genetics

A small number of genes that influence conduct have been identified. According to a study of a large group of adopted children, only 4 percent of these children had a birth parent who had committed a serious criminal offense. This same 4 percent of children, however, would end up being responsible for 70 percent of the crimes later attributed to the entire group of adopted kids. This statistic may demonstrate the large role genetics may play in behavior.

A mental illness in a parent may affect their child in two ways. First, if a parent has a mental disorder that is partly genetic in origin, the child may have inherited those genes. Second, the erratic, abnormal actions of the mental disorder in a parent may also contribute to the child's behavioral problems—a double whammy.

If your child has CD and you discover that CD runs in your family, this realization doesn't mean your child is simply a bad seed and nothing can be done about it. It is important to understand that many factors can influence the way in which genetics play a role in a child's behavior.

Prenatal Factors and Birth Complications

Pregnancy and delivery problems are also common in children with CD. Risk factors include low birth weight of a child, a mother's poor diet during pregnancy, and exposure of a child to heavy metals such as lead before or after birth. A pregnant woman's tobacco or marijuana use and alcohol consumption may also contribute to her child being affected by CD. Researchers have also suggested, however, that the risk of CD may be linked to a mother's genetic predisposition to this behavioral disorder rather than to any brain damage from these lifestyle factors, or it may be linked to both a mother's genetics and her habits during pregnancy.

ASSOCIATED DISORDERS

ADHD and ODD are both risk factors for CD. Some experts think that ODD may actually lead to CD—a child's verbal abuse becomes physical, aggressive abuse as he ages. Almost 50 percent of children with ADHD could also be diagnosed with CD and ODD according to experts. The reasons for this statistic include common factors such as impulsivity, poor self-regulation, and temperament. Understanding and treating ADHD, ODD, and other behavior problems may help your child with his CD symptoms. The following percentages represent how many children with CD are also bothered by other disorders.

- 80 percent of children with CD also have ADHD. (See Chapter 1 on page 7.)
- 10 to 30 percent of children with CD also have ODD. (See Chapter 2 on page 31.)

- 50 percent of children with CD also have depression. (See Chapter 7 on page 141.)
- 40 percent of children with CD also have anxiety disorder. (See Chapter 5 on page 101.)

As you can see, the percentages of children with CD who have another behavioral or mental disorder are high, complicating the care of CD children. The good news is that treating one of these associated disorders may significantly improve CD symptoms as well. (See Chapter 7 on page 141 for more information on the physical or mental disorders that may accompany CD.)

DIAGNOSIS

If your child has CD but you are not familiar with this disorder, the only thing you may see is your child misbehaving. Teachers and school psychologists are more likely than parents to identify an established behavioral disorder through witnessing a child's actions. It might be the school psychologist or school counselor who recommends that parents seek outside professional help. They might recommend having your child be seen by his doctor, an outside child psychologist, or a psychiatrist.

Who can make the definitive diagnosis of CD? There are several possibilities. The first is your family doctor, who perhaps has known you and your child for several years. Tell her about your child's behavior at home and the information you have learned from his teacher and counselor. Has she had other patients like your son? Would she feel comfortable treating your child herself, or can she refer you to another professional who has had more training and experience? She will likely know the professionals in your town who are best qualified to help your child. These professionals could include a *pediatrician,* who specializes in diagnosing and treating children's physical and mental health; a *child psychiatrist,* who is specially trained in mental and behavioral problems of children; or a *pediatric neurologist,* who specializes in brain and nervous system problems in children. All three are qualified to make a diagnosis, recommend behavioral therapies, and prescribe medications.

School Counselors and Psychologists

School counselors and school psychologists can play important roles in helping teachers to understand and deal with troubled children who act out in class and seem unable or unwilling to learn. They can also serve as a bridge between school and family. While most schools have at least one counselor on staff, they may share a school psychologist with several other schools, serving a population of five hundred to seven hundred students. Therefore, many school counselors and psychologists may not have the time to help children with complicated problems such as CD.

Although school counselors and school psychologists may collaborate with each other to help a particular student, they are different and have different jobs and backgrounds. School counselors promote a student's academic, social, and emotional development, either one-on-one or in small groups. On the other hand, school psychologists can perform these duties but have specialized training to address mental health and behavioral problems.

School counselors and school psychologists have different educational backgrounds. A school counselor has to earn a bachelor's degree in school counseling, psychology, or education, followed by a master's degree in school counseling. School psychologists must earn a bachelor's degree in psychology, education, or a related field. Next they complete a certain number of graduate classes to earn an education specialist degree, or they can complete more classes and training to earn a doctoral degree in education.

Schools across the country vary greatly in the services they offer. Ask your child's teacher or principal about those offered by your school and your school district. These services are free and can be quite helpful.

Each of these doctors may start with a physical exam to look for signs of any physical disorders that may contribute to his CD symptoms. She may order lab tests and, on occasion, brain scans. She will take a medical and behavioral history of your child and his relatives. She may ask you to complete questionnaires like the one at the beginning of this chapter. She may also give your child various tests to assess the presence of behavioral or learning problems.

Based on all this information, she may diagnose your child with CD and perhaps other disorders. Then she can recommend behavioral therapy and psychological counseling by skilled colleagues who will work with you and your child. She may decide to prescribe medications that often improve CD symptoms. Finally, she can send a report to your child's teachers and principal so that your child may qualify for certain school services.

On the other hand, your doctor may recommend a *child psychologist,* who can also diagnose CD and treat your child with behavioral therapy.

Simples Changes to Try

Here are some simple, basic changes you can make at home. Choose the ones that seem appropriate for you, your child, and other family members. You can report your success and failures to your child's doctor.

- Although it may be difficult, during moments of bad behavior try to stay calm, cool-headed, and under control.
- Avoid harsh physical discipline. It doesn't improve a child's behavior and may make it worse.
- Eliminate or reduce the time your child spends viewing violent TV shows, movies, or video games. These can reinforce the idea that violent behavior is acceptable and appropriate. After watching a violent show, movie, or game, a child will often exhibit more aggressive behavior.
- Engage in physical exercise with your child through fast walking, jogging, or dancing to music of your child's choice.
- Have a code word that you and your child can use to tell him to calm down. If he responds to the word and calms down, then he will receive praise and perhaps a small reward. The reward will depend on the age of the child.
- If there are multiple adults in your household who set rules, consistency among caregivers is important.
- Keep a close eye on your child's activities.

While this person does not have a medical degree and cannot prescribe medication, she has a doctorate in child psychology in addition to both an internship and residency. Undoubtedly, she has seen many children like your child. She will interview parents or caregivers and the child. She may also ask you to complete several questionnaires.

Similar to a medical doctor, a child psychologist may take a history of your child's behavior since birth and ask if other relatives have a history of behavioral or mental disorders. If she hasn't already received information from your child's teacher and counselor, she will ask to see

- Participation in sports may reduce symptoms of CD, as exercise may make your child less aggressive by altering brain chemicals. Speak to the sport's coordinator or coach regarding your child's behavior.
- Reduce family stress by taking time to choose an activity for the whole family that is fun and relaxing for everyone. For yourself, practice deep breathing and relaxation exercises, which you can find online. Get enough sleep. Save your energy for things you can control.
- Seek support from organizations such as the National Alliance on Mental Health, Big Brothers Big Sisters of America, and school or church groups that offer positive interactions and model appropriate behavior. Adults in these organizations may help your child feel welcome, appreciated, and admired, and may establish strong relationships with him. Make sure you speak to the program's coordinator regarding the behavior your child may exhibit. These are things your child may not be able to get currently at home or school, where adults are only critical.
- Set aside fifteen minutes every day for parent or caregiver and child to play together. The child chooses the activity, which might be playing catch, reading or drawing together, playing a game, or watching an appropriate TV show or sporting event.
- Stay positive. Catch your child doing something positive and give him praise.

Let your doctor know what you have tried and whether or not it was successful in calming your child down or improving your relationship with him.

their observations and any learning tests your child has already taken. She may consult with a medical doctor, who can prescribe medication in addition to the behavioral therapies.

What about costs? Both psychologists and psychiatrists are expensive (psychiatrists more so than psychologists) because of their schooling and training. Check with your insurance company or Medicaid to see how much of these costs they will cover.

Getting the definitive diagnosis of CD along with other accompanying disorders will open doors to school services like special education. Therefore, it's important to find the right doctor to help you and your child who will also work with your school. (See Chapter 8 on page 153.) Once you have the diagnosis you can talk to your doctors about ways to treat your child.

TRADITIONAL TREATMENT

Your doctor has a couple of tools in her toolbox to improve your child's troubling behavior. Let's start with traditional treatments that are well studied and regarded by experts in child behavior. Your child needs all the help he can get and may need a couple of different types of therapies, including behavioral therapy, medication, and natural treatments.

Therapy

Therapy for CD may include psychotherapy, cognitive behavioral therapy, family therapy, parent training classes, or peer group therapy. Similar to ODD treatment, the methods used to treat your child depend on many things, including his age, the severity of his symptoms, and how much he will cooperate.

Psychotherapy

Psychotherapy, or *talk therapy*, is a treatment in which problem behaviors, feelings, and thoughts are discussed and changed through conversations with a therapist. The therapist also works with relatives and teachers to change the patient's environment, which influences his abnormal behavior. While waiting for your appointment with a therapist you could try to employ the changes suggested in the inset on page 66.

Cognitive Behavioral Therapy

Cognitive behavioral therapy is a form of psychotherapy in which negative patterns of thought about yourself and your world are challenged and changed to improve your behavior. Doctors who treat children with CD have learned that these kids feel threatened by many situations and react with aggression and anger even if there is no threat. For example, if your child views his peers as threatening, he may physically attack them. Changing his view of these interactions will make him less likely to overreact and thus improve his behavior.

Family Therapy

Family therapy is a form of psychological counseling that involves all family members. It focuses on improving communication between family members. Family therapy views an individual child disorder as part of family disturbances. A therapist may interact with the whole family but may also work with groups within the family.

As the family sessions go on, you may learn that there is a family member who abuses your child either physically, emotionally, or sexually, or abuses drugs and alcohol. If this person is unable to change, you may have to consider other options. Ask this person to either change his behavior through counseling or leave your house, or take your child and live in a quieter, more peaceful home. Your therapist can help you with these very difficult decisions.

Parent Training Classes

Parent training classes for parents or caregivers teach better ways to discipline children. If you find yourself yelling at or hitting your child because he misbehaves, parent training classes will help you to find other, better ways to discipline him. Ask your doctor to recommend a class. Often behavioral clinics or university hospitals will offer such classes at reduced rates. Take advantage of these.

If parent training classes are advised, try to find a course that reflects the demographics and history of your family, if possible. This advice is particularly relevant for children of cultural backgrounds that are associated with high rates of behavioral disorders while also being underserved by the healthcare establishment. The perspectives and needs of an African American family, for example, which has lived under a specific set of socioeconomic conditions for generations, will likely be different than those of families from other backgrounds.

Peer Group Therapy

Peer group therapy with other children like your child may help him to develop better social and interpersonal skills. In peer group therapy, children learn problem-solving techniques, using games and stories from real-life situations to learn self-control. Friendships may form that can help your child with social skills. These groups may be offered through a behavioral clinic, university, or medical center. Ask your doctor to recommend one that is appropriate for your child. (Similar to our advice regarding parent training classes, if your family is from a community that is overrepresented and underserved in regard to behavioral disorders, try to find a peer group that understands your child's background.)

In conclusion, you can see why it's important to find the right professionals to help you—someone who cares about your child but is firm, can work with both you and your child, and has insight into the behavioral therapies available in your location.

Medication

Unfortunately, there is no formally approved medication to treat children or teens with CD, but medication for other accompanying disorders such as ADHD or depression may be quite helpful.

Keep in mind, the following medications are strong. All have the potential to cause side effects. Severe side effects are rare but possible. Behavioral therapy should be tried first or at least alongside medication first. Ask your doctor if a medication she prescribes might have side effects. Ask whether taking this medication requires follow-up blood tests or blood pressure measurements. Just as important, you should ask how soon before you might see improvement. When you fill the prescription at your pharmacy, remember that your pharmacist can answer questions you may have at that time. When you get home, read the package insert that lists helpful information about this drug.

Be aware that some foods or supplements can interfere with the effectiveness of medications or increase the likelihood of their producing side effects. For example, grapefruit contains a chemical called furanocoumarin, which interferes with the metabolism of many medications. As such, these medications cannot be eliminated from the body as efficiently as they should and consequently will accumulate in the body, causing problems.

Anticonvulsants

Divalproex sodium (Depakote) is an anticonvulsant medication that may be recommended. This medication improves impulse control, depression, and aggressive behavior in children with conduct disorder. It should be monitored by your doctor, who will keep track of your child's blood levels of the medication, liver tests, blood counts, and clotting tests.

If your child suffers from aggression and mood swings, lithium may help to reduce the frequency of these issues. If your child is on lithium, he must be monitored for side effects and have his blood levels measured regularly. He will require extra attention and time from his family.

Antidepressants

If your child is depressed and aggressive, he may benefit from an antidepressant such as fluoxetine (Prozac). Some doctors prefer bupropion (Wellbutrin) for children with ADHD and depression. A child taking an antidepressant should be monitored for restlessness and thoughts of suicide.

Beta-Blockers

Beta-blockers such as clonidine (Catapres) may control impulsivity and aggression. The child's vital signs, dizziness, sedation, and dosage should be carefully monitored.

Non-Typical Antipsychotics

Risperidone is a drug used to control aggression and improve other symptoms of conduct disorder. Children with ODD and CD with or without ADHD are candidates. The doctor will want to monitor your child's weight, blood pressure, glucose, lipid profile, and A1C, so regular doctor visits are important. Many doctors recommend only short-term use of risperidone.

Stimulants

If your child also has ADHD and is impulsive and acts without thinking, *stimulant* or *non-stimulant medications* for ADHD may help and, in turn, improve his CD. These medications include stimulants such as Dexedrine and Ritalin. In a group of children aged four to seven years old with CD and ADHD, stimulant therapy decreased inattentiveness, aggressive behavior, and irritability. (Please see page 26 in Chapter 1 for side effects of these drugs.)

As you can see, there are excellent behavioral therapies and medications to help your child. The next section discusses other ways to help your child, each of which can be used alongside behavioral therapy or medication.

COMPLEMENTARY TREATMENT

Part Two of this book suggests effective natural ways to improve your child's symptoms of CD. Keep in mind that these interventions may become more difficult as the child grows older and more rebellious. Younger children are usually easier to influence, so the younger you start tracking down the causes of your child's behavior, the better. But it is never too late to try. Some of the natural interventions described in detail in Part Two include:

- **addressing environmental factors.** Like children with ADHD, some children with CD are sensitive to things they breathe in or are exposed to in their environments. Keep in mind that allergies are more common in those with mental illness than in those without. Sensitivities to substances such as pollens, molds, and animal dander are related to both ADHD and CD. Chemicals such as secondhand tobacco smoke, cleaning supplies, perfume, gas fumes, wet paint, and many others can also provoke behavioral and health-related symptoms in children. Heavy metals such as lead can also play a major role in both ADHD and CD.

- **the use of helpful programs or devices.** If your child has attention problems, a special video game that is fun to play and has been shown to improve problems with attention may help. In addition, regular summer camps or special camps for children with ADHD and learning disabilities might be appropriate for a child with CD. These camps can vary in length from a few days to weeks. There may be scholarships available to pay for them as well. Keep in mind that "boot camps" for children with CD could cause more harm than good if they are too restrictive or abusive in any way. Check out what goes on at any camp you may be considering. (See Chapter 12 on page 225 for more information.)

- **changing your child's lifestyle.** Lifestyle changes can greatly improve your child's behavior and school performance. Regular exercise improves attention, grades in school, aggression, depression, and sleep by changing chemicals in the brain. Getting good quality sleep for enough hours improves behavior and school performance, too.

- **focusing on nutrition.** The human brain needs fifty or more different essential nutrients every day to perform its work of learning and behaving normally. You can improve nutritionally poor diets by avoiding excessive sugar, corn syrup, salt, refined foods, and food additives, which contribute to both ADHD and CD. Good diets are made up of nutritious foods that everyone needs for success. Micronutrient supplements of vitamins, minerals, and fatty acids have improved behavior, conduct, and learning in children and adults with ADHD and CD. Even juvenile and adult offenders given micronutrients have shown improvements in behavior.

CONCLUSION

As stated at the beginning of this chapter, in about 40 percent of cases of childhood-onset conduct disorder, the child develops into a troubled adult with antisocial personality. Such children do not recognize right from wrong, are aggressive to others, and disregard the rights of others, showing no remorse when they do. They may also end up committing crimes and even spending time in prison. On the brighter side, about 60 percent of children with CD have more promising futures. With the proper help and treatment, they may grow up to be responsible individuals, hold down good jobs, have families, and contribute to their communities.

As you may know from firsthand experience, raising a child with conduct disorder is extremely challenging and frustrating. His behavior affects all members of your family. You are anxious and worried about not only his current behavior but also his future and the future of your family. Parenting such a child requires a lot of patience. It also requires determination to find skilled professionals who can diagnose his condition, identify any accompanying disorders, and then help him with the right therapies.

The experts won't have a crystal ball to predict your child's future, but they should be able to give you some educated ideas about his future based on their experiences with similar children. You will also need to work with your child's teacher and school personnel on both behavioral and learning issues. Providing as stable a home and family life as possible is just as important, of course.

If your child has mild CD and is treated early, his future may be bright. However, if he has untreated childhood-onset conduct disorder and his home life is characterized by parental abuse, financial hardships, and a lack of supervision, his prospects for a good life decrease. Whatever the age of your child, he needs to learn how to better respond to his environment so that he doesn't react with aggression to every situation he views as a threat. Treatment with behavioral therapy, medication, or natural treatments as described in Part Two should improve both his behavior and his ability to learn.

By acting now you may be able to decrease your child's risk as a teenager and adult for developing other behavioral or mental disorders. You may also help him to avoid the school-related problems associated with CD, such as failing and dropping out. The message is clear: By seeking help for your young child now, he can be properly diagnosed with any psychological or learning problems that may accompany his CD and get them treated.

4.

Obsessive-Compulsive Disorder

Obsessive-compulsive disorder, or *OCD,* is a behavioral disorder that affects children, adolescents, and adults. According to the National Institutes of Mental Health, a person with OCD has "uncontrollable, recurring thoughts (obsessions) and/or behaviors (compulsions) that he or she feels the urge to repeat over and over." These symptoms may persist throughout life and, if severe, be disabling at any age. When they are severe, they may interfere with all aspects of life, including school, personal relationships, and work.

Although OCD can develop in adulthood, a majority of cases begin in childhood. OCD in children is usually diagnosed between the ages of five to twelve, although it may appear as early as four years old. This condition occurs in roughly 1 to 2 percent of youths in the United States. Male children are more likely to be affected by OCD than are female children. They are also more likely to experience symptoms related to unwanted and disturbing thoughts. Females are more likely to report the onset of symptoms during puberty or pregnancy. Their symptoms more often include aggressive obsessions and feelings of uncleanliness.

Common obsessions associated with OCD are a fear of germs or contamination, and unwanted or forbidden thoughts involving sex, religion, or harm. Compulsive activities typically include excessive cleaning, hand washing, or other rituals.

Left untreated, childhood OCD may lead to other serious behaviors such as anxiety, panic attacks, depression, or even drug or alcohol abuse. However, OCD in children is treatable, and remission is possible through the use of a combination of medication, behavioral therapy, and natural therapy.

QUESTIONNAIRES

The following questionnaire, adapted from a questionnaire used by Columbus Nationwide Children's Hospital, can help you to determine the likelihood of your child having OCD. It is accompanied by a questionairre regarding your child's sleep habits.

Table 4.1. Obsessive-Compulsive Disorder Questionnaire

Symptom	Frequency			
Common Obsessions and Compulsions	**Never**	**Occasionally**	**Somewhat Often**	**All the Time**
How often does your child display a fear of dirt, germs, or contamination?	0	1	2	3
How often does your child display a need for symmetry, order, or precision?	0	1	2	3
How often does your child display religious obsessions?	0	1	2	3
How often does your child display a preoccupation with bodily waste?	0	1	2	3
How often does your child think of lucky or unlucky numbers?	0	1	2	3
How often does your child have sexual or aggressive thoughts?	0	1	2	3
How often does your child fear illness or harm coming to himself or his relatives?	0	1	2	3
How often does your child display a preoccupation with household items?	0	1	2	3
How often does your child voice his displeasure with intrusive sounds or words?	0	1	2	3
How often does your child perform grooming rituals, such as hand washing, showering, or teeth brushing?	0	1	2	3

Common Obsessions and Compulsions	Never	Occasionally	Somewhat Often	All the Time
How often does your child perform rituals, such as going in and out of doorways, needing to move through spaces in a special way, or writing, erasing, and rewriting text?	0	1	2	3
How often does your child perform checking rituals, such as making sure an appliance is off, a door is locked, or his homework is done?	0	1	2	3
How often does your child perform rituals to undo contact with a "contaminated" person or object?	0	1	2	3
How often does your child perform touching rituals?	0	1	2	3
How often does your child perform rituals to prevent harming himself or others?	0	1	2	3
How often does your child order or arrange objects?	0	1	2	3
How often does your child perform counting rituals?	0	1	2	3
How often does your child hoard or collect things of no apparent value?	0	1	2	3
How often does your child perform cleaning rituals related to the house or other items?	0	1	2	3

Table 4.2. Sleep Disorder Questionnaire

Does your child show daytime sleepiness or fatigue?	Yes	No
Does your child snore at night?	Yes	No
Does your child stop breathing for a second or more at night?	Yes	No
Has any doctor told you your child's tonsils or adenoids are enlarged?	Yes	No

EVALUATING YOUR RESPONSES

If you answered "never" or "occasionally" to the majority of questions in Table 4.1, then your child probably does not have OCD. After all, anyone can have repeated "bad" or "disturbing" thoughts or engage in certain rituals every once in a while without having OCD. We all check and recheck things at times, like making sure you have your wallet or house keys. If you answered "somewhat often" or "all the time" to the majority of questions, however, then your child may, in fact, have OCD. In addition, if you answered "yes" to any of the questions in Table 4.2, then your child could be a experiencing a sleep disorder alongside his OCD.

TYPES

While the official medical definition of OCD does not list specific subtypes, research suggests that OCD can present in a few different patterns, which are based upon the type of symptoms involved. Common types of OCD include those that are centered on hoarding, ordering/symmetry, contamination/cleaning, checking, and obsessive thoughts without compulsions. These symptoms can vary from mild to extreme.

Many parents have trouble understanding the unfamiliar terms used by physicians and therapists to describe OCD symptoms. The following section should help to bring you up to speed with these terms. Be sure to ask any professional you see to explain these symptoms further if you still feel in the dark after discussing them during an appointment. Ask that these questions be answered, if possible, in a way you can understand.

SYMPTOMS

If your child displays any of the following symptoms, depending on their degrees of severity, they may cause him and his loved ones great distress. According to researchers from Yale and the National Institutes of Health, symptoms of OCD in children may be *mild, moderate, severe,* or *extreme* based on their frequency and how much they interfere with a child's life at home, at school, and with friends. A child's OCD may be considered mild if symptoms occur for less than one hour a day. It is also considered mild if symptoms do not interfere with social life or school performance. A child's OCD is considered moderate if symptoms occur for one to three hours a day or frequently interfere with normal day-to-day activities. In children with moderate OCD, symptoms definitely interfere with school and peer relationships, but the condition is still manageable.

If a child's symptoms occur for more than three to eight hours a day or are very intrusive in day-to-day life, causing substantial problems in school performance and with others, his OCD may be considered severe. If a child's symptoms occur for more than eight hours a day, causing near-constant thoughts that lead to compulsive activities and are incapacitating, his OCD is classified as extreme.

Where does your child fall on the OCD spectrum? Understanding the severity of the problem will help you know when it's time to seek help from a professional. When you discuss your child's symptoms with his teacher or doctor, or read about OCD, these are some of the terms you may encounter most commonly.

Anxiety

Anxiety is a feeling of worry, nervousness, or unease about an upcoming event or something with an unknown outcome. Children with OCD are often anxious and may also meet the criteria for an anxiety disorder. Treating an anxiety disorder may help OCD symptoms.

Body Dysmorphic Disorder

Body dysmorphic disorder, or *BDD,* is an obsession in which a person imagines that his body or one of its parts is defective or repulsive or may become so. If he actually has a minor physical defect, he may see it as much worse than it truly is.

Catastrophizing

Catastrophizing refers to an obsession in which a person irrationally imagines that everything will end in worst-case outcomes—e.g., a dark sky will lead to a tornado, someone not showing up on time has had an accident, a relative who has a cold will die of pneumonia, etc.

Compulsions

Compulsions refer to actions a person feels required to perform, even if it makes no sense to do so. A person with compulsions may try to stop himself from engaging in this behavior but find that he cannot. The effort to stop may lead to anger and frustration until he does what he feels he must do. He may spend a large part of his time carrying out these actions repeatedly.

Family members may be included in his rituals. For example, a person who constantly washes his hands may insist that his mother wash hers and throw a serious tantrum if she doesn't. In addition to excessive hand washing, compulsions might include setting up objects in a certain formation, knocking on a door exactly three times before entering, and so on. These compulsions will vary from person to person.

Obsessions

Obsessions refer to any worrisome thoughts, ideas, or pictures that enter a person's mind and make him feel uncomfortable or nervous. He may not want to have these thoughts or images, but they keep coming back nevertheless. He may feel like he is stuck in an endless loop of these thoughts and have great difficulty turning them off.

Remission

Remission occurs when a child with OCD no longer meets the criteria for OCD. While adults tend to have lifelong OCD, in children with OCD, full remission is often possible.

Somatic Symptoms

Somatic symptoms are physical symptoms that may not have a physical cause. They may be the focus of obsessions that center on how a person feels. Examples include frequent headaches, stomachaches, or other forms of pain. To the person experiencing these symptoms, the pain is very real, even though his doctor may not be able to find anything that is physically causing such discomfort.

Tics

Tics may be described as sudden involuntary twitches or movements (e.g., blinking or widening of the eyes, scrunching of the nose, opening of the mouth, etc.), or sounds that an individual makes repeatedly (e.g., sniffles, snorts, certain words, etc.). Tics may be present in children with OCD.

Tourette's Syndrome

Tourette's syndrome is a type of psychological disorder that involves involuntary repetitive movements, sounds, or twitches. While it is a separate disorder and may be present on its own, it may also occur alongside OCD.

Trichotillomania

Trichotillomania is a specific OCD behavior in which a person pulls out his own hair. The hair being pulled could be the hair on his head, eyebrows, or any other part of the body. This behavior is commonly caused by stress or anxiety.

OBSERVING YOUR CHILD'S BEHAVIOR

You may have seen troubling behaviors in your child that you haven't understood. Now, after reading about obsessions and compulsions, you may realize that your child appears to have these symptoms. You may have noticed that he performs certain actions over and over. He may lay objects out in a particular pattern and have "meltdowns" if anyone interferes with his carefully constructed designs. He may check his school bag for the umpteenth time just to be sure he has what he needs for school. Your child may have rituals that he shows repeatedly, but he may not want to share the thoughts that lead to these rituals. Your teacher may have noticed similar actions in the classroom. It is helpful to know how your child's OCD presents both at home and at school.

Family Life

All children do things at various times that irritate their parents or caregivers. As your child has grown and developed, he may have had times when he repeatedly did some annoying things. You may have laughed the first few times because his actions made no sense and seemed silly. Finally, you may have said, "Stop! Don't do that!" He may have then stopped his actions, only to resume behaving in a frustrating manner after a few minutes had passed. You may have yelled, "I said stop! Don't do that." After several repetitions of his behavior and your responses, in frustration and anger, you may have spanked him and sent him to his room. By this time, he may have turned hysterical, feeling an even greater need to perform the banned behavior in order to calm his anxiety. When left alone in his room, he may have repeated this behavior to calm himself down.

When your child repeats the same poor behavior over several days and you see it has become a daily compulsion, you may feel confused, frustrated, and helpless. Over time he may add other compulsions to his daily activities. You may wonder, "What am I doing wrong?" The fact is that you have done nothing wrong. What you can do is seek professional help to identify what the problem is and learn how to control, modify, or eliminate your child's OCD.

Triggers

Triggers are actions that provoke obsessive-compulsive behavior in your child. If OCD is a condition you have witnessed in your child, we would suggest you write down your observations of his behavior in a notebook. Then you can share your observations with your child's teacher, doctor, or therapist. Sometimes when you take time to watch your child as a casual observer might and record these observations in your notebook, some important things may become more apparent to you.

For example, you may see which events trigger an episode. Does an episode occur after a particular meal or snack? Is there a person in the family or your home that seems to set your child off? Is he more likely to have obsessive episodes if he is tired? Does he show more obsessive-compulsive behaviors when he is stressed? These observations will help you better understand his problems.

Sleep Symptoms

The following observations are also important to include in your notebook: Does your child show daytime sleepiness? Does he snore in his sleep at night? Does he breathe noisily during sleep? Does his breathing stop for a few seconds or even longer? Is his sleep restless? Have you ever been told by a doctor that your child's tonsils are enlarged? If you answered "yes" to any of these questions, be sure to consult the section on sleep in Chapter 9. (See page 167.) It is important to tell your child's doctor or therapist about any sleep-related issues he may be experiencing.

Origins of Symptoms

In your notebook of observations, be sure to include whether or not a parent or sibling has ever been diagnosed with OCD. A family history of OCD is important information. Moreover, think about the time your child started having obsessive thoughts and behaving compulsively. Did these new thoughts or behaviors follow a traumatic event, like a death, illness, or accident experienced by someone close to your child? Did they follow a severe, damaging storm that caused all family members to be anxious and afraid? Was he severely embarrassed at school by a teacher or student? Did his problems start after he had an illness? Did the experience leave him overly worried about germs and cleanliness or about parts of his body? This information may be very important when you talk to your child's doctor or therapist.

School

In addition to recording your own observations, it is helpful to acquire the observations and insights of your child's teacher. Getting a teacher's input regarding how your child performs in school can tell you whether or not he displays similar troubling symptoms in more than one setting. Of course, a school setting is completely different from a home setting. School represents a highly structured environment made up of a classroom full of other students and an adult, the teacher. Your child may feel threatened by all these children and the unfamiliar adult. Some of the children may tease and bully him because of his strange behavior. He may find his lessons and learning stressful. Stress makes OCD symptoms worse, but at school he has no bedroom to which he might escape from all the pressure.

Visit with the Teacher

You may want to have a discussion with your child's teacher before school starts in the fall. Explain any problems he shows at home so his teacher will be aware of symptoms that may occur in class. If his symptoms are mild, his teacher may not recognize them and therefore may not realize when he is struggling. After a few weeks of school, check back with the teacher to see how things have been going.

If your child has an experienced teacher, then that teacher has probably taught a number of children with OCD, can identify the various behaviors related to the condition, and knows how to reach your child. Asking the school counselor and perhaps the principal to sit in on parent-teacher conferences may be helpful. Each may offer suggestions from their different perspectives.

Observations by the Teacher

Your child's teacher may tell you that your child wants to wash his hands or organize his possessions repeatedly. If he constantly asks to go to the restroom, this request may be caused by his need to wash his hands again, or he may need a few minutes alone in a less stressful environment. The other students may tease him about his frequent bathroom trips, adding to his anxiety and increasing his need to go back to the restroom.

The teacher may notice that your child needs a good deal of reassurance, has to arrange his school bag in a certain way, is not be able to switch easily from one task to another, or constantly retraces his actions. If he has a disturbing thought while going upstairs at school, he may want to retrace his steps over and over until he gets rid of the thought, even if he's late to a class. This may make him look like he has a conduct problem.

Your child's teacher may remark that your child erases and rewrites his work again and again because he wants each letter to be perfect. You may have noticed this same behavior at home when he takes forever to finish his homework. The erasers on his pencils may be worn down to the metal. This ritual may wear holes in the paper and make him late in turning in an essay or test. Ask his teacher if letting him work on a laptop might help him complete his work better and quicker.

In-School Triggers

Ask your child's teacher if there is a time of day when his behavior is worse than at other times. In other words, do his symptoms appear mostly in the early morning, right before lunch, or after lunch? Is he worse after any snacks that are given to him? Is he worse before a big test, an oral presentation, or some other stressful classroom event? Knowing which events trigger symptoms in your child is important information.

School Performance

Ask about grades and test scores, and how he is doing in each of his subjects. Is he behind his peers in class or below national norms on routine testing? Is he currently failing any subject? Does he turn in his homework on time? Is it complete or has it been hastily put together? What does he need to do to improve his ability to learn? How can you help?

Sleepiness

If your child's teacher tells you he acts tired or even falls asleep in class, this is valuable information. You may have noticed this daytime sleepiness at home as well. If the teacher doesn't say anything about fatigue, be sure to ask. As you will learn later in the following section, telltale signs of daytime sleepiness may indicate the presence of a sleep disorder.

Other Possible Disorders

Some of your child's actions in class may make him look like a child who has ADHD, CD, or a learning disability. For example, if he thinks he must cap and recap his pen four times or his mother will get sick, then he will pay attention only to this ritual and not what is going on in class. His teacher will think he is inattentive or suffering from ADHD. If your child struggles with perfectionism, then it may take him a while to complete his work, which may give the impression of his having a learning disability. He may, in fact, actually have one or more of these conditions, as they are common in children with OCD. Nevertheless, if these other conditions are ruled out by a professional, your child's symptoms may all be attributable to his OCD.

The Next Step

Be sure to record all the different things your child's teacher shares with you about your child's behavior in school. Then you can take your notebook with you to an appointment with your child's doctor or therapist. If the teacher recommends you consult your child's doctor, follow up on this advice. If his doctor or therapist asks for information from the school, sign the papers for the school to release these details.

Once you have seen your child's doctor and a plan of action with a behavioral therapist has been put together, consider letting your child's teacher and school know. (Remember that you are trying to achieve the best possible outcome for your child in all his environments.) If the therapist wants you to stop giving in to your child's compulsions, she will no doubt want his teacher to do the same. You and your child's teacher should be on the same page. In addition, you should ask the

Video Game Addiction

The concept of video game addiction as a diagnosable disorder has not yet been fully accepted by the research community. In 2013, however, the American Psychiatric Association's *Diagnostic and Statistical Manual of Mental Disorders* (DSM-5), which healthcare professionals use to diagnose mental disorders, included a condition called "Internet gaming disorder" as one worthy of further research, stopping short of calling it a unique mental disorder due to a lack of sufficient evidence. (Despite its name, the condition refers to video games played on any electronic device and not simply those played online.) In 2019, the World Health Organization (WHO) chose to list Internet gaming disorder as a new disorder in its *International Classification of Diseases* (ICD-11).

Although the debate is ongoing as to whether video game addiction should be treated as an official disorder, there are symptoms of gaming addiction for which concerned parents can look. According to the DSM-5, video game addiction may be present if you notice five or more of the following symptoms in your child over the course of twelve months.

- A preoccupation with video games
- Withdrawal symptoms such as irritability, anxiety, and sadness
- A need to increase time spent gaming
- Unsuccessful attempts to stop gaming
- A loss of interest in other activities
- Psychosocial problems due to excessive gaming

teacher and therapist to discuss the therapist's goals and plans for both home and school settings.

RISK FACTORS

You are probably wondering, "Why does my child act as he does? He does things that make no sense—some of them rather weird—over and

- The deception of family members, therapists, or others regarding the amount of time spent gaming
- The use of gaming to escape or relieve negative moods
- Jeopardizing or losing a significant relationship or educational opportunity because of time spent gaming

Furthermore, researchers have suggested that people who are addicted to video games tend to suffer from poor impulse control, symptoms of ADHD, symptoms of OCD, and decreased cognitive functioning.

The cause of gaming addiction is thought to be related to the neurotransmitter dopamine, which affects pleasure. (Dopamine also plays a role in learning, attention, reinforcement, and sensorimotor integration.) The playing of video games increases dopamine, which makes the player happy. Constant increases in dopamine, however, can also result in increased tolerance to this chemical. In other words, the more a gamer plays, the more dopamine is required to create the same level of happiness, and thus the longer each gaming session will need to be.

Currently there is no test to confirm video game addiction, and many professionals feel that gaming addiction is merely a symptom of a different disorder rather than a disorder in itself. Nevertheless, if you suspect your child is addicted to video games, talk to his doctor and follow the treatment methods recommended by the American Academy of Pediatrics. Cognitive behavioral therapy or even medication may be warranted. In the meantime, try to strike a balance between screen time and other means of relaxation for your child, which may include playing board games, listening to music, going for walks, or reading.

over again. What's more, he seems to know they don't make any sense!" So, what is going on in your child's brain?

No one knows the exact cause of OCD, and it may be different for different children. Understanding what goes on in the brain of someone with OCD is quite technical and not completely understood even by experts. But one researcher, Luke Norman, PhD, put it this way: "In OCD, the brain responds too much to errors, and too little to stop signals." In other words, the brain gets stuck in an almost endless loop of "wrongness," in which a thought goes round and round without an ending. It's like being on a merry-go-round that won't stop until someone steps on the emergency brake.

Brain Abnormalities

Brain abnormalities are common in children with OCD. With modern technology, brain scans have shown these differences in the brains of children with OCD. For example, the prefrontal cortex of the brain plays an important role in controlling our actions and acts as the center of decision making. But in children with OCD, this area of the brain is different. An overactive *neural circuit*—i.e., a group of interconnected neurons in the brain that performs a particular function—between important parts of the brain is thought to be partly responsible for OCD symptoms. Imbalances of neurotransmitters—i.e., brain chemicals that help brain cells to communicate with each other—are also thought to play a role. In fact, "bad" and "intrusive" thoughts may be caused by an imbalance in the neurotransmitter GABA, which is responsible for inhibiting the activity of certain brain cells. Low serotonin, another neurotransmitter, is suspected of contributing to OCD. The reason that certain antidepressants are helpful in controlling OCD symptoms is that they increase serotonin levels in the brain.

Differences in your child's brain may account, at least in part, for his OCD. Traumatic experiences in his life and his environment may also trigger the onset of this condition.

Diet

Although there are few studies that address a possible association of poor diet and OCD, it is safe to assume that if your child's diet is deficient in vitamins, minerals, and other basic nutrients, his brain will not work well. You could think of necessary nutrients as a deck of playing cards. If you don't have all fifty-two cards in the deck, the game you've chosen to play may be unplayable. The brain requires roughly fifty nutrients to function properly. If your child is missing one or more, his "game" might be off, too! These nutrients are used to make brain cells, brain fibers, and neurotransmitters, which carry messages from one brain cell to another. If these nutrients are low in your child's diet, he is going to struggle with learning or behavioral problems because his brain is starving for the right dietary components.

The central role nutrition plays in various behavioral and mental disorders is discussed further in Chapter 10. (See page 185.)

Genetics

Like many disorders discussed in this book, OCD may have a genetic component. Children with a parent or sibling with OCD are more likely to develop OCD than is a child with no family history. For example, one study reported a 12 to 18 percent greater incidence of this behavior in children with parents and siblings who had OCD. Therefore, a child with OCD is genetically more likely to have the disorder, and he likely has the added disadvantage of having a close relative who displays OCD behavior in his home environment. In identical twins, 80 percent of both children had OCD, while in fraternal twins the rate was 50 percent. These statistics suggest a strong genetic component for OCD. As you have read earlier, however, genes may be turned on or off by various environmental factors.

Hyperthyroidism

The thyroid is a butterfly-shaped gland that lies just below the larynx. It secretes the hormones *triiodothyronine*, or *T3*, and *thyroxine*, or *T4*. These hormones are required for your body and brain to work normally. Either too little thyroid hormone (hypothyroidism) or too much thyroid hormone (hyperthyroidism) can cause adverse symptoms, including behavioral problems. According to an early report of child and adolescent OCD, too much thyroid hormone may contribute to OCD, and medication to reduce thyroid hormones may improve symptoms of OCD. More research is needed, but a simple blood test to determine thyroid hormone levels could rule this possibility out.

Infection

If your child's OCD behavior seemingly appeared out of nowhere following an infection, he may be affected by a condition known as *pediatric acute-onset neuropsychiatric syndrome,* or *PANS*. If your child's OCD symptoms appeared out of nowhere following a strep throat infection in particular, he may be affected by a condition known as *PANDAS,* which is short for *pediatric autoimmune neuropsychiatric disorders associated with streptococcus disorder.* Both PANS and PANDAS are controversial disorders that suggest that the onset of OCD may be the result of a bacterial infection, such as an infection with the bacteria that causes strep throat, leading to a misdirected immune response that attacks the brain and causes OCD symptoms. A child with PANS or PANDAS, however, may experience symptoms that include not only obsessive-compulsive thoughts and activities but also other types of behavioral changes, such as sudden separation anxiety, fear, or panic attacks; constant screaming, irritability, or mood changes; or hyperactivity. This sudden, disturbing array of symptoms may terrify the child and his parents. A desperate, horrified parent may report, "My previously calm, happy child is possessed by the devil!"

You may suggest PANS or PANDAS to your child's doctor as the cause of his acute-onset OCD, but try not to insist on this diagnosis. It is a physician's job to consider numerous possible diagnoses before rushing to judgment. Working with your child's doctor as a partner will get you better results than attempting to dictate the outcome of the appointment, even if it is glaringly obvious to you that PANS or PANDAS is the root of your child's problem. Although PANS and PANDAS are becoming more widely recognized in the medical community, your child's doctor may still be extremely resistant to the idea that a bacterial infection could be behind your child's symptoms. Once you've explained how suddenly these symptoms arose and how drastically your child's behavior has changed, your child's doctor may be more receptive to the possibility.

Thankfully, if a diagnosis of PANS or PANDAS is made, the solution may be fairly simple: a prescription for antibiotics that will kill the bacterial infection affecting your child's brain. Nevertheless, your child may need to undergo some form of psychotherapy to reduce the severity of his symptoms before the antibiotics eliminate his infection.

Trauma

What has taken place in your child's life may have triggered the onset of his OCD. A traumatic event is defined by experts as "exposure to actual or threatened death, serious injury, or sexual violence" or some other adverse experience. Some studies have reported that, in some children with OCD, there is an association between a traumatic event and the onset of OCD. Flashbacks, nightmares, and hyperawareness may occur following the event, leading to obsessive thoughts. Symptoms may involve fear and anxiety, or even depression, anger, or aggression. Some of these symptoms and thoughts would be normal in any person who has experienced trauma. But your child's response to a troubling event is much like that of a soldier who has come back from combat and now has post-traumatic stress disorder (PTSD). OCD children, however, may also become obsessive as a result of trauma.

ASSOCIATED DISORDERS

As if parents or caregivers weren't stressed enough by their child's OCD, a child with OCD could have other disorders as well. There are a number of common disorders that are associated with OCD.

- 25 percent of children with OCD also have Tourette's syndrome.
- 31 percent of children with OCD also have an anxiety disorder separate from OCD. (See Chapter 5 on page 101.)
- 39 percent of children with OCD also have major depression. (See Chapter 7 on page 141.)
- 51 percent of children with OCD also have ADHD. (See Chapter 1 on page 7.)
- 51 percent of children with OCD also have ODD. (See Chapter 2 on page 31.)

As you can see, accompanying disorders are extremely common in children with OCD. It's important to diagnose whether or not these are present, as treatment of them may also improve OCD symptoms. (See Chapter 7 on page 141 for more information on the physical or mental disorders that may accompany OCD.)

If your child has a sleep disorder, it can adversely affect his brain, due to a temporary lack of oxygen during sleep. This issue can trigger symptoms of a variety of conditions, including ADHD, ODD, and OCD. Obstructive sleep apnea (OSA) occurs when a person is unable to breathe in enough oxygen while sleeping because the airway is temporarily blocked for a very brief period. In other words, he stops breathing momentarily—for a few seconds to as long as a minute—depriving his brain of oxygen. This result is known as *hypoxia,* or low oxygen. Then breathing resumes and oxygen levels increase.

The temporary blockage may arise because of enlarged tonsils or adenoids, or for other reasons. It may occur many times in a night and is believed to cause brain alterations resulting in OCD or other behavioral disorders. (See Chapter 9 on page 167 for further information on sleep.)

DIAGNOSIS

You may think, "I suspect my child has OCD because I see his obsessions and compulsive behaviors every day. Why do I need a diagnosis?" There are a few reasons. First, you want to identify your child's behavioral disorder. Having a definitive diagnosis will help you get special education services from his school. Next, a healthcare professional can uncover any other disorders that might be present. Finally, having a diagnosis will lead to treatment from the professional you see. Be sure to bring the notebook containing your observations and what your child's teacher has observed to your appointments.

Start by finding out if your family doctor has had experience in helping children with OCD. If your child's doctor does not have experience in this area, ask to be referred to other local doctors who have been trained in helping children like yours. If you suspect your child might have PANS or PANDAS, you could ask his doctor to refer him to a medical center or clinic in your city. You should also request that your child's thyroid hormone levels be measured.

Discuss your child's sleep at night and the possibility of obstructive sleep apnea. Make sure your child's doctor examines your child's tonsils and adenoids. If they seem to be enlarged, she may refer you to an ear, nose, and throat specialist (ENT doctor). Your family doctor may recommend a pediatrician, pediatric neurologist, allergist, or pediatric psychiatrist, all of whom would have had training and experience in treating children with OCD or conditions that can contribute to OCD and could prescribe medication. You may be referred to a child clinical psychologist, who cannot prescribe medications but is an expert in behavioral therapy. Any of these professionals will need to work with your child's teacher and school.

To be diagnosed with OCD, your child's symptoms must be continual, severe, and disruptive. There may be questionnaires for you to complete, or your therapist may simply ask about different symptoms. You may also be asked to complete questionnaires for other disorders so that your child's doctor has a total understanding of your child's behavior and whether he has "pure" OCD or OCD with other behavioral disorders. (For more information on finding the right professionals to diagnose and treat your child, see Chapter 8 on page 153.)

Once you have a diagnosis, you will want to discuss possible treatments. There are medications, behavioral therapies, and natural treatments. Keep in mind that untreated OCD will frequently get worse.

TRADITIONAL TREATMENT

Treatment options for OCD include therapy, which involves talking to a therapist to manage mental health problems, and medication. Your child may require both. According to experts, the best OCD treatment is a combination of therapy and medication. Much will depend, however, on your child's diagnosis and age. Some doctors prefer to recommend only therapy because of a child's age. If he also has ADHD, then medication for that condition may be helpful. (For more information on ADHD, see Chapter 1 on page 7.)

Therapy

Find a therapist with whom you and your child feel comfortable—someone with whom your child will feel free to share personal problems and thoughts. He may be embarrassed by his thoughts, of course, and may hesitate to share them with the therapist or even with you. There are three common psychotherapies for children and their families. The first type of therapy is called *cognitive behavioral therapy,* or *CBT*. It is based on how your child feels emotionally, and how he thinks and behaves. The second type is *exposure response prevention,* or *ERP,* which is a type of cognitive behavioral therapy that helps children to turn off their "bad" thoughts or repeated rituals. The third type is called *family therapy,* in which the whole family learns how each member can help your child who has OCD.

Changes to Try Now

As you wait for the day of your appointment with a therapist, here are some suggestions that might help your child now.

- Don't accommodate or enable your child, as doing so will reinforce his behavior.
- Family plans should not be altered to accommodate your child's abnormal behavior.
- If your child demands that you, too, wash your hands repeatedly, refuse to do so.
- It's important not to model or encourage OCD behavior. If you suspect other family members also have OCD, seek treatment for them, too.
- There will be times when your child "melts down." During such times, do not give in to his demands.
- Make it clear to your child that you will not allow OCD to control his life or yours.
- Don't participate in any of your child's rituals or offer excessive reassurance.
- A child with OCD should be treated in a consistent manner by parents and other family members—everyone should be on the same page. If a child's caregivers lack consistency, he will be even more anxious and his symptoms may worsen.
- Set limits. For example, if he wants to repeatedly wash his hands, allow him to wash them three times only, but no more.
- Small rewards and brief sincere praise for improved behavior will provide incentives for your child to work through his problems. Rewards may include earning points toward playing a favorite game, time to play electronics, or your child's choice of movie on family night.

Cognitive Behavioral Therapy

Cognitive behavioral therapy, or CBT, can be very effective in helping people with OCD, with as many as 75 percent of patients improving. What is cognitive behavioral therapy? Keep in mind that almost all of us have intrusive thoughts that don't make sense or are even alarming from time to time, but most people are able to end these thoughts and not get stuck in an endless loop. The idea behind cognitive behavioral therapy is that your thoughts, feelings, and actions are interconnected. Cognitive behavioral therapy can teach your child how to recognize his fears and obsessive thoughts and avoid his repetitive behaviors. In other words, his thoughts create feelings, which create behaviors, which create thoughts, and your child is lost in an endless loop. Treatment focuses on what happened when he first started having troubling thoughts and how he can avoid responding to them now.

For example, perhaps a child with OCD hears a noise in the night and immediately concludes that there is a burglar downstairs. He feels terrified. A normal person might conclude, "That's just the cat downstairs knocking over an object. He's always getting into something," or think, "It's just my dad coming in late from work. I'm glad he's home." In either case, a normal person would roll over and go back to sleep. The child with OCD, however, keeps thinking about the burglar and the worst-case scenario of the intruder coming upstairs and harming or killing him and his family. With thoughts like those, it's hard to go back to sleep.

Your child's therapist might try to uncover any original traumatic event that seems related to the onset of his OCD—if there was one. The event would have caused high levels of anxiety and fear at the time, and the memory of it would still cause these reactions now. For example, a child may be terrified of germs because his grandmother died from COVID, which he knows is a virus. He had not washed his hands when he saw her last. He now thinks he needs to wash his hands constantly so he or others won't get sick like his grandma did. A therapist may help the child decide how many times washing his hands would be enough. The child is taught that the more he checks or carries out his compulsions, the less certain and the more anxious he will become.

If your child gets relief from cognitive behavioral therapy but the OCD reappears sometime later, he can always enter therapy again.

Exposure Response Prevention

Exposure response prevention, or ERP, is a type of cognitive behavioral therapy that helps children with OCD. It is composed of two major parts: exposure and response prevention. In part one, the child with OCD is exposed to the environment that causes him great anxiety. In other words, he faces his greatest fear. Then the response prevention by the therapist keeps the child from acting on his immediate compulsion. For example, if a child repeatedly wants to wash his hands after touching something dirty, such as a used kitchen towel, he is prevented from doing so by his therapist or parent. He learns that nothing terrible happens. The child learns to tolerate the anxiety the dirty towel brings without washing his hands twenty times. Some therapists believe that this is the most effective way to treat OCD. Parents will want to make sure that their child's school subscribes to this type of therapy in order to ensure consistency across home and school environments.

Family Therapy

In family therapy, a therapist will discuss a troubled child's behavior and feelings with his family members. Parents and siblings should receive an explanation in simple terms of what is going on in the child's brain and how each family member might help to improve matters.

Medication

If your child has mild OCD, he may be able to manage it without medication. Children with moderate, severe, or extreme OCD, however, often need medication. It's important to understand that there is no magic pill that will cure your child's OCD, but there are medications that can control OCD symptoms, especially when combined with psychotherapy. Unfortunately, when he stops using medication to treat his OCD, his symptoms may return.

Antibiotics

Antibiotics are used only if your child has been diagnosed with PANS or PANDAS, in which case his doctor will prescribe an antibiotic to treat the underlying infection. Otherwise, antibiotics will do nothing to treat typical OCD.

Antidepressants

The type of antidepressant recommended for OCD is called a *selective serotonin reuptake inhibitor,* or *SSRI.* SSRIs increase serotonin levels in the brain, calming brain activity and improving OCD symptoms. There are four of these antidepressants that have been approved by the FDA for children with OCD: clomipramine (Anafranil), fluoxetine (Prozac), fluxamine (Luvox), and sertraline (Zoloft). These drugs come with some age restrictions. For example, Prozac can be used in children at age seven or older, while Anafranil may be used only by children who are ten years old or older. Your child's doctor will know which medication is appropriate for your child.

Ask your child's doctor about possible side effects. After all, these are all strong drugs that alter brain chemistry. Nevertheless, they have been found to be safe and effective for children with OCD. They rarely cause severe side effects. When you pick up your child's prescription, be sure to read the guide that comes with the medication. Common side effects of SSRIs include feeling anxious, indigestion, diarrhea, and loss of appetite leading to weight loss. Dry mouth is also common but may improve over time.

In very rare instances, your child could develop suicidal thoughts from taking an SSRI. If this is to happen, it will usually occur in the first few months, or when the dosage is either increased or decreased. Notify your child's doctor immediately if your child reports having such thoughts. Don't stop the use of antidepressant without guidance from the prescribing doctor.

Keep in mind that SSRIs work slowly. Be patient, as it may take as long as ten to twelve weeks for your child to realize the benefits of an SSRI fully. Your child's doctor may need to adjust the dose, but don't adjust it yourself. In addition, if one antidepressant doesn't work for your child, your child's doctor may try a different one. While you are waiting for him to respond to a medication, you can work with his behavioral therapist. You could also try one of the natural treatments found in Part Two of this book.

If your child has an accompanying behavioral disorder, such as ADHD, your child's doctor may prescribe a stimulant drug for his ADHD in addition to his antidepressant for OCD. If he suffers from depression, taking one of the antidepressants for OCD should help both his OCD and his depression. You can see now why it is important to find a doctor who is experienced and knowledgeable about medications for OCD and other related disorders.

COMPLEMENTARY TREATMENT

In addition to psychotherapy and medication, you may find natural alternatives to be quite helpful. Part Two of this book explains how to use natural therapies to help your child. These therapies include:

- **addressing environmental factors.** Treating your child for the things he breathes in or is exposed to in his environment may help. Sensitivities to pollen, molds, and animal dander may be related to OCD, ADHD, and depression. Chemicals in a child's environment may also trigger episodes of OCD.
- **changing your child's lifestyle.** Improving your child's sleep may be helpful. Sleep disorders are discussed thoroughly in Chapter 9. (See page 167.) It provides ways to help your child get to sleep, stay asleep, and wake up bright and alert.
- **focusing on nutrition.** Your child needs to be fed an optimal diet to enable his brain to work properly. A diet lacking in nutrients combined with an excessive amount of nutrient-poor foods may leave his brain starving for a healthy diet. Your child will need to avoid foods, beverages, and candy that contain food additives such as high fructose corn syrup and artificial sweeteners, as well as excess regular sugar. Feed your child a healthy diet full of fresh fruits, veggies, whole grains, lean meats, eggs, fish, nuts, seeds, and legumes. A micronutrient supplement of vitamins, minerals, and fatty acids may alleviate your child's OCD and help him to learn in school.

Choose the above natural treatments based on what your family can afford or put into action.

CONCLUSION

OCD is a chronic mental disorder that may begin to affect a child in childhood and then continue into adolescence and adult life if left untreated. If moderate, severe, or extreme, OCD can disturb a child's family life, interfere in his learning and behavior at school, and cause problems with his peers and classmates. In addition, the presence of accompanying mental or behavioral disorders may be as high as 90 percent in individuals with OCD. These disorders include depression, anxiety disorders, panic attacks, post-traumatic stress disorder, ADHD, eating disorders, and drug or alcohol abuse. Therefore, it's important to treat OCD early, before it completely dominates a child's life.

Thankfully, OCD can be treated and sometimes completely cured with treatment. The treatments discussed in this chapter, which include medication, psychotherapy, and natural therapies, can be quite helpful and should lead to some noticeable improvement at the very least.

5. Anxiety Disorders

Many children have fears and worries. (Fears and worries related to school are the most common examples.) If your child experiences these feelings persistently, however, he may have an *anxiety disorder.*

Anxiety disorders have two components: a strong negative emotion and an element of fear. There are actually several different anxiety disorders, each involving an excessive form of fear. For example, there is generalized anxiety disorder, which consists of a variety of worries. Separation anxiety disorder refers to excessive worry about separation from parents or guardians. About 7 percent of children in the United States (4.4 million) have been diagnosed with anxiety. Girls are more likely to be diagnosed with anxiety than are boys. If your child's anxiety interferes with schooling, home life, or recreational time, he may have an anxiety disorder and need special care.

Most parents are quick to brush off their child's anxiety, immediately telling him to relax whenever he starts to display anxious behavior. Although it may not seem like it, this reaction is typically the result of good intentions, as parents seek to avoid overreacting and making things worse. In the face of their child's distress, they hope to help by invalidating it, saying, "There's nothing to worry about!" If you suspect your child exhibits nervous tendencies, however, it is important not to dismiss his feelings. If he frequently displays anxiety in regard to certain activities, it is usually not helpful to say, "Don't be such a worrywart. You will be fine!" The good news is that childhood anxiety disorders are highly treatable and he very well could get to a point where he feels fine.

QUESTIONNAIRE

The following questionnaire can help you to determine whether your child has an anxiety disorder. The symptoms you are evaluating should be present for at least six months in a child usually older than four years of age. They should also be present in more than one setting—whether at home, in school, or somewhere else with friends or relatives.

Table 5.1 Anxiety Disorder Questionnaire

Symptom	Frequency			
Anxiety	**Never**	**Occasionally**	**Somewhat Often**	**All the Time**
How often is your child very afraid when away from parents?	0	1	2	3
How often does your child exhibit extreme fear over a specific thing or situation, such as a dog or insect, or going to the doctor?	0	1	2	3
How often is your child very afraid of school or other places where there are people?	0	1	2	3
How often is your child very worried about the future and bad things happening?	0	1	2	3
How often does your child have repeated episodes of sudden, unexpected, intense fear that comes with symptoms such as heart pounding, trouble breathing, or feeling dizzy, shaky, or sweaty?	0	1	2	3

EVALUATING YOUR RESPONSES

If you answered "somewhat often" or "all the time" to one or more of these questions, then your child may have an anxiety disorder. If you answered all these questions with "never" or "occasionally," then your child probably doesn't have an anxiety problem. After all, almost all children will be anxious in certain situations, but if the problem becomes overwhelming and disabling, it needs to be investigated by a professional.

Anxiety has four different degrees of severity: *mild, moderate, severe,* and *panic.* A child with mild anxiety may not have moderate or severe symptoms, but they still may impact his emotional, social, and academic abilities. A child who has mild anxiety may continue to have symptoms such as shyness and social anxiety throughout childhood and into adulthood. They may leave him with inadequate coping skills and later develop into a more severe problem.

A child with moderate anxiety experiences more frequent symptoms than does a child with mild anxiety, but he is still able to function on a daily basis better than a child with severe anxiety. He may feel on edge, unable to control his worries, or unable to relax for several days or the majority of the week. These symptoms may disrupt his life. If he develops better ways to cope using self-help strategies or the help of behavioral therapy, he will have better success in managing his moderate anxiety for the rest of his life.

A child with severe anxiety has symptoms that are intense and persistent, completely disrupting his life. Depression may also occur alongside severe anxiety. He may experience extreme fatigue, increased heart rate, and feelings of panic, and may withdraw socially.

Panic-level anxiety is the most extreme form of anxiety disorder. It frequently consists of unexpected panic attacks that strike often and regularly. During a panic attack, a child may experience a sudden onset of extreme fear, heart palpitations, rapid breathing, nausea or dizziness, and fear of death. Needless to say, it is a terrifying experience, especially for a child. Determining the severity of your child's anxiety symptoms is an important step in choosing what to do about his condition.

TYPES AND THEIR SYMPTOMS

Fears and anxieties are normal and common in young children. As reported by parents, one quarter of children are nervous, fearful, or anxious. Younger children express more anxiety than do older children, and girls display more anxiety than do boys. The anxiety levels of some children, however, are powerful enough to suspect a disorder.

The word "anxiety" is often used in such a wide-reaching, general way that it can be difficult to understand the experience of a person who has been diagnosed with an anxiety disorder. By getting a better picture of different types of anxiety disorders and their symptoms, it is possible to grasp what it means to suffer from one of these conditions.

Generalized Anxiety Disorder

If your child worries excessively about a variety of general issues, which may include his grades, family, relationships with his peers, and performance in sports, he may suffer from *generalized anxiety disorder,* or *GAD.* This condition can cause the sufferer to feel restless, nervous, tired, and unable to concentrate or sleep well.

Fight-or-Flight Response

When confronted by what it perceives as dangerous circumstances, a person's brain sends messages to a part of the nervous system called the *sympathetic nervous system,* which triggers the flight-or-fight response in an effort to deal with the situation. This response helps keep us safe by preparing us to run away or stay and fight when faced with danger.

The flight-or-flight response has helped to keep humans safe since the Stone Age. It involves a chemical release in the brain of the neurotransmitters *adrenaline* and *noradrenaline.* These chemical substances cause the heart to speed up, increase breathing, dilate pupils, and decrease salivation—all beneficial reactions if you are being chased by a tiger! If you are fearful of relatively harmless things or situations due to an anxiety disorder, however, these reactions tend to make things much worse, increasing unwanted chemical changes in your body and brain, and intensifying your anxiety.

When it comes to children who are being raised in communities in which there may be ongoing violence, anxiety is often a natural part of their lives. For a child living in such conditions, it may be difficult to distinguish an anxiety disorder from the anxiety created by real-life threats.

Panic Disorder

If your child suffers from repeated attacks of intense fear or terror that come on suddenly and peak quickly, he may suffer from *panic disorder.*

These periods are typically marked by feelings of impending doom, heart palpitations, shortness of breath, and chest pain. Understandably, they can also place the affected person in a state of constant worry about when the next attack might happen.

Phobias

A *phobia* is an intense, irrational fear of a specific object or activity. Examples of phobias include fears of animals, storms, heights, water, blood, spiders, darkness, medical procedures, and many other possibilities. A child with a phobia will try to avoid situations that trigger it or suffer through his phobia with great anxiety. He may cry, throw a tantrum, or have a headache or stomachache. By the age of ten, phobias usually diminish or go away completely.

Selective Mutism

If your child is consistently unable to speak in certain situations, such as at school or in another public setting, but can speak without any trouble in other situations, such as at home with a family member, he may have *selective mutism.* This condition, of course, can pose a serious problem to important aspects of a child's life—in the recent example, the academic and social aspects of his life.

Separation Anxiety Disorder

If your child is older than three and is fearful when you leave the room or go out of sight, he may have *separation anxiety disorder,* or *SAD.* This type of behavior is normal in very young children, but as a child ages, this fear should disappear. Separation anxiety disorder is most common in children aged seven to nine. A child with SAD may suffer from extreme homesickness and feelings of misery at not being with loved ones. He may demand more attention from his parents. In more severe forms of this disorder, the child may refuse to go to school, camp, or sleepover at a friend's house. He may worry about bad things happening to his parents or have a vague sense of something terrible happening in their absence. He may have fears of illness, accidents, kidnapping, or physical harm. New situations may trigger his anxiety.

Social Anxiety Disorder

If your child intensely fears social or performative activities, he may have *social anxiety disorder.* He may be unable to start a conversation with a peer or to maintain a friendship. He may dread an upcoming piano recital and perform poorly at it (or not at all), although he could play the piece perfectly at home. Having to speak in class may fill him with dread, and actually speaking in class may seem to last a lifetime to him. He may even dislike using a phone because he doesn't know how to have a conversation and is embarrassed by long periods of silence. This disorder is marked by elevated anxiety about being judged negatively by others and feeling embarrassed.

Internalizing Behaviors

Internalizing behaviors are characterized by inward-directed feelings and are often associated with anxiety disorders. They include being withdrawn, nervous, or irritable; feeling lonely, sad, or afraid; sleeping more than usual; eating more or less than usual; not talking; and experiencing headaches or other physical symptoms without any physical basis.

OBSERVING YOUR CHILD'S BEHAVIOR

Although a moderate amount of anxiety can be healthy to experience, too much is not. For example, moderate anxiety may motivate your child to study hard for a test because he is fearful of getting a bad grade. Similarly, some anxiety can help a child to practice before an athletic performance. Of course, a fear of heights will keep your child safe by keeping him away from dangerous elevations. Excessive, uncontrollable anxiety, however, is debilitating. A child who is filled with anxiety over taking a math test may be able to focus only on his fear, not how to solve the math problems, consequently failing the test.

Physical symptoms may accompany severe anxiety. These include increased heart rate, dizziness, blushing, fatigue, nausea, sweating, and stomach upset. Cognitive reactions may include thoughts of being hurt, feelings of incompetence or inadequacy, images of monsters or wild animals, difficulty concentrating, self-critical thoughts, and more. Anxiety may also affect a child's behavior. He may avoid certain situations, cry or scream, bite his nails, clench his jaw, suck his thumb, or fidget. Simply put: Uncontrolled anxiety can terrorize a child.

Family Life

If your child has excessive anxiety, you are most likely already aware of it. It can disrupt the lives of every member of a family. A child with excessive anxiety may:

- Worry so much about school that he is unable to eat breakfast. This lack of nutrients only adds to the problems he'll face every morning in class.
- complain of a stomachache or headache to avoid school. If you insist on his going to school, he cries and screams.
- say, "Don't leave me!" every time a parent must leave him for a while, such as at school during the day or with a babysitter for an evening, or even for a brief time, such as to run out and quickly grab something at the grocery store. If this behavior happens in public, it may be quite embarrassing to the child's parents.
- be so stressed and anxious about a performance that he forgets what he is supposed to perform or even runs out of the room.
- be irrationally terrified of spiders, dogs, or other animals.

School

If your child has an anxiety disorder, he will no doubt display associated symptoms at school. Your child's teacher may have commented that he shows some or all of the following signs of anxiety.

- trouble concentrating in class or completing classwork
- being self-conscious and avoiding certain situations
- physical symptoms such as a racing heartbeat, fast breathing, tense muscles, sweaty palms, queasy stomach, or trembling hands or legs
- missing class time due to coping problems at school
- talking with a school counselor or therapist frequently

There are many ways a teacher can help a child with excessive anxiety. A good teacher will be in close contact with the affected child's parents to learn which techniques work at home and discuss effective techniques she has used in school. Your child's teacher will also need to know if any other disorder, such as ADHD, has been diagnosed, or may recommend testing for other disorders.

A teacher can help a child with an anxiety disorder by:

- giving him a daily schedule, so he knows what is going to happen that day.
- allowing him extra time to complete his work.
- checking his assignments to see if he has written them down correctly.
- modifying assignments and reducing workload when necessary.
- promoting relaxation techniques and allowing for breaks.
- setting aside a safe, calming space, and allowing him to speak with a counselor when needed.

You may find yourself wondering, "Why does my child act this way? Where did I go wrong? Why is my child so different from other kids I see?" To answer these questions, we must discuss the many factors that can contribute to anxiety disorders.

RISK FACTORS

The causes of childhood anxiety are not completely understood, but it appears to be related to a combination of risk factors. Understanding these factors can lead to actions that will improve your child's anxiety disorder.

Brain Abnormalities

Our brains perform in an amazingly complex way, with many different areas of the brain, circuit pathways, and neurotransmitters all working together—hopefully in harmony. Children with anxiety disorders may have various abnormalities in their brains. First, brain-imaging studies have shown structural differences between the brains of children with anxiety and the brains of children without anxiety. It appears that the amygdala and the closely related *superior temporal gyrus* of a child with an anxiety disorder are larger in volume than the same brain structures of the average child. The amygdala detects and organizes reactions to normal dangers in the world. An overexcited amygdala is implicated in children who are behaviorally withdrawn, anxious, or depressed. Certain brain circuits associated with social and emotional processing are also affected by this issue.

According to research, the brain reaches 80 percent of its full development by the age of three. Any trauma experienced during this period or beyond can cause it to develop abnormally in its attempt to handle the trauma. This reaction explains why prolonged trauma in early childhood can cause a child to have fewer of the skills required to function well at home, school, and in his community.

As they are in many of the other disorders discussed in this book, the neurotransmitters adrenaline, noradrenaline, and others are involved in anxiety disorders. The neurotransmitter *gamma-aminobutyric acid,* or *GABA,* also plays important roles in anxiety disorders.

Diet

Anxiety disorders often go hand in hand with a poor diet. A child who is anxious may be a picky eater and end up having a diet that is nutritionally inadequate. This poor diet can cause the brain to react negatively, generating anxiety or other mental or behavioral disorders. Similarly, a child with obesity and anxiety likely has a nutritionally poor diet. A high incidence of anxiety disorders occurs in people with obesity. A high-calorie diet composed of excessive sugar, fat, and calories can be a disaster physically, mentally, and emotionally. Keep in mind that Americans are well fed but poorly nourished. (See Chapter 10 on page 185 for more information on diet.)

Familial Factors

Brain scientists suspect that fear and fear conditioning can be shaped in young children by stressful events, which may occur due to familial issues. Familial dysfunction is especially prominent in children with anxiety. Anxiety runs in families, and many familial factors may affect the development of anxiety. These factors may include marital stress, poor parenting practices, child abuse, and the views a family has about its anxious child. When a family consistently answers a child's needs with rejection, is overly controlling or overprotective of a child, or models anxious behaviors to a child, these factors can contribute to the child's anxiety disorder. Families that are affected by low income and food insecurity, and which likely live in dangerous neighborhoods, are naturally more stressed than most, which may contribute to anxiety in their children.

Genetics

Studies of families and twins report that anxiety tendencies are, at least, partly inherited. A child of a parent with an anxiety disorder is

Tips for Parents from the Child Mind Institute

As a parent, you are no doubt interested in reducing your child's anxiety—you want to make your child feel better. In the process, however, you may react to his anxiety in the wrong way and actually increase his fears. Here are some tips from the Child Mind Institute that are designed to help you lower your child's anxiety effectively.

- Your goal should be to help your child manage his anxiety, not to eliminate sources of anxiety in his life. He needs to learn coping mechanisms so he won't overreact to stress.
- Don't plan his life around his anxieties. Helping your child avoid stressful things just reinforces the idea that there is something to be worried about and increases his anxiety. Help him face his fears.
- Don't promise he won't fail his math test. Just reassure him that if he studies hard and prepares well, then you will be proud that he did his best.
- Listen to and respect his feelings without empowering them. If your child is worried about going to the doctor because he is due for a shot, let him know that no one likes shots and you realize he is scared, but he will get through it and you will be there to encourage him.
- Don't ask leading questions such as, "Are you worried about the upcoming exam (or recital, speech, or some other event)?" Instead

about five times more likely to have an anxiety disorder than a child whose parents do not struggle with anxiety. A child's anxiety disorder, however, may be different from that of his parent. For example, a child may have separation anxiety while his parent has social anxiety. Interestingly, a twin with an anxiety disorder may have a different type of anxiety disorder than that of his twin sibling.

Studies have reported that about one-third of anxiety disorders are due to genetic factors. Multiple genes appear to affect children with anxiety disorders. For example, specific gene studies have identified various genes that code for serotonin, a calming neurotransmitter, involved in anxiety disorders. Other genes related to anxiety are associated with the

ask open-ended questions about such subject matter, such as, "How do you feel about your upcoming exam?"

- Don't suggest, whether by the tone of your voice or your body language, that there is something to be afraid of. Suppose he has an experience with a large dog that jumps up on him and scares him. The next time you and he see a dog, don't express anxiety. Remain cool and calm. You want to help him avoid the idea that every dog is a threat, so don't reinforce his fears.
- Encourage your child to engage in life and deal with his anxiety. The more he learns to get through an anxiety-provoking situation, the more his anxiety will decrease and his confidence will grow, allowing him to handle stressful times in the future.
- Think things through with your child. What is the worst that could happen? For example, if he gets a poor grade on a test, the world won't end. He can work harder for the next test. You can ask him, "What would you do if you have to wait for me to pick you up after soccer practice?" He might reply, "I could tell the coach my mom is late. He would call you or wait with me." Having a plan can reduce his anxiety in a healthy, effective way.
- Model healthy ways of handling anxiety for your child. Let your child see you manage and tolerate stress in your life and feel good after it has subsided.

dopamine system. In light of anxiety's genetic component, it is important to remember that, although we can't change our genes, our diets and environments can turn genes on and off.

Environmental Toxins

Very low levels of lead are well known to cause all kinds of learning and behavioral problems in children, including anxiety. Lead acts as a destructive neurotoxin that damages the brain, sometimes permanently. No level of lead is safe. (See page 213 for more information on lead.)

Exposure to airborne toxins can also cause mental disorders. Air pollution has been associated with anxiety and depression in children, adolescents, and adults. (See page 214 for more information on air pollution.) Exposure to airborne allergens such as pollen, dust, and mold can also cause behavioral symptoms, including anxiety and depression in children. Finally, environmental chemicals that most people can tolerate may bother sensitive children. These chemicals include perfumes, scented products, and gasoline. (See page 219 for more information on environmental chemicals.)

Sleep Problems

Your child's sleep patterns can be extremely revealing when you are trying to determine whether or not he has an anxiety disorder. Not surprisingly, children with anxiety disorders often have nighttime fears, suffer from insomnia, and refuse to sleep alone. Following good sleep hygiene is a crucial part of any attempt to alleviate these problems. (See page 171 for more information on sleep hygiene.)

Research also suggests that some children with anxiety disorders have obstructive sleep apnea, a condition in which the affected individual stops breathing momentarily during sleep. This breathing problem may occur repeatedly over the course of a night, disturbing brain chemistry and functioning. Removing the tonsils and adenoids of a person with obstructive sleep apnea may have a significant effect on his sleep and behavior. (See page 173 for more information on obstructive sleep apnea.)

A sleep disorder known as restless legs syndrome may also be present in children with anxiety disorders. In this disorder, the affected child's legs twitch, jerk, and feel weird, keeping him awake. He may complain about these symptoms at bedtime, only to have them dismissed by his parents as "nothing," or as an excuse to avoid going to sleep. The problem, however, is very real. These movements continue throughout the night, disturbing his sleep and affecting his brain. Measuring levels of serum ferritin, a marker of iron sufficiency, is vital part of remedying the problem. If the affected child's iron level is low, his doctor can prescribe a simple iron supplement, which should help to alleviate symptoms of restless legs syndrome and possibly reduce his anxiety. (See page 174 for more information on restless legs syndrome.)

Thyroid Problems

Levels of thyroid-stimulating hormone, an indicator of proper thyroid functioning, may be low in some children with anxiety disorders. Treating the problem with thyroid hormone is a manageable and helpful solution. When you take your child to visit his doctor, ask about thyroid testing.

ASSOCIATED DISORDERS

Other conditions are very common in kids with anxiety disorders, affecting about 75 percent of such children. According to research:

- approximately 56 percent of children with anxiety disorders also have childhood depression. Children with depression experience persistent sadness, feelings of worthlessness, irritability, and other similar symptoms. (See Chapter 7 on page 141.)
- approximately 25 percent children with anxiety disorders also have attention-deficit/hyperactivity disorder, which includes symptoms of inattentiveness, impulsivity, and hyperactivity. (See Chapter 1 on page 7.)
- approximately 21 to 45 percent of children with anxiety disorders also have oppositional defiant disorder. As a result, they may display symptoms such as anger, irritability, defiance, or vindictiveness. (See Chapter 1 on page 7.)

(See Chapter 7 on page 141 for more information on the physical or mental disorders that may accompany anxiety disorders.)

DIAGNOSIS

As is the case with the other disorders discussed in this book, there is no lab test to diagnose a child with an anxiety disorder. You may suspect that your child has an anxiety disorder after completing the questionnaire included at the beginning of this chapter, but you will still need an official diagnosis by a doctor, psychologist, or psychiatrist.

To begin, make an appointment with your family doctor, who may interview you and your child, and perhaps give you and your child questionnaires to complete. Your family doctor may also ask for information from your child's teacher about your child's ability to cope in class.

Your doctor should ask questions about your child's sleep habits, examine his tonsils and adenoids, and ask about the possibility of his having restless legs at night. As previously explained, restless legs syndrome indicates a need to get a reading of your child's serum ferritin level, a measurement of iron, and, if low, treat the problem. She may also measure your child's thyroid hormone levels, as low levels may contribute to anxiety. Finally, make certain to ask her to test for lead.

Your child may be referred to a behavioral therapist for further diagnosis and treatment. Behavioral therapy can be very effective in helping your child to manage his anxiety successfully. Medication can also be quite beneficial and may make behavioral therapy easier and shorter.

TRADITIONAL TREATMENT

In your efforts to have your child's anxiety disorder treated properly, you will likely end up seeing a therapist who is trained to help patients like your child. There are a couple of therapies that can benefit your child. Medication can be very helpful as well.

Therapy

Your child's doctor may suggest that your child see a child psychologist or psychiatrist, who will select a behavioral counselor, who is a specially trained therapist, for your child. She will act as is your child's "coach," guiding him to develop the skills he needs to manage his anxiety.

Cognitive Behavioral Therapy

Cognitive behavioral therapy is the most effective way to treat your child's anxiety. It usually consists of about ten sessions with your child, each lasting about an hour, and six more sessions with you. Your child may be part of a group of children similarly affected, or he may be treated alone. Check with your health insurance so you know how much of this therapy will be covered.

Therapy begins by helping you and your child gain some distance from the anxiety and start thinking of it as a "bully in the brain." Your child may be asked to give it a name—for example, "Mr. Bully" or "Mr. Pain in the Rear." The therapist will then tell your child that he is going to learn techniques to handle his bully, making the child feel more in control.

The therapist may also encourage the child to realize how his anxiety is affecting his life. She may list all the things he is unable to do and the feelings he has because of his bully. Perhaps he can't sleep in his own bed or enjoy sleepovers. Perhaps he feels overwhelming anxiety before and during school. Maybe he stays indoors all the time because he is terrified he might see a dog outside.

Exposure Therapy

Next, the therapist will help your child to face his fears. This strategy is called *exposure therapy.* By this time, the therapist will have gained your child's trust. She will design a plan that begins with exposure to low-anxiety events—perhaps a series of pictures—and then to more anxiety-inducing situations, and finally to a thoroughly stressful event. Some of this training may take place in the therapist's office and then progress to an outdoor setting. Your child will learn to manage his anxiety and control his fears as he and his therapist face these fears together. By the end, he should feel a sense of mastery over his anxiety as he notices it diminishing.

If your child is also on medication to reduce anxiety, he may make more progress in behavioral therapy.

Medication

The best way to treat an anxiety disorder is with a combination of an antidepressant and behavioral therapy. If your child's doctor decides that medication is appropriate for your child, it's important that she find the right one. The best medication for anxiety is antidepressants, especially those known as SSRIs, or selective serotonin reuptake inhibitors. These drugs are widely used for depression in both children and adults with excellent results.

Antidepressants

SSRIs are perhaps the best form of medication for many children with anxiety disorders. They are usually well tolerated and have few side effects. Another one of their advantages is the fact that they start working quickly—after the first week or two. The child then begins to feel better and is able to make more progress in behavioral therapy. The FDA has approved SSRIs for children that include escitalopram (Lexapro), fluoxetine (Prozac), fluoxamine (Luvox), and sertraline (Zoloft). (Although SSRIs are usually well tolerated, please see page 97 for more information on possible side effects.)

Benzodiazepines

Benzodiazepines are tranquilizers that are often given to children with anxiety disorders. They should be only used short-term, perhaps for a month or two, and can be extremely effective in children experiencing severe distress. In the long run, however, the effectiveness of this type of medication does not last. Sometimes children who use benzodiazepines don't want to stop taking them; they like how this type of medication makes them feel and don't want to switch to an SSRI, which may be a better choice in the long run.

Warnings

Your child's teacher may have reported to you that your child has trouble paying attention. This inattentiveness may seem to point to ADHD, and certainly some children with anxiety disorders do have ADHD. Perhaps your child's doctor has ordered a stimulant drug for your child's inattentiveness and the issue has improved. Some children with inattentiveness, however, are distracted in the classroom by their anxiety, not due to ADHD. Some experts warn that stimulant medications may cause stomachaches or trouble sleeping, and they may make your child's anxiety worse.

These experts advise against the use of the drugs clonidine and guanfacine, warning that these medications do not truly treat anxiety, although they may make a child calmer. These experts also point out that some doctors prescribe antipsychotic medications without evidence that these medications help anxious children.

No doubt you see how important it is to find the "right" doctor for your child—one who is well trained and experienced in selecting the best medication for your child's condition.

COMPLEMENTARY TREATMENT

There are several effective natural therapies that can be used alongside behavioral therapy and medication. There is no reason you cannot complement traditional medication and behavioral therapy with these methods. Part Two of this book describes various natural, medication-free ways to treat your child's anxiety and discusses them in depth. Consult the section on sleep and diet in particular for ways to reduce symptoms of an anxiety disorder. (See pages 167 and 185.) These options include:

- **addressing environmental factors.** What your child inhales from the air he breathes or ingests through the water he drinks may affect his daily behavior. (See Chapter 11 on page 211 for more information.)

- **changing your child's lifestyle.** Lifestyle changes, including adequate sleep, aerobic exercise, and a healthy diet, can make a huge difference in your child's anxiety, mood, and ability to cope with everyday life. (See Chapter 9 on page 167 for more information.)

CONCLUSION

A child with anxiety has excessive worries and fears. If he has an anxiety disorder, he may have one of several types—generalized anxiety disorder, separation anxiety disorder, panic disorder, social anxiety disorder, etc. Depending on the severity of his anxiety, he may definitely be a troubled child.

Since anxiety problems tend to run in families, you may identify with his problems and realize how your own problems with anxiety have negatively impacted your life. This realization may motivate you to get help for your child so he won't suffer as you have. The good news is that your child can be helped. Please do not feel embarrassed by your need to get help from experts. Both behavioral therapy and medication have been shown to reduce anxiety in children effectively and assist them in managing their fears. In addition, complementary treatments, such as lifestyle changes and nutrition, may help to address the root problems of his anxiety disorder and get him on the road to recovery.

6.

Autism Spectrum Disorder

Autism spectrum disorder, or *ASD,* is referred to as such because its symptoms can vary in kind and severity from person to person, thus forming a spectrum. It is a serious, troubling condition that affects children in two predominant ways. First, autistic children have trouble communicating and socializing with others. Second, autistic children have limited interests and engage in repetitive behaviors. Signs of autism include avoiding eye contact; having little interest in other children, parents, or caregivers; delayed language ability; and throwing a tantrum if there is even a small change in routine. An autistic child may also be interested only in one or two toys or objects, or repeatedly rock back and forth or wave his arms.

Autism is thought to affect approximately 1 in 44 children in the United States. In 2000, the rate was about 1 in 150. Each year this rate seems to increase dramatically, which may be due to better diagnoses or other unknown factors. Autism spectrum disorder is found worldwide and affects all races, economic classes, and genders, although males are about four times more likely than girls to have ASD. In regard to the onset of autism, a child may develop normally until about eighteen months to two years of age, at which point he may regress and stop meeting developmental milestones. The earlier ASD is diagnosed and treated, the better the outcome—and the outcome can be positive in some children.

Keep in mind that some children with ASD are talented in unique ways. They may display amazing math skills that few other children and adults possess. They may have outstanding—even genius-level—musical ability. Even without these special talents, some autistic children are able to go to high school and even graduate from college. They may go on to have jobs and families and lead relatively normal lives. In some cases, however, an autistic child's symptoms are so severe that he may need residential care.

SYMPTOMS

Symptoms of ASD usually appear in the first three years of life and are hard to miss. As such, you likely already know whether your child is autistic and therefore do not require an ASD questionnaire to determine whether you should seek an official diagnosis. Nevertheless, if you have begun to suspect ASD in your child and have yet to see a professional about it, the presence of certain symptoms in your child should let you know it is time to see his doctor for a proper evaluation. According to the Child Mind Institute, a leading independent nonprofit organization dedicated to children's mental health, your child may be affected by autism spectrum disorder if he:

- doesn't like to cuddle or hug.
- likes to play alone.
- doesn't answer to his name.
- doesn't want to give, share, or show off things he likes.
- doesn't use motions to communicate.
- doesn't understand how others feel.
- cannot show how he feels.
- doesn't understand relationships.
- has trouble reading and using body language.
- speaks later than normal.
- hasn't spoken a word by eighteen months old.
- cannot say two-word phrases by two years old.
- speaks differently than other children.
- sounds like a robot when speaking.

- speaks in a very singsong way.
- repeats the same action over and over again.
- focuses on small details and nothing else.
- struggles with changes in his routine.
- puts toys in order instead of playing with them.
- gets extremely focused on specific topics or objects.
- is overly sensitive to sounds, lights, textures, or smells.
- feels uncomfortable around loud noises or bright lights.
- needs more sensations to feel comfortable.
- tries to bump into things or constantly touch or smell things.

The severity of ASD is based on communication impairments and repetitive patterns of behavior. Some experts refer to mild, moderate, severe, or very severe ASD. The American Psychological Association, however, uses levels to describe the differences in autism severity.

Children at level 1 are able to speak in full sentences and engage in limited conversation with others. They may try to make friends but are often unsuccessful in their attempts. They may find it difficult to switch from one activity to another. They may also have trouble with organization, which interferes with their abilities to be independent. These children require a moderate degree of support.

Children at level 2 have marked deficits in verbal and nonverbal social communication. They are inflexible in behavior, have difficulty coping with change, show repetitive behaviors, and have narrow interests. They require substantial support.

Children at level 3 require very substantial support. They are severely inflexible in behavior, have extreme difficulty with change, and are markedly dysfunctional in all areas.

TERMINOLOGY

The following terms are those you are likely to hear most when discussing autism with people in the medical field.

Asperger Syndrome

Individuals with *Asperger syndrome* usually have milder symptoms of autism disorder. They typically do not have problems with language or intellectual disabilities, though they may experience social challenges and display unusual behaviors and interests.

Autism Spectrum Disorder

As explained at the outset of this chapter, the term "spectrum" is used due to the broad range of symptoms associated with ASD and their levels of severity, which can vary greatly.

Developmental Milestones

There are five major areas of ability that are used to describe how a typical child develops. These areas include physical growth, brain skills (cognitive skills), emotional and social development, language development, and sensory and motor development. For example, in terms of physical growth at one year, a child needs to weigh within a certain weight range to be considered "normal." In addition, a "normal" baby is expected to smile by a certain age, within a range of weeks, which shows emotional development. Moreover, a child is expected to talk using any number of words within a range by the time he reaches a particular age, which confirms language development.

Echolalia

Echolalia is the repetition of certain sounds or phrases uttered by another person, which sounds like an echo. Children with echolalia repeat certain words or sounds they have just heard, or something they heard hours or even days before. This condition is not uncommon in children before the age of two. In older toddlers and children it may be a sign of autism and should be brought to the attention of a doctor.

Pervasive Developmental Disorder

Pervasive developmental disorder, or *PDD,* was one of a few disorders that were incorporated into autism spectrum disorder in 2013. PDD is a disorder in which children show delays in socialization and communication skills. These symptoms can appear in early infancy, but they typically show up at around the age of three. Children with PDD tend to have problems using and understanding language, and may experience difficulties related to people, objects, or events.

Sensory Processing

Sensory processing refers to the way in which your brain processes the information taken in by your senses—vision, hearing, touch, taste, and smell. A child with ASD often overreacts or underreacts to the sensory information being processed by one or more of his senses. For example, he may overreact to loud noises. If you raise your voice, his reaction may be one of anger, frustration, or even violence because your voice is so loud. He may overreact to bright lights or clothing that feels uncomfortable to him. His clumsy motor skills often interfere with normal activities, such as putting on a shirt and buttoning it.

Stimming

Stimming refers to repetitive or unusual movements or noises. It may occur in normally developing children under the age of three. If the condition continues beyond this age and is apparent on a daily basis, you should report it to your child's doctor. Forms of skimming include rocking, flapping of hands, flicking of fingers, and snapping of fingers. Children may bounce, jump, twirl, or walk on tiptoes. They may pull their own hair. Stimming seems to help some autistic children and teenagers cope with emotions and overwhelming situations. It changes their brain chemistry slightly, calming them down.

OBSERVING YOUR CHILD'S BEHAVIOR

In previous chapters we discussed common behavioral disorders and the observations made by parents and teachers that may point to such disorders. As mentioned earlier, if your child is on the autism spectrum, you will likely be aware of this fact by the time you read this book and familiar with the behaviors of ASD, having observed them in your child. Moreover, there is such a wide range of behaviors associated with ASD that many of the observations we could note here may not actually describe your child.

At this point you may find yourself wondering, "Why is my child autistic? Is it my fault?" Years ago, doctors would tell parents that autism was caused by bad parenting. "Experts" even referred to certain mothers as "refrigerator moms" due to a perception that these mothers were cold and uncaring. What a terrible thing to tell parents who are struggling to help their troubled child. Although there is still much to be learned about what causes autism, modern medicine points to genetic abnormalities and environmental factors as its main risk factors, not cold mothers.

RISK FACTORS

ASD is an amazingly complex disorder. Because it can be so severe and disabling to a child, causing extreme anxiety in his family and tremendous difficulties in school, substantial funding has been made available by both private donors and organizations and governments around the world to study this disorder. Thanks to this funding, scientists and doctors continue to piece together the puzzle that is ASD.

Brain and Body Abnormalities

Extensive imaging studies have identified structural abnormalities in the brains of children with ASD. No one pattern appears in every autistic person, however. One difference is an increased volume of the *cerebrum,* which is the largest part of the brain and accounts for two-thirds of the total weight of the brain. The cerebrum integrates sensory impulses, directs motor activity, and controls intelligence.

The *hippocampus* of the brain is also enlarged in some autistic children. This structure is responsible for forming and storing memories. The amygdala, which is involved in the experiencing of emotions, may also be different in size—larger in some, smaller in others. The *cerebellum,* located at the base of the skull between the cerebrum and brain stem, controls balance, movement, and other complex motor functions. It may be smaller than normal. Finally, autistic children may have extra *cerebrospinal fluid,* which surrounds the brain and spinal cord for protection and supply of nutrients. This extra fluid may make their heads slightly larger than normal, beginning as early as six months of age and continuing through age three. Your child's doctor may have actually measured the circumference of your infant child's head as part of a check-up.

Researchers have also documented multiple abnormalities throughout the bodies of children with ASD. These abnormalities are both *physiological* and *metabolic*. Physiological functions refer to the ways in which the parts of the body work together. Metabolic functions refer to the chemical reactions in the body's cells that convert food into energy.

Diet

Parents often report that their child with ASD eats only a few foods. If these foods aren't offered, the child revolts and refuses to take even a bite of another food. This scenario is called *selective eating*. Children who fit this description tend to prefer highly processed foods and eat fewer fruits, vegetables, and whole grains. Therefore, they also tend to have nutritionally poor diets and weight-related health issues. In other words, these children are overfed but undernourished. Approximately fifty nutrients are needed for the brain to function normally, so a child's dietary preferences may certainly be listed among the risk factors for brain dysfunction.

One study compared the benefits of medication and standard treatment with the benefits of a micronutrient supplement that consisted of thirty-six vitamins, minerals, antioxidants, and amino acids. Both groups improved, but those taking the supplement experienced lower activity levels, less anger, more spontaneity, less irritability, and far fewer side effects. This outcome suggests the children were deficient in multiple nutrients, and that supplementing these nutrients had a very positive effect. (See Chapter 10 on page 185 for more about nutrient supplementation.)

Environmental Toxins

While genetics seem to play a huge role in ASD, scientists think that exposure to certain environmental chemicals may also play an equally important part. These exposures may impact a child at conception or during pregnancy, infancy, or the first few years of life. Chemical exposure may account for a child who develops normally and then starts to regress. Chemicals that have been studied in connection with ASD include pesticides, phthalates, polychlorinated biphenyls (PCBs), solvents, and others. Some of these chemicals seem to be more harmful than others.

Researchers have also studied certain genes that may be affected by these substances. They concluded that there may be a subset of children who are prone to experiencing complex interactions between their genes and certain environmental toxins, which may lead to the development of ASD.

Genetics

The involvement of genetic abnormalities in ASD is well accepted by experts. Approximately one hundred genetic abnormalities have been associated with ASD, with different affected genes resulting in different symptoms. In relation to the previous section on environmental factors, a variety of mental disorders have been attributed in part to genes that increase a person's susceptibility to certain harmful substances in the environment.

We can see the influence of genetics in autism spectrum disorder by looking at ASD rates in families. For example, when one identical twin is affected by ASD, there is a 90 percent chance that the other twin will also have it. The chance of a fraternal twin being affected by ASD if his twin is autistic ranges from 0 to 24 percent. The ASD rate in non-twin siblings of children with ASD has been estimated to be between 2 and 6 percent. Furthermore, the risk of autism spectrum disorder for a family member of a child with ASD is five to ten times higher than average.

Infections and Immune System Dysfunction

Many experts have reported evidence that infection may play a role in causing or contributing to autism. During a mother's pregnancy, an infection during any one of the three trimesters can increase the child's autism risk by approximately 37 percent. Infection in a baby or toddler can also increase autism risk by about 54 percent. In fact, a baby who experiences at least one infection during the first year of life is more likely to develop autism than a child who does not experience an infection during this period.

This connection may be explained by the fact that some severe infections can directly damage a child's brain cells or cause damage due to inflammation. It could also be explained by the fact that the use of antibiotics to treat infections leads to a depletion of good bacteria in the intestine, and what happens in the gut is very much linked to what goes on in the brain, as modern medicine has discovered.

Research has also linked dysfunctional immune systems with autism. Children with ASD may have abnormalities in their white blood cells, decreased lymphocytes (a type of white blood cell), imbalances in different immunoglobulin (antibody) levels, or an autoimmune disorder, in which the immune system attacks a person's own cells. Some of these issues have been linked directly to particular genes.

Sleep

Sleep problems can be a major issue for many autistic children. In fact, anywhere from 50 to 80 percent of autistic children have sleep problems. Moreover, their brains seem to be especially sensitive to sleep problems. They may have more trouble settling down at bedtime and their melatonin levels may be too low to bring on sleep. Addressing and resolving sleep problems can help the child and his exhausted parents.

When addressing sleep problems, the best place to start is with good sleep hygiene, which means improving your child's bedtime routine so that he falls asleep more easily. A child with ASD, however, may have an actual sleep disorder. Restless legs syndrome is a disorder in which a person's experiences uncontrollable leg movements and strange sensations in the legs. These issues delay the onset of sleep and disturb sleep throughout the night. Thankfully, restless legs syndrome is often easily remedied. The problem has been linked to a low level of iron in the blood, which, if confirmed by a doctor, can be treated with iron supplements.

Obstructive sleep apnea is another sleep disorder children with ASD may have. In this condition, breathing momentarily stops and then quickly restarts during sleep. These breathing interruptions occur many times a night, which can result in behavioral problems during the day. The most common causes of obstructive sleep apnea are enlarged tonsils and adenoids. A study of autistic children with obstructive sleep apnea reported much-improved behavior after a tonsillectomy. The sooner the need for a tonsillectomy was observed and the surgery was performed, the better the outcome was in relation to obstructive sleep apnea. (See Chapter 9 on page 167 for more information on sleep problems.)

One interesting phenomenon seen in about 17 percent of autistic children is that they may show improved symptoms when sick with a fever. Children with severe autism seem to make the most gains, in fact. The reason for this occurrence is not yet understood and, unfortunately, when the fever goes away, so do the improvements.

ASSOCIATED DISORDERS

Identifying associated disorders is critical in autism because treatment of one or more of these disorders may improve autism symptoms, thereby improving the lives of the autistic child and his parents.

- Roughly 30 to 80 percent of children with autism meet the criteria for ADHD. Children with ADHD are inattentive, hyperactive, and impulsive. (See Chapter 1 on page 7.)
- Approximately 40 percent of children with ASD are diagnosed with an anxiety disorder. Children with anxiety disorders are excessively worried, tense, and fidgety, and may struggle to concentrate. (See Chapter 5 on page 101.)
- As children with ASD get older and more self-aware, depression may become a problem. Approximately 20 percent of people with ASD suffer from depression. (See Chapter 7 on page 141.)

In addition to the brain-related conditions associated with ASD, autism has been linked to a number of physical conditions as well. Unfortunately, it can be very difficult for a child with ASD to communicate these issues to his caregiver. The resultant frustration may lead to repetitive behaviors, irritability, aggression, or other similar outcomes. According to the Children's Hospital of Philadelphia, the following conditions have been reported in connection with ASD.

- Gastrointestinal issues commonly affect people with ASD, causing them considerable discomfort. These problems include diarrhea, constipation, gaseousness, and abdominal pain, and may result in eating problems, disturbed sleep, or discomfort lying down.

- Approximately one-third of children who fall on the spectrum of autism have epilepsy. It may be difficult to recognize a seizure in a child with ASD, as it may be mistaken for other repetitive behaviors common to autism. An autistic child may also be unable to communicate the fact that he is having a seizure and not simply exhibiting some other habit associated with ASD. *Childhood absence epilepsy,* or *CAE,* in particular, may be easily confused with ASD. When a child with CAE experiences what is known as an absence seizure, he may be found staring blankly and being completely unresponsive to his surroundings, only to return to normal awareness ten to twenty seconds later. During the seizure, the child's eyelids may flutter and he may engage in repetitive movements such as chewing motions or finger rubbing.

- Children with ASD are more likely than the average child to be overweight or obese. In one survey of children's health, 19 percent of children with ASD were overweight, while 23 percent were obese. Nevertheless, this same survey also showed that 14 percent of typically developing children were overweight and 15 percent were obese, which indicated that weight was a problem for a large number of children in general.

- Ear infections tend to occur more in children with ASD than they do in other children. In one study, researchers found that this tendency appeared in lower-functioning autistic children at an earlier age than it did in their higher-functioning peers. They also found that ear infections were more common in autistic children with low-set ears, who also had higher scores on scales measuring autism symptoms. This correlation may suggest that intermittent hearing problems due to recurring ear infections may affect language and social development.

- Allergies are extremely common in children and adults in the United States, but they are even more common in children with autism. For example, reporting has shown food, respiratory, and skin allergies to be higher in children with ASD (11.25 percent, 18.73 percent, and 16.81 percent, respectively) compared with children without ASD (4.25 percent, 12.08 percent, and 9.84 percent, respectively). The wheezing, congestion, and itchiness associated with allergies can make children with ASD miserable and distracted.

(See Chapter 7 on page 141 for more information on the physical or mental disorders that may accompany ASD.)

DIAGNOSIS

ASD can vary greatly from one child to another, prompting one expert to say, "If you've seen one child with autism, you've seen *one* child with autism." It is important, therefore, to find an experienced doctor who has seen many children with ASD to diagnose and treat your child. If your child's doctor suspects he has a disorder on the autism spectrum, ask her if she has the qualifications to help your child (i.e., any experience treating children with ASD or extra training in diagnosing and treating ASD.) If she does not, ask her to refer you to a specialist who has the training and experience required to treat your child. This specialist could be a child psychiatrist, child psychologist, pediatric neurologist, or developmental pediatrician. It could even be a physician trained in complementary or functional medicine who uses both traditional treatments and nontraditional therapies, which may include methods that focus on nutrition.

You may want to seek diagnosis and treatment at a local medical center, academic facility, or children's health clinic. Whoever you see should answer your questions, take your concerns seriously, and make you and your child feel comfortable. Look for an expert clinician who can spot subtle differences between a child with ASD and one who seems to have ASD but may have an entirely different disorder. For example, a child may have a language disorder that can masquerade as autism. A child who is withdrawn may have social and communication problems that are not part of ASD. A skilled, experienced doctor will be able to make the correct diagnosis and recommend a treatment program.

Medical History

Your child's doctor may start by asking you about the pregnancy period, how your child was after birth, and his developmental milestones as he got older. (Please be completely honest with the doctor about any bad habits that might have affected the child via the mother during pregnancy, such as drug use or smoking.) Abilities that were apparent in infancy may not be by the time your child is evaluated for ASD, but it is still important to inform your child's doctor of them. She will also want to know if your child has had repeated infections and, if so, whether his behavior changed after these incidents. Finally, she will inquire about any family history of ASD or other medical or behavioral disorders.

If your child lives in potentially dangerous environmental conditions (e.g., near a highway, toxic waste site, power plant, petrochemical plant, etc.), let his doctor know, as this information may contribute to her understanding of his disorder. The EPA has acknowledged that underserved communities in the United States are the most exposed of all US communities to toxic environments.

Finally, if you know of or suspect the presence of mold in your home, inform your child's doctor of this fact during the interview.

Screening

Screening may start with questionnaires to be completed by parents or caregivers. The Modified Checklist for Autism in Toddlers (M-CHAT) is a commonly used questionnaire that is designed to raise a red flag in connection with a child who may have autism. Another screening tool is the Autism in Toddlers & Young Children (STAT) questionnaire, which asks questions in more detail than the M-CHAT. These tools do not lead to an official diagnosis of autism but rather indicate that further evaluation is needed.

Physical Exam

Your child's doctor should also complete a careful physical exam of your child and ask pertinent questions. If your child has problems eating, she should examine his mouth. Is the structure of the mouth and teeth normal? She should also look for enlarged tonsils and adenoids, which may interfere with his sleep. She should inquire about past illnesses that have required antibiotics and ask about his diet. If he eats only a few foods, what are these foods? Finally, she should inquire about any sleep-related problems he may have.

Cognitive Testing

Diagnosis may also involve cognitive testing, which evaluates how a child thinks. Moreover, if a child misses a question on a test, he may become so upset he has a tantrum. This reaction also reveals useful information to the doctor. Cognitive testing can tell a doctor what a child can do and what he can't. It's important for a doctor to know her patient's talents and what he does well so his therapy can build on these abilities and use this cognitive growth to help him to do new things.

Other Diagnostic Tools

Your child's doctor may use a diagnostic tool such as the Autism Diagnostic Observation Schedule, which consists of a series of activities that involve both the examiner and the child being evaluated. In the version designed for toddlers, activities are based mainly in play between the child and his tester. There is also a version for older kids, which deals more with communication. These "tests" do not have right or wrong

Tips for Parenting a Child with ASD

Although children with ASD can vary greatly in terms of symptoms and their severity, the following tips can be of help the caregiver of a child with almost any form of ASD.

- Provide positive feedback to your child. If he does something well, praise him, tell him you love him, and give him a hug. Be specific in your praise so he knows what he has done that pleases you. If appropriate, a small reward, such as a sticker, may make him happy.
- Provide consistent a schedule for your child to follow. As you know, he may become extremely upset if you don't. Children with ASD like structure.
- Build time for play into his schedule. What does he like to do when he is not engaged in therapeutic or learning activities?
- Keep in in mind that changes will probably not occur overnight with therapy. Be patient.
- Take your son on errands, such as grocery shopping, knowing that doing so may cause stress for both of you but will also have positive effects.

answers but are simply meant to evaluate social skills, communication, and repetitive behaviors.

Your child's doctor may also interview you and any other people who have close contact with your child, including teachers. She may even visit the school to observe your child firsthand.

TRADITIONAL TREATMENT

Although treatment may not seem possible with ASD, it is. The following treatment options, which include behavioral therapy, physical therapy, feeding therapy, occupational therapy, and speech and language therapy, can be of benefit to your child. Medication may also be required, of course, and there are even some natural complementary treatments that may help to improve your child's ASD symptoms.

- Join a support group, which will give you the opportunity to share your experiences with others and to hear about their experiences. Members can support and learn from each other. A group may even invite experts to provide advice at some meetings.
- Take a break from your child, if possible. Let other caregivers take over so you can rest, sleep, or do "normal" activities. Check with your local college to see if it has a student who is studying psychology or social work and could come to your house to supervise your child as a learning experience. In addition, try to get someone to do some household chores for you on occasion in order to ease your burden.
- Deal with your stress. Parents of children with ASD are generally more stressed than parents of children with other disorders. You may need someone to talk to—a psychologist or social worker, your pastor or rabbi, or perhaps a close friend who is a good listener. You could also take up an exercise, even if it's just fast walking or biking around the block, which will increase your breathing and heart rate, releasing feel-good chemicals in your brain, and encourage optimal of delivery of nutrients throughout your body. Of course, try to eat a healthy diet and get enough sleep. In other words, look after yourself.

Therapy

There are many types of therapy that can be beneficial to children with ASD. Your child's doctor may be able to recommend someone she has worked with before who has successfully helped many children like your child. Keep in mind that if one type of therapy doesn't work for your child, there are others that might.

Behavioral Therapy

Behavioral therapy can be extremely helpful in the treatment of ASD. A behavioral therapist can teach parents how to manage the problematic behaviors exhibited by their autistic child, and if that child happens to have another behavioral disorder that has gone undiagnosed, such as anxiety or ADHD, she can spot it and then treat it as well.

Feeding Therapy

Many children with ASD have feeding problems. If you struggle with feeding your child, ask your child's doctor if she can recommend a feeding therapist. This person may be a psychologist, occupational therapist, or speech therapist who is specifically trained in feeding children like yours.

As children with ASD frequently have problems with their senses, they may taste food differently and the textures of certain foods may bother them as well. For example, they may dislike lumpy foods that require chewing or smooth foods that feel strange to them. If your child struggles to chew and swallow, a therapist can help with those problems. She may examine his mouth to see if there are any structural problems that need to be addressed by a different specialist. This information may reveal why feeding your child is so difficult.

If your child will only eat unhealthy foods like cookies, crackers, or chips, you will need help and support in changing his diet to include healthy fruits, vegetables, and whole grains. This change is important because he needs many different nutrients for his brain and body to work properly. These nutrients are not typically found in sufficient amounts (or at all) in junk food. He probably won't accept these changes easily, but your therapist will have strategies that can help.

Make sure that your family sets a good example. Your child won't understand why all of you eat what he can't have, such as French fries, candy, soft drinks, chips, and other non-nutritious foods. Simply don't keep these items in the house.

Proper eating is important not only for good nutrition but also for socialization skills. If you can change your child's diet, you may find great improvements in his health and behavior. A feeding therapist will help you set up a plan to accomplish this task successfully.

Occupational Therapy

Occupational therapy benefits more people than simply those who require help with work-related activities. They teach people how to do everyday tasks, whether these people are adults who have had strokes and are unable to do simple tasks or young children with ASD. They work in concert with speech therapists and physical therapists with similar goals in mind for children.

An occupational therapist, or OT for short, will suggest age-appropriate activities that will promote small muscle coordination and strength. Depending on your child's ASD, she may be able to improve his ability to do such tasks as putting his clothes on, using cutlery, or drinking from a glass. These therapists engage in play with your child to encourage new skills, which may also benefit his social development and language skills.

Physical Therapy

As you know, most children with ASD show problems with language, communication, and behavior. Approximately 75 percent of children with ASD also have trouble with motor coordination, including deficits in large muscle coordination, motor planning, gait, and postural control. Many of these abilities are delayed, and these delays become especially noticeable as the child grows older. A physical therapist may be a helpful member of your child's group of therapists, and working on motor skills may boost language and cognitive skills as well. It's important for your child to exercise throughout his life for both his physical and his mental health.

Some communities have "swim and gym" programs for preschoolers who have muscle and coordination problems. A trained graduate student may take your child into a swimming pool to help him work on splashing, kicking, and floating. In a gym, your child may do balance exercises, throw and catch balls, or do floor exercises. Sometimes a community will offer therapeutic horseback riding. Horseback riding is a form of physical therapy because the rider must react and adjust to the horse's movements.

Play Therapy

Children with ASD often play differently than other children. For example, they may focus on a part of a toy, such as the wheels of a toy car, not the whole toy. Keep in mind that how a child with ASD plays is also a form of self-expression. You may think of this play as his "words." Play can help your child to learn and connect with his therapist, parents, and other family members.

Play therapy typically takes place on the floor. The therapist tries to interact with the child on the child's own terms. In other words, she plays with the child in whatever way he is playing. Then the therapist adds something, perhaps another toy, to their play. She may introduce language into their game. The goal is to create play that alternates between the child and her, which encourages communication and focus. Play therapy may take place for up to twenty-five hours a week and should be practiced in the home too. All areas of development may improve with play therapy.

Integrated play groups are composed of a therapist, your child, other children like him, and other children without ASD. The latter children can show their peers how to lead and how to play. Eventually, the goal is for the children to take over, leaving the therapist as an observer. Over time, your child will learn how to play with other children, improving his socialization skills. Integrated play also allows your child opportunities to enrich his vocabulary.

Speech and Language Therapy

A child with ASD often has some form of speech difficulty. He may be unable to communicate with words, grunting, shrieking, humming, babbling in world-like sounds, or uttering foreign-sounding words he has made up. He may use real words but talk in a singsong manner or like a robot.

The earlier speech therapy starts, the better the outcome will be. Your pediatrician may recommend a speech and language therapist, who will help your child to understand what is being said to him and be able to speak comprehensibly in response. Just think how difficult your world would be if you couldn't understand others or have them understand you. It would be scary and extremely frustrating, and you could very well become angry and destructive.

If a child with ASD has difficulty sucking, chewing, or swallowing food or liquids, a speech and language therapist may address the issue by examining the structures of his mouth and the coordination of his mouth muscles as he eats or drinks, similar to the way in which a feeding therapist would examine him.

Your community may offer a language program for preschoolers who have severe language delays or whose speech can't be understood. It may be run by the department of speech at a university or specialized school. As part of this program, children can learn how to repeat the words and short sentences presented by their teacher and others.

Parental Training Classes

Another form of behavioral therapy is for parents of children with ASD. Your child's doctor may recommend you attend parental training classes, either alone or as part of a group. No, your parenting skills did not cause your child's autism, but he didn't come with an instruction manual when he was born, so knowing how to use established, effective parenting strategies with your autistic child can make a real difference in his life and yours.

Medication

More than half of children with ASD are on one or more prescription medications. Abilify and Risperdal are the only two medications approved by the FDA specifically for children with ASD. Many children with ASD also have hyperactivity, anxiety, depression, or aggression, which can be helped by another medication. So, if your child has both ASD and ADHD, he may benefit from Abilify or Risperdal and a stimulant medication. Figuring out which medications to use for your child's ASD and other disorders can allow you to send him to school or take care of him at home instead of having to put him in residential care. If your child is uncontrollable, with violent meltdowns that present danger to himself, his family, or others, medication can help.

Abilify (aripiprazole) works by balancing levels of the neurotransmitters dopamine and serotonin to improve thinking, mood, and behavior. Abilify is reported to reduce symptoms such as aggression, tantrums, rapidly changing mood, and self-injurious behavior in approximately eight weeks. It is often prescribed before Risperdal, which has more serious side effects.

Risperdal (risperidone) is another medication that may help your child. It's an antipsychotic medication that helps children with extreme behavioral problems, including anger, irritability, and aggressiveness. Like Abilify, it improves aggression, temper outbursts, and self-injurious behavior by rebalancing the neurotransmitters dopamine and serotonin. As recently mentioned, Risperdal can have serious side effects, including substantial weight gain and metabolic, neurological, or hormonal changes, which can be harmful. Weight gain could reach almost twelve pounds in about as many weeks and occur alongside increased blood sugar and blood lipids (fats).

Moreover, Risperdal use may result in a condition called *tardive dyskinesia,* which is characterized by repetitive, involuntary movements—and the longer treatment lasts, the greater the risk. It may also increase the level of the hormone *prolactin* in the body, leading to breast enlargement, production of breast milk, and bone loss. These side effects could be permanent.

Some experts point out that other treatments, such as behavioral therapy, should be tried first before the use of medication, except in cases of children in severe crisis. When it comes to medication, the benefits may outweigh the risks. You can see why it's important for you to keep in close contact with the prescribing doctor and your pharmacist. Baseline values of height, weight, vital signs, prolactin levels, and levels of blood fats and sugar should be established before beginning medication and then monitored over the course of treatment.

If your child responds well to behavioral therapy, he may be able to switch to a milder medication or even go without. If your child is taking medication for a behavioral disorder, however, never stop usage of this medication suddenly. Your child's doctor can explain how you can gradually reduce the dosage so your child can safely stop taking the medication.

COMPLEMENTARY TREATMENT

Children with ASD often need all the help they can get. There is no reason the following therapies can't be used in association with traditional ones. Just keep your child's doctor informed of the complementary treatments you try and their results. These alternative methods may include:

- **addressing environmental factors.** The air your child breathes and the water he drinks may affect his daily behavior. Research has shown that environmental toxicities may be a major cause of ASD, as they may interact with genetic predispositions. (See Chapter 11 on page 211 for more information on the connection between environmental factors and behavioral disorders.)

- **helpful programs and devices.** There are summer camps designed for autistic children. Your child's doctor may be able to recommend one, but you will still have to do some research on your own to identify which camp would be a good fit for your child. If you can talk with other parents who have used a particular camp, then do so. The information you get from them can be invaluable. A camp will likely offer different lengths of stay. The shortest length—perhaps a week—may be the best choice for your child as a first-time camper. If it goes well, next time you can opt for a lengthier stay. (See Chapter 12 on page 225 for more information on summer camps.)

- **lifestyle changes.** Lifestyle changes, including getting restful sleep, doing aerobic exercise, an eating a healthy diet can make a huge difference in your child's mood and ability to cope with life. Sleep is especially important when it comes to ASD. Addressing sleep issues can sometimes bring huge improvements in ASD symptoms. If a healthy diet is difficult to achieve for your child due to his ASD, a micronutrient supplement may allow him to get the nutrients he needs. Such supplements have been found helpful in connection with children with ASD. Supplementation could be a challenge as well, however, as your child may have trouble swallowing pills. In this case, you may wish to try a liquid supplement. (See Chapters 9 and 10 on pages 167 and 185 for more information on sleep and nutrition, respectively.)

CONCLUSION

Raising a child with ASD is a challenge for which no parent is truly prepared. Your child's problems may be so severe that he is extremely difficult to manage at home or school. Conversely, his ASD may be quite mild, allowing him to attend school and have healthy relationships.

Many children with ASD can improve—some a lot—with the right guidance and treatment. Ask your child's doctor for recommendations when trying to find the best professionals for your child both in diagnosis and treatment. You may need a team of experts to assist in his treatment, at least at the beginning. As you learn more about ASD and how to address your child's problems, you may be able to do much of his therapy at home.

7.

Associated Disorders

As you have seen mentioned throughout Part One, many behavioral disorders are associated with other disorders or conditions. Moreover, treatment of an associated disorder typically improves the symptoms of a child's primary disorder, and vice versa. For example, discovering why your child has aches and pains may help solve his behavioral issues. If your child has ADHD and is sensitive to dairy, he may get stomachaches or headaches when he drinks milk. Removing dairy from his diet may result in not only the disappearance of these aches but also the improvement of his ADHD symptoms, sometimes dramatically.

Similarly, a child who has conduct disorder may also be obese. His weight should be a red flag that his diet is poor. Changing his diet by removing excess sugar, fat, and fast foods and replacing them with healthy foods should help him to lose weight while also improving his behavior.

This chapter addresses problems that are commonly associated with the behavioral disorders described in this book, which include aches and pains, depression, gut issues, learning disabilities, and obesity. Not only is it important to improve these conditions, but learning about them may help you to understand your child's main disorder more fully.

ACHES AND PAINS

Most children have minor aches and pains from time to time, which might mean an occasional headache or perhaps a stomachache before a big event. Perhaps he occasionally complains about having sore legs at night. If these events are relatively rare, you probably don't think much about them, particularly if he is up and about before long and feeling fine. If he experiences aches and pains more often, however, you may have already taken him to his doctor to rule out anything serious. If his doctor assured you that nothing was seriously wrong—that the aches and pains might be "growing pains" or simply psychosomatic—and recommended over-the-counter medication as treatment, you may have been relieved. Don't forget, though, that your child's aches and pains are real, whatever their origins may be, and if they continue it may be time for you to play detective.

Keep a careful record of what your child eats and drinks, and of any exposures he might have to substances to which he may be sensitive. Include in this record any headaches, stomachaches, or muscle aches he might experience. Do you see any pattern? Do his aches occur after he has eaten a certain food, or when he is has been exposed to perfume or other scents? When he avoids this food or scent, do his headaches disappear? If so, keep him away from the substance that seems to set off his symptoms for a week or so and see what happens. Is his behavior any better? Then reintroduce the suspected trigger and see if he gets worse in any way.

The relationship between food sensitivities and behavior has been studied for decades. For example, in a study of children with ADHD who were placed on a diet of just a few hypoallergenic foods—a "few foods" diet (see page 208)—the behavioral symptoms of these children improved dramatically, and so did their headaches, stomachaches, and muscle aches. Other improvements included reductions in bedwetting, migraines, and seizures. When the children had certain common foods reintroduced into their diet, their behaviors and physical symptoms returned.

DEPRESSION

Feeling sad or down sometimes is a normal part of life for both adults and children. On the other hand, if your child has been feeling sad, uninterested in things he used to enjoy, or hopeless in certain situations, then you should take these emotional changes seriously. If this mood continues longer than a few weeks, he may suffer from depression.

Childhood depression is fairly common. It is estimated that 3.2 percent of children aged three to seventeen years (approximately 1.9

million kids) have been diagnosed with depression in the United States. Symptoms of childhood depression may include:

- changes in eating patterns (either eating more or eating less than normal).
- changes in energy levels (either being tired and sluggish or tense and restless more than normal).
- changes in sleep patterns (either sleeping more or less than normal).
- engaging in self-injury or self-destructive behavior.
- feeling sad, hopeless, or irritable much of the time.
- feeling worthless, useless, or guilty.
- having a hard time paying attention.
- not wanting to do or enjoy fun activities.

If your child is depressed, he may not talk about his feelings, so it is important to look for the signs of this condition. Depression is a serious illness that can affect every aspect of your child's life. He may be so depressed that he is inattentive in school and his grades drop. He may become socially isolated because he lacks the desire to play with friends. He may refuse to do family chores or participate in family activities, preferring to spend his time alone in his room. And because depression often affects sleep and diet, it can also lead to physical health problems.

Very few young children commit suicide, but it does occur, and the risk gets higher as children grow older. If your child starts talking about taking his life or says the world would be better without him, call his doctor immediately. Then put all prescription drugs out of his reach, place any guns in the house in a locked cabinet, and be sure he has no way of opening this cabinet.

It is common to have depression along with ADHD, ODD, CD, or an anxiety disorder. Improving your child's depression may also improve the symptoms of his behavioral disorder, and vice versa.

A child's family situation can be a major driver of childhood depression. For example, if either parent is depressed, the child is at greater risk of depression. So far, genetics do not seem to be the reason for this elevated risk. Rather, it may be caused by stress within the family. Of course, the basic personality of a child may make him more susceptible to depression. Not surprisingly, a loss of a beloved family member, such as a parent, sibling, grandparent, or pet, can also trigger depression. Poor sleep patterns and an unhealthy diet may also promote depression. In fact, low levels of zinc, folate, and magnesium can play a role in a child becoming depressed, so it is important not to allow sugary junk foods to replace nutrient-dense foods such as vegetables, fruit, and whole grains in your child's diet.

POOR GUT HEALTH

Your child's intestinal tract (gut) and brain are in constant communication with each other, sending signals back and forth. This connection is called the *gut-brain axis*. The state of your child's gut plays a major role not only in his physical health but also in his mental health and behavior.

In the large intestine, there are roughly more than 40 trillion microorganisms, or microbes. Yes, that's trillion with a "t." The total accumulation of microbes in your gut is known as your *microbiome*. The microbiome includes bacteria, fungi, and other microorganisms. Bacteria are the largest and most commonly studied component of the microbiome. In fact, there are more than a thousand different species of bacteria in the human gut. These microbes play different roles in the body, most of them important for good health, though some can lead to disease. The composition of your microbiome largely depends on your diet.

As a baby grows, the microbes in his microbiome begin to grow in number and diversify in type. Breast milk contains certain bacteria that help the baby to digest the milk, which provides nutrients for the growth and development of the baby's body and brain. The milk also feeds the baby's microbiome.

As the baby grows and eats whole foods, fiber also feeds the microbiome. Certain bacteria digest some forms of fiber, producing critical nutrients for gut health. Some microbes also produce vitamins and amino acids, and alter byproducts of metabolism. Microbes also improve the strength of the intestinal mucosa, or gut wall, and influence the immune system's response to infection.

Perhaps most importantly for this discussion, gut microbes affect the central nervous system, controlling brain function and behavior, which, in turn, affect the gut. The gastrointestinal tract, through the microbiome, is sensitive to emotions such as anxiety and sadness. For example, anxiety can cause stomach upset as a result of the gut-brain axis. Research also reveals that gut microbe populations are different in some children with psychological disorders such as ADHD, autism, anxiety, and depression.

So, how does a child's microbiome become altered? Certainly, diet is one reason. If your child eats too much sugar and too little fiber, his bad bacteria will thrive while his good bacteria will diminish, disturbing the gut-brain axis. (Unfortunately, artificial sweeteners also have a negative effect on good gut bacteria, so don't consider them a good alternative to sugar when it comes to microbiome health.)

Another reason a child's microbiome may become unbalanced is the use of antibiotics. Studies have shown that children who were exposed to prenatal antibiotics in the womb, or to antibiotics from infancy to about the age of two, were 10 to 50 percent more likely to exhibit sleep disorders, ADHD, conduct disorder, anxiety disorders, learning problems, or other behavioral disorders when they got older. The hypothesis is that the antibiotics kill off good bacteria and upset the balance in a child's intestine, affecting the expression of genes responsible for dopamine, which is related to ADHD, autism, and other disorders.

Of course, let's not forget that antibiotics have saved millions of lives over the years. They are a crucial weapon against severe, uncontrolled bacterial infections. Unfortunately, they are being improperly used in children. In fact, the CDC states that one in three prescriptions for antibiotics is unnecessary. Many common infections in young children, such as recurrent ear infections, are often caused by viruses, not bacteria, but are still treated unnecessarily with antibiotics. Antibiotics do not kill viruses, but they do disturb the microbiome and thus upset the immune system. Studies have reported that children with ADHD or autism often have a history of recurrent ear infections. Recurrent infections coupled with antibiotic use weaken the immune system, allowing for more ear infections and creating a vicious circle of infection.

If your child was developing normally, experienced a series of ear infections that were treated with antibiotics, and then began to have behavioral problems, these behavioral issues may be associated with the ear infection and antibiotics. Perhaps he also developed digestive problems such as diarrhea, nausea, or vomiting during the same period. These conditions could easily have been caused by antibiotics.

If your child has had multiple rounds of antibiotics, there are a few things you can do to help him to restore his gut balance. A good diet is essential to the restoration of a healthy microbiome. His diet should contain very little added sugar but lots of vegetables, fruit, and whole grains. Vegetables, fruit, and whole grains are especially important to have in the diet, as most are good sources of *prebiotics,* which are a specialized plant fiber that acts as food for healthy bacteria in the gut. Foods high in prebiotics include leeks, asparagus, onions, shallots, Jerusalem artichokes, garlic, legumes, beans, bananas, and grapefruit.

Your child's diet should also include low-sugar, dye-free yogurt that contains multiple species of probiotic bacteria. Similarly, you could give him probiotic supplements, which are over-the-counter supplements of "good" bacteria that can help to reestablish a balanced microbiome in your child's gut. These methods can alleviate the intestinal problems associated with antibiotics and may also improve the behavioral disorders caused by an imbalanced microbiome. When purchasing a probiotic supplement, make certain that it contains greater than 70 billion colonies of bacteria and at least five different types of bacteria.

You can inquire with your doctor or pharmacist about which probiotic product would be best for your child.

LEARNING DISABILITIES

Does your child struggle in school even though he basically is bright in other areas of his life? Does he make an effort to get passing grades only to fall short again and again? Is he is frustrated? Are you and his teacher frustrated? Parents and teachers often lash out at this type of child because they don't understand why he cannot learn like most other kids. They often say, "You would learn if you'd try a little harder," which is never helpful. A child who has trouble learning may become convinced he is dumb and hate going to school, where everyone around him seems to learn effortlessly. Other children may even tease him because of his learning problems.

What you (and perhaps your child's teacher) may not know is that your child may have a *specific learning disorder,* or *SLD.* A child with a specific learning disorder has difficulty in one or more areas of learning without his overall intelligence being affected. According to experts, SLDs are some of the most common disorders facing kids today. The American Psychiatric Association states the prevalence of SLDs to be 5 to 15 percent among school-aged children.

There are several specific learning disorders, including *dyslexia,* or difficulty with reading; *dyscalcula,* or difficulty with math; and *dysgraphia,* or difficulty with writing. Approximately 79 percent of children with learning disabilities also have behavioral disorders. For example, almost half of children with ADHD are also affected by SLDs. Specific learning disorders tend to make behavioral problems worse, and vice versa. It's not hard to imagine how having ADHD would make learning more difficult, or how a child who is struggling to read may become inattentive, overactive, or even act out.

According to the CDC there are some general symptoms of learning disorders that should set off your alarm bells. Does your child have difficulty telling his right from his left? Does he reverse letters, words, or numbers? Does he have trouble recognizing patterns or sorting items by size or shape? Is staying organized difficult for him? Does he have trouble remembering what was just said or what he just read? Does he have trouble with coordination? Does he struggle with tasks involving his hands like writing, cutting, or drawing? Does he struggle to understand the concept of time? It is surely not difficult to recognize how all these symptoms would cause severe problems in the classroom and at home.

To find out what causes SLDs, it is important to recognize what does not cause SLDs: laziness, lack of effort, being unintelligent, being a bad child, or poor parenting. A specific learning disorder occurs because a child's brain is slightly different from the brains of his peers, and it's no one's fault. No one knows exactly what causes SLDs, but there are a few commonly recognized risk factors.

- **environmental exposure.** Exposure to high levels of environmental toxins such as lead increases the risk of specific learning disorders.
- **genetics.** SLDs run in families, although adults may not realize they have always struggled with learning until their children have been diagnosed. Experts report that 30 to 40 percent of moderate to severe learning disabilities are caused by genetics.

- **malnutrition.** A lack of micronutrients during pregnancy, infancy, or childhood is a risk factor for learning disabilities. A poor diet makes it very difficult for a child's brain to grow, develop, and perform normally.
- **physical trauma.** Head injuries or brain infections during pregnancy or early childhood increase a child's risk of specific learning disorders.
- **prenatal and neonatal risks.** If your child did not grow appropriately in your uterus, was born prematurely with a very low birth weight, or was exposed to alcohol, cigarette smoke, or drugs as an infant, his risk of acquiring a specific learning disorder is elevated.
- **psychological trauma.** Psychological trauma or abuse in early childhood may affect brain structure and development, leading to a specific learning disorder.

If you suspect your child has a learning disability, it's important to intervene as early as possible. First, your child's doctor should test his vision and hearing to rule each of them out as the possible cause. Next, you could ask for a meeting with your child's teacher and perhaps his school's guidance counselor. Your child may have a series of tests conducted by a team of professionals, which might include a psychologist, special education teacher, occupational therapist, or social worker. Once a diagnosis has been made, a treatment plan can be devised to help.

As you learned earlier in Part One, public schools in the United States are obliged by law to provide an Individualized Education Program (IEP) for any student with a learning disorder who meets certain criteria. Your child's IEP then sets learning goals and strategies that your child's school can use to support his learning.

By law, schools must come up with ways to accommodate children with learning disorders. A child with an SLD may be allowed more time to complete assignments or tests, seated near the teacher to promote his focus on tasks, or placed in a smaller classroom taught by a special education teacher. Other accommodations may include the use of computer applications to support writing, being given fewer math problems or assignments, or the use of audiobooks to supplement his reading.

Therapy for SLDs varies. For example, some children benefit from occupational therapy, which can improve motor skills and thus treat problems with writing. In addition, a speech therapist can help children who have difficulties with language. Your child's doctor may prescribe medication to boost attention and concentration, and reduce anxiety and depression. A doctor who practices "functional" or "integrative" medicine may be able to suggest dietary changes, supplement use, eye exercises, neurofeedback, or other treatments that might be beneficial to your child.

If your child has a learning disorder, assure him that he is not lazy or dumb but simply needs to learn a little differently than others do. Emphasize to him that you and his school are going to help him. Focus on his strengths and encourage him to pursue interests that give him confidence and pleasure. Remind him that you love him for who he is, no matter what, and give him lots of hugs.

OBESITY

Obesity is truly an epidemic in the United States and around the world. Approximately 14.4 million American children and adolescents may be considered obese. The term "obesity" is used to describe children and adults based on both height and weight. Body mass index, or BMI, is the numerical expression commonly used by the medical community to determine a person's weight status (e.g., underweight, normal, overweight, or obese).

Obesity seems to impact behavioral health and is associated with sleeping disorders, anxiety, depression, and low self-esteem. Children who are affected by the disorders described in Part One of this book are more likely to be overweight or obese than children who are not. For example, children with ADHD are more likely to be obese than non-ADHD children. Is this because they are impulsive and reach for a sugary treat without thinking? Perhaps a child with ODD is obese because he is so obstinate that he refuses to make good food choices and simply eats whatever he wants. The same could be true for a child with conduct order.

It is also not surprising that children with OCD, anxiety, or depression often turn to food as a way to ease their minds. Like those who act out, they may be addicted to sugar, which temporarily makes them feel better by increasing the feel-good neurotransmitter dopamine in the brain. But this "sugar high" is soon replaced by a low—along with a strong craving for more sugar.

Problems start early. For example, "acting out" behaviorally at twenty-four months of age is associated with higher weight at twenty-four months of age and through to the age of twelve. Obese boys at age three have more conduct problems than do boys of normal weight. By age five, obese boys have more conduct problems, hyperactivity and inattentiveness problems, peer relationship problems, and total difficulties.

Again and again, obesity and behavior seem to be connected, but this connection is a complex one. Do behavioral disorders lead to overeating, or does obesity by itself lead to behavioral disorders due to the fact that obese children tend to lack the healthy nutrients necessary for normal brain functioning? Although we may not have definitive answers to these questions, we can still address a number of the underlying reasons that children are overweight or obese.

Diet and Exercise

As you undoubtedly already know, consumption of high-calorie, low-nutrient foods and beverages contributes to excessive weight gain. Unfortunately, these foods and beverages are practically everywhere—at the grocery store, on just about every street corner, in vending machines, at sporting events, and almost anywhere else you might find yourself. Obvious examples of nutritionally poor foods with excessive calories are candy and dessert. Perhaps more important to point out are examples of nutritionally poor high-calorie beverages, which include soft drinks, sports drinks, and even fruit juices with no added sugar.

While fruit juice sounds like a good choice, it's actually not that healthy. The American Academy of Pediatrics recommends that no fruit juice be given to children under the age of one, as it fills them up but provides very few nutrients. It further recommends that children not be given fruit juice in baby bottles, as constant exposure to the sugar in juice is detrimental to their developing teeth. For young children, it recommends less than four ounces of juice each day, and no more than a cup for children aged seven to eighteen. Ultimately, it favors whole fruit instead of juice for children of any age, which contains many different vitamins and minerals, and should satisfy the desire for something sweet. Whole fruit also provides fiber, which promotes a feeling of fullness, thus helping to discourage overeating.

Sugar-free beverages are a problem, too, as they make you think that drinks must taste sweet. Moreover, calorie-free beverages have been shown to lead to weight gain, not weight loss. In addition, artificial sweeteners have been known to upset the healthy balance of bacteria in the gut. (See Chapter 10 on page 185 for more on nutrition and its role in behavioral disorders.)

Finally, children who don't exercise much are more likely to gain weight than those who do because they don't burn as many calories. A sedentary lifestyle of watching television or playing video games coupled with a poor diet puts a child at risk of becoming overweight or obese.

Familial Factors

If a child is overweight and comes from a family of overweight people, his genetics may be causing him to gain weight more easily than the average child. Alternatively, it may be nurture, not nature, at fault. Perhaps his relatives are unintentionally teaching him to indulge in unhealthy foods, too often splurging on desserts, candy, and sugary beverages. Of course, if his family members tend to sit around instead of engaging in any sort of physical activity during their free time, his weight may be related to a lack of exercise.

Whether or not your child is overweight, it is a good idea to encourage family exercise, even if that means taking a brief walk around the block. You could also ride bikes together, or play bean bag toss or Frisbee with him.

Finally, a child's risk of obesity is increased by parental or familial stress in the home. Children might overeat to deal with the emotions brought on by stress. In many cases, food is also used as a replacement for love.

Socioeconomic Factors

If you live in a community with limited resources and limited access to supermarkets, you may buy foods that are convenient, such as foods that don't spoil quickly—e.g., frozen meals, crackers, cookies, and potato chips. Furthermore, if your neighborhood is unsafe, opportunities to exercise may be limited.

Medications

Did you know that some prescription drugs can increase the risk of obesity? Ask your doctor if any of your child's prescription medications could lead to excessive weight gain.

CONCLUSION

Understanding each of the previously described issues may prove extremely helpful when it comes to improving your child's behavior. Conditions such as depression, learning disabilities, obesity, and poor gut health are commonly associated with the behavioral disorders discussed earlier in Part One. Treating these associated conditions can make a real difference in your child's life, as well as in the lives of his family and school peers.

The point of identifying these related problems is to understand your child as a whole, not simply in terms of his behavioral disorder. In doing so, you may see better overall improvement.

8.

Finding Professional Help

You may need a particular professional or a team of professionals to help your child, depending on his needs. This team of professionals might include your child's current medical doctor, another medical doctor trained specifically for children like yours, a psychologist or behavioral therapist, a speech therapist, a nutritionist, or maybe an educator who can advise you on learning problems.

It is important, however, not to relinquish control of the care of your child completely to the healthcare professionals on your team, which often happens, especially if you're a person of color or a member of an underserved community. These healthcare professionals should be seen as partners in the care of your child, but the ultimate decisions regarding your child's care should almost always be your own.

THE RIGHT PROFESSIONAL

If the description of one of the disorders discussed in Part One of this book seems to fit your child to a T, then you should begin your child's healthcare journey with a trip to his primary doctor, who will evaluate his overall state of health. If your child's primary doctor is not the right person to treat his disorder, she may refer you to another medical doctor or psychologist who specializes in helping children like yours.

Another way to find the right healthcare professional for your child is to ask friends who have similar issues with their children for recommendations. Special educators who see countless troubled children every day may also be able to provide you with a few suggestions. Try not to be embarrassed about asking for help. You are all your child has to rely upon, so don't hide behind self-consciousness. Of course, you may find the right doctor for your child by doing some online research based on the information you've acquired from this book, but remember that this information is not meant to allow you to diagnose your child yourself. It is only meant as a guide to point you in the right general direction. You are still looking for a doctor to diagnose your child, not just to treat him.

Unfortunately, some doctors, due to time restrictions, listen to parents for only a few minutes and then reach for their prescription pads. Prescription medications can be quite helpful, and you may want to choose this avenue to keep your family from fracturing, or to keep your child from being expelled from school. Medication is sometimes necessary and may be used as a quick answer to an urgent problem, allowing a family the time to take a breath and figure out what the next step should be in solving the issue in a more holistic way. In other words, a prescription isn't necessarily the right or complete answer. More often, it is just a bridge to a better, more in-depth solution. Therefore, a doctor's approach to the use of medication should be considered when you are trying to find the right professional for your child.

What you are looking for is the best doctor for your child's wellbeing, which may not be your family doctor or pediatrician, but her office is generally the right place to start your search. During your visit, it may become clear that this professional isn't the right person to treat your child's disorder. Nevertheless, don't be discouraged. Keep in mind that not all doctors are the same. Yours might not have the right training to address your child's condition. The only way to find out is to ask questions, which may include:

- What do you think is going on?
- Have you treated many children with this condition before?
- If you have treated children like mine, how did they do?
- Do you look at the role of diet and nutrition in treatment?
- Do you keep up with the medical literature on my child's condition?
- Would you be comfortable treating my child for this disorder?

Remember that you are in charge, even if you don't feel that way. If you encounter any resistance when you ask questions such as those recently noted, it may be a sign that the doctor to whom you are speaking isn't the right doctor for this issue.

Of course, finding the right doctor is the goal of every family that is dealing with behavioral disorders, but what are the qualities that make a doctor the right one? Finding a doctor who will truly listen to you and see you as a partner in your child's treatment is crucial to your child's success.

Perhaps the easiest way to determine if a doctor is the right one for you and your child is simply to ask the doctor. If the answer is "yes," then your next step is observation of how your child and the doctor communicate, taking note of the doctor's questions and your child's responses to them, and of your child's questions and the doctor's responses to them. In addition, pay attention to the healthcare provider's openness to change, and do not allow the same methods to be tried repeatedly without observable positive results.

One simple word—"listening"—is at the heart of your child's success in his treatment with his healthcare provider, but what does it mean to listen?

First, a healthcare provider should not interrupt you. It is important that you are permitted to describe your child's situation in as much detail as you feel is necessary. Effective listening is evident when a doctor is concentrating on your words, not trying to hurry you along, and making sure you are completely finished with your explanation. Too often, healthcare professionals seem to be thinking as you are talking, meaning they are hearing their own voices in their heads and not yours. While you are speaking, they are already formulating an answer so they can quickly move on to their next patients.

A good doctor will summarize what you have said so that you know it has been understood accurately. Once you are confident in the doctor's understanding, the doctor should offer his opinion and treatment recommendations, and ask you for your comments on these recommendations. In doing so, he is showing consideration for your opinion on his approach and treating you as a partner in your child's treatment, which will truly be a team effort.

How his doctor responds to your input also plays a factor in your knowing whether you've made the right choice. If his doctor seems dismissive of certain concerns of yours (for example, the belief that particular foods affect your child's disorder) or replies to your suggestion of a left-of-center theory for your child's condition by saying, "I'm sorry but you are wrong, but we can add this medication to your child's treatment and see if it helps," it might be time to find a doctor who will listen seriously to you.

This approach, however, does not mean you should continue to search for a doctor until you find one who is willing to go along with your every suggestion. It simply means that the right doctor is the one who understands that parents with behaviorally challenged children are willing to look down any and every avenue for a solution, even if it seems far-fetched. Most avenues will be dead ends, and you must acknowledge this fact, but all dialogue between you and your child's doctor should be welcome and respected by both parties.

Specially Trained Doctors

There are three organizations that teach healthcare providers how to maximize patient visits in their practices, training them in effective listening and treatment of their patients. They practice both traditional medicine and nutritional/environmental medicine, often called integrated medicine or functional medicine.

- The American Academy of Environmental Medicine (AAEM)
  www.aaemonline.org
- The Academy of Integrative Health & Medicine (AIHM)
  www.aihm.org
- The Institute for Functional Medicine (IFM)
  www.ifm.org
- The American Association of Integrative Medicine (AAIM)
  www.omicsonline.org/societies/american-association-of-integrative-medicine

You can look on the websites of these organizations to find how to locate one of their certified providers. You may be looking for a certified medical doctor (MD), osteopathic physician (DO), or advanced nurse practitioner, but you may end up needing another certified professional such as a nutritionist/dietician, chiropractor, or naturopath on your team. In fact, many healthcare providers are affiliated with other types of healthcare professionals, allowing for a comprehensive approach to care.

THE APPOINTMENT

When you schedule an appointment with a doctor who may potentially treat your child, tell the receptionist what you are looking for in a doctor. In other words, be specific so you don't end up wasting your time or anyone else's. Find out how much time an appointment lasts. If you think you may need more than just a few minutes of the doctor's time, ask for two back-to-back appointments or schedule the last appointment of the day. If a doctor is booked for months, ask to be referred to someone else. Of course, before you book any appointment, find out if the office accepts your health insurance.

When your child sees a doctor, this doctor should take a complete health and family history and perform a physical examination. Healthcare providers with additional training at any of the above institutions previously mentioned may perform more than the usual work-up.

A comprehensive medical history can yield 90 percent of what's needed to make a diagnosis. But please understand that taking a medical history is both an art and a science, which is why a doctor's listening skills are of crucial importance. Prior to being seen, you may even be asked to complete a health history form online or in the doctor's waiting room. Filling it out online may be best, as it will allow the doctor more time to review it before your appointment.

It is also important to make a list of questions you would like to ask the doctor, which will ensure you have all your concerns addressed. Do try to be reasonable with your list of questions, though. You and your family aren't the only ones dealing with serious matters, and the other patients would appreciate the same amount of attention. If you find you have too many questions, prioritize a smaller number of them and save the rest for your child's follow-up visit.

Child's History and Family's History

Your child's doctor will start by asking why you and your child are there. She may ask if other blood relatives have mental or behavioral problems. If so, don't be upset at this type of questioning. If his doctor is doing her job correctly, she is supposed to ask these questions. They are meant to be probative, attempting to discover the root cause of your child's disorder, which is not always done in traditional medicine. She may also ask about your child's time in his mother's womb, including information on his mother's life and experiences before becoming pregnant and during pregnancy (including any toxic exposures), as well as the birthing experience.

His doctor should also inquire about the health and behavior of your child during infancy. Was he an easy baby or a difficult one? Was he breastfed or bottle-fed? His doctor may ask about developmental issues—for example, when your child first rolled over, sat up, stood, walked, or talked. He might inquire about your child's favorite forms of play, whether he plays well with siblings or other children, the amount of TV he watches each day, and the amount of exercise he gets each day.

His doctor may also ask about your child's nutritional intake in a typical day, and especially about his junk food intake. He will likely inquire about your child's favorite foods, the types of cravings he has, whether he takes a multivitamin or any other supplement, and whether he is taking any prescription medication (and the reason it was prescribed). His doctor will want to know how school is going for your child, perhaps requesting information from your child's teacher about his relationships with classmates, how he performs on standardized tests, and what his behavior is like in class.

Offer any information you can about your child's teacher and any other professionals he may have seen. Let your child's doctor know if a behavior rating scale has been filled out by your child's teacher, what the results were, and what the teacher's comments were regarding your child's behavior with peers in class. If your child has seen a psychologist or psychiatrist—either at a school, clinic, or private practice—his doctor will most likely ask for a summary of any written opinions and the results of any computer tests that may have been taken by your child during one of these meetings (e.g., the CPT). She may also inquire about any therapies that have been tried, where they were tried, and the results they yielded.

At this point, it is probably clear that a ten- or fifteen-minute doctor's appointment would not allow for all this vital information to be discussed. In fact, in an ideal world, if you've found the right healthcare provider, the first visit should last for at least sixty minutes. Acquiring as complete of a picture of your child's background as possible will help his doctor to put together a profile that can determine important pieces of his behavioral problem.

Physical Exam

The second part of your child's appointment should be a physical exam. Not surprisingly, children with hearing or vision problems often have trouble paying attention, so these issues should be tested. His doctor may have facilities in her office to test these issues, or you may be referred to a vision or hearing doctor. She may ask your child to read from an age-appropriate book and then monitor if your child appears happy, calm, and capable while doing so, or unhappy, nervous, and clumsy. She will also ask your child questions to assess his speech development.

Allergies often create many physical signs and symptoms in a child, and may contribute to his behavioral difficulties. He may have pale skin, red earlobes or cheeks, dark circles under the eyes, a stuffy nose, "allergic gape" (i.e., the mouth remaining open because the nose is stuffy), rashes on any parts of the body, or "geographic tongue," in which the surface of the tongue has red patches of various shapes and sizes, making it look like a map. The existence of any of these signs suggests that your child might have allergies.

Children and teens with ADHD and CD are likely to weigh more than children who are not affected by these behaviors. If your child is overweight or obese, his weight might be evidence of a poor diet of too many calories and too few nutrients, and of a lifestyle without enough exercise.

Your child's doctor should take his blood pressure. This reading is especially important for children of color, who are associated with higher rates of hypertension, also known as high blood pressure—although the rates of hypertension in Caucasian children have been rising. If your child's blood pressure is elevated, it may mean that he is developing hypertension, which can be caused by a high intake of salt. Salt intake itself doesn't cause behavioral problems, but the salty foods in a child's diet may indicate nutritionally poor eating habits, which have been associated with behavioral problems.

Evidence of a deficiency in essential fatty acids includes dry hair, dandruff, dry skin, follicular keratosis (tiny hard bumps on the backs of the arms or front of the thighs), and broken nails. Your child's doctor may ask about any excessive thirst or frequent urination he may be experiencing, as these symptoms can also suggest a fatty-acid deficiency.

Of course, these symptoms can also point to diabetes, the presence of which may be determined by a blood test.

If your child has sleep problems, his doctor will want to check his tonsils and adenoids. If they are enlarged, she may refer him to an ear, nose, and throat doctor. If they are severely enlarged, she may recommend a sleep evaluation by a sleep expert. It's important that sleep problems be identified and treated. (See Chapter 9 on page 167.)

After his doctor has collected all the information she requires, she may make a diagnosis such as ADD, ADHD, ODD, or CD. These labels help doctors and patients to communicate. They are also important to use in a school setting, where these diagnoses open the door to special education classes.

When making a diagnosis, a good doctor will consider the child as a unique individual. Two children may have the same symptom—hyperactivity, for example—but for entirely different reasons. One child may have sensitivities to artificial colors, while another may have a high level of lead in his blood. Likewise, two children may have identical biological abnormalities but display completely different signs of them. One child who is sensitive to milk may suffer from fatigue and irritability, while another child who is sensitive to milk may wet the bed.

Your child is an individual and must be considered as such when analyzing his symptoms and history in relation to possible behavioral disorders.

Blood Tests

To help identify important pieces of your child's behavioral puzzle, ask his doctor if she will consider ordering one or more of the following blood tests. If she is resistant to ordering these tests, ask her why this is.

Serum Ferritin

Ferritin is a protein that binds to iron. This test will tell your child's doctor whether or not his iron stores are low and would benefit from iron supplementation. Iron deficiency can occur in anyone, including infants and young children. It has been associated with ADHD, restless legs syndrome, depression, gastrointestinal distress, OCD, conduct disorder, and anxiety disorders. Iron supplements, however, should never be given to a child unless a laboratory test has confirmed a low iron level. Iron supplements should be kept out of reach of children.

Acanthosis Nigricans

Although type 2 diabetes is known as adult-onset diabetes, this condition is being diagnosed in younger and younger people, including children. One sign of emerging type 2 diabetes with which many people are unfamiliar, but which a doctor may discover, is the appearance of a dark area (or ring) on the back of the neck that makes it look as though the affected person hasn't washed his neck. This dark area may also occur in armpits. Known as acanthosis nigricans, it is one of the earliest physical indicators that may be seen without there being any lab evidence of type 2 diabetes. Although acanthosis nigricans is associated with type 2 diabetes, the exact mechanism behind this sign is unknown.

Children exhibiting acanthosis nigricans are usually overweight or obese, which is often the result of a poor diet that consists of lots of sugar-rich foods. Although acanthosis nigricans is not a cause of difficult behavior, its presence can point to nutritional problems, which can result in behavioral disorders.

Serum and RBC Zinc

Zinc is an important mineral, as it is necessary for many chemical reactions, including those in the brain. Low zinc has been reported in children with ADHD. Some depressed patients have low zinc levels and may improve with zinc supplements. Low zinc is also related to skin disorders such as eczema and acne. Zinc supplements should be used cautiously, as too much zinc can cause a copper deficiency. Sometimes a zinc ointment can be useful for skin disorders.

Serum and RBC Magnesium

Magnesium is another mineral that is not consumed in high enough quantities in the United States. It is very important for protein synthesis, the proper functioning of muscles and nerve cells, normal glucose levels, and normal blood pressure. Children with ADHD or conduct disorder tend to have lower levels of magnesium than do children without either of these issues. Magnesium is important for relaxation and sleep. Magnesium supplementation has shown to improve ADHD symptoms. In addition, combination vitamin D and magnesium supplementation has shown to improve conduct problems and anxiety.

Vitamin D_3 (25-Hydroxyvitamin D)

In 2012, doctors at Johns Hopkins University School of Medicine recommended that all children be screened for vitamin D_3 deficiency, especially those who are obese, have darker skin, have a diet low in vitamin D_3, or spend little time outdoors. Note the emphasis on the D_3 form of the vitamin, as it is the most bioactive, which means it is the most effective at the cellular level. If your child is at high risk of vitamin D deficiency, then lab tests for vitamin D should be ordered and retaken every six months until his vitamin D level is greater than 30 ng/ml. Low vitamin D has been linked to ADHD, depression, anxiety, and behavioral problems.

Blood Lead

Lead is a highly toxic heavy metal. No amount of lead is safe for humans. Lead in children has been associated with ADHD, CD, ODD, anxiety, stomachaches and headaches, juvenile delinquency, and learning disabilities.

TSH and Thyroid Hormones

Both abnormally high levels of thyroid hormones (hyperthyroidism) and abnormally low levels of thyroid hormones (hypothyroidism) are notorious for causing changes in behavior. Signs of hyperthyroidism include weight loss, hyperactivity, increased appetite, hair loss, and hand tremors. Hypothyroidism often presents with a loss of attentiveness, weight gain, decreased activity and appetite, and thickening of the skin.

A low thyroid level is the most common thyroid condition in children, but high levels can cause behavioral problems, too. Abnormal levels of thyroid hormones may require correction in children with ADHD, juvenile delinquency, ODD, mood problems, OCD, or anxiety.

If any of the previously mentioned substances show up in abnormal amounts on lab tests, ask your child's doctor what these results mean and how you may correct them.

Referrals

Your child's doctor may refer him to other professionals to assist in your child's diagnosis, treatment, and management. For example, if your child is having sleep problems, his doctor may refer him to a sleep clinic for evaluation, diagnosis, and treatment. (Learning about and enforcing good sleep practices or treating a sleep disorder can make a huge improvement in your child's health and behavior.) If depression or any other condition outside your healthcare provider's area of expertise or comfort zone is diagnosed, she will also refer your child to a professional who can provide appropriate care.

WHAT TO DO IF YOU CANNOT AFFORD TO SEE A DOCTOR

If you cannot afford to see a doctor for your child's behavior problems, there may be help available to you. Most children who are uninsured will qualify for a publicly funded option such as Medicaid or the Children's Health Insurance Program (CHIP). These programs are run by the federal government and states, and may vary in eligibility requirements and coverage from state to state. For more information on finding healthcare for your child, you may call 1-877-KIDS-NOW (1-877-543-7669) or go to InsureKidsNow.gov. Your county health department may also be a helpful resource in your search for local medical care for your child. Finally, you may look for Federally Qualified Health Centers, or FQHCs, which are community-based centers that provide care on a sliding fee scale according to a person's ability to pay.

CONCLUSION

The right doctor can help you to identify important puzzle pieces in your efforts to solve your child's behavioral disorder. Oftentimes it takes a team of different doctors to find all the necessary puzzle pieces and put them in the correct places.

At the outset of your quest to improve your child's behavior, your child's doctor will take his medical history, which will include any relevant details about both your child and his close relatives. She will also perform a physical exam, order blood tests, and interpret results. She will then likely make a diagnosis and suggest treatments. She may also recommend other professionals to assist in your child's treatment. With each step along your child's healthcare journey, never forget that any professional you see should consider you a partner in your child's treatment.

PART TWO

Complementary Treatments

9.

Lifestyle Factors

Lifestyle habits can not only help your child to lead a long, healthy life but also improve his behavior. These habits include getting enough high-quality sleep and exercising. (Of course, a healthy lifestyle also includes proper nutrition, but that subject is so dense that we have dedicated Chapter 10 to it.) If you help your child to establish beneficial routines early, you will be giving him an invaluable gift for life.

SLEEP

Research suggests that a lack of restful sleep may be associated with behavioral disorders. Unfortunately, sleep problems are very common in children and can leave them to deal with all kinds of behavioral and learning problems throughout the day. Most of the time, the connection between sleep and behavioral disorders goes unrecognized. If your child has trouble sleeping, be sure to tell his doctor, who may not ask about the issue.

Some treatments for sleep problems are easy to carry out, while others are more difficult. For example, if your child has restless legs syndrome (see page 174), his iron level may be low. If it is low, his doctor may prescribe an iron supplement, which may improve your child's sleep problems and thus his behavior. Such treatment is easy. If your child shows signs of obstructive sleep apnea (see page 173), his doctor may order a sleep study, which will be time consuming and expensive but may prove worth the time and money. If you suspect your child may be suffering from a sleep condition, the following questionnaire can help to confirm this suspicion.

Questionnaire

The following sleep questionnaire is an adaptation of the pediatric sleep questionnaire (PSQ) developed at the University of Michigan. For the purposes of this book, we've included questions about the various behavioral disorders discussed in Part One. If you are unsure about your answers, try observing your child over a few nights as he sleeps and then fill out the questionnaire again.

Table 9.1. Pediatric Sleep Questionnaire

SYMPTOM	Answer		
Snoring	**Yes**	**No**	**Do Not Know**
Does your child snore more than half the time?			
Does your child always snore?			
Does your child snore loudly?			
Breathing	**Yes**	**No**	**Do Not Know**
Does your child breathe heavily or loudly?			
Does your child have trouble breathing or struggle to breathe?			
Has your child ever stopped breathing during the night?			
Does your child breathe through his mouth during the day?			
Does your child have a dry mouth in the morning?			
Waking	**Yes**	**No**	**Do Not Know**
Does your child wake up unrefreshed in the morning?			

Does your child have problems with daytime sleepiness?			
Has a teacher commented that your child appears sleepy during the day?			
Is it hard to wake your child up in the morning?			
Does your child wake up with headaches in the morning?			
Has your child stopped growing at a normal rate at any time since birth?			
Does your child have nasal allergies that keep him awake at night or cause him to wake up often?			
Behavioral Issues	**Yes**	**No**	**Do Not Know**
Does your child occasionally wet the bed?			
Has your child been diagnosed with ADHD?			
Has your child been diagnosed with OCD?			
Is depression or anxiety a problem for your child?			
Has your child been diagnosed with conduct disorder?			
Does your child have learning disabilities?			

EVALUATING YOUR RESPONSES

If you answered "no" to the first fifteen questions, then your child probably does not have a sleep problem. If you answered "yes" to a few or more of these sleep questions, then your child may have a sleep problem. If your child has one or more of the behavioral issues mentioned in the last section of the questionnaire as well as a sleep problem, improving his sleep may also improve his daytime behavior.

Why Sleep Is Essential

Did you know that your child's behavior and physical health depend on the amount and quality of sleep he gets each night? Sleep is a crucial factor in a child's ability to behave, learn, think, and reason normally. After all, nature has designed humans to spend about one-third of their lives sleeping, and for good reason.

Solving your child's sleep problems will improve not only the quantity and quality of his sleep but also his daytime behavior and learning ability, sometimes dramatically. Good sleep helps to clear the mind, restore a feeling of wellbeing, and make a person feel ready to face the world. A day in school will go better because sleep improves attention and memory, strengthening neural pathways and helping to make new ones. Enough high-quality sleep is also important for your child's immune system, helping to keep him free of infections and diseases. It also aids in healing and cellular repair. Finally, sleep is necessary for proper growth and development.

Stages of Sleep

In order to appreciate the importance of deep sleep, it is helpful to understand the various stages of sleep, of which there are three.

- **Stage 1. Wakefulness to light sleep.** During this short period of sleep, a person's heartbeat, breathing, and eye movements slow down. Muscles relax. Brain waves slow down.
- **Stage 2. Deeper sleep.** During this period of sleep, a person's heartbeat and breathing slow down further. Muscles relax even more. Body temperature falls and eye movements stop.
- **Stage 3. Deep sleep.** All body and brain functions slow down even more during deep sleep. Waking from a deep sleep typically leaves a person groggy, sleepy, and confused.

Deep sleep is so important because it is when the "housekeeping" of the brain occurs. During deep sleep, the brain rids itself of waste products created throughout the day. If these waste products are not adequately removed from the brain during sleep, it will have trouble functioning optimally the next day. It's like trying to make meals in a kitchen full of garbage and dirty plates from the previous day—it would go a lot more smoothly if all the debris were thrown away.

If your child's brain does not enter deep sleep, the processing of cleaning up after itself will not occur properly, and he will likely show problems emotionally and behaviorally. He will certainly have trouble learning at school.

Sleep and Behavior

The quantity and quality of a child's sleep can play a major role in the behavioral disorders discussed in Part 1. An insufficient quantity of sleep may result from your child's bedtime being too late to allow for sufficient sleep before he has to get up, or from your child's inability to fall asleep. Most children in the United States do not get enough sleep. If your child is three to five years old, he needs eleven to fifteen hours of sleep every night. If he is five to fourteen years old, he needs nine to thirteen hours of sleep every night. (Infants and young children need more sleep, while older children need less.) Many children get only seven to eight hours of sleep every night, and sometimes even less. In terms of the quality of your child's sleep, it depends upon the amount of deep sleep he experiences during sleep.

If your child has a behavioral disorder, it may make his falling asleep more difficult, shortening his hours of sleep. For example, a child with ADHD may experience a rebound effect from his daytime stimulant medication as it wears off, becoming hyper and unable to sleep as his symptoms return. If your child has ODD or CD, he may simply refuse to go to bed at a set time. If your child has OCD or anxiety, he may have trouble drifting off because of his worries. Unfortunately, when a behavioral problem causes an insufficient quantity of sleep, this lack of sleep can contribute to the severity of the behavioral problem, and thus a vicious circle is created.

Sleep disorders also lead to problems in both quantity and quality of sleep. These disorders include poor sleep hygiene, restless legs syndrome, and obstructive sleep apnea.

Poor Sleep Hygiene

Poor sleep hygiene simply refers to poor sleep habits. Think of sleep hygiene as you would dental hygiene. If your child doesn't brush and floss his teeth, he will get cavities. Similarly, if your child has poor sleep hygiene, he won't get enough high-quality sleep each night, which will lead to poor behavior during the day.

Good sleep hygiene includes making sure your child's bedroom is dedicated to sleeping only. Your child should avoid spending hours lying on his bed and doing other activities before bedtime. His brain needs to associate his bed with sleep.

It is important to set a bedtime that is enforced. Your child's bedtime should give him enough sleep to wake up feeling refreshed and ready to go at a specific time the next day. For example, if your child has to get up at 7:00 AM and needs ten hours of sleep, then his bedtime should be 9:00 PM, and he should start getting ready thirty to sixty minutes before this time. It is also helpful to keep consistent bedtimes and wake times every day, including on the weekends.

The time before your child gets into bed should be spent winding down from his day by engaging in a set routine, which may include laying out clothes for the next day, taking a warm bath or shower, cuddling, playing with toys, reading, listening to quiet music, or working on a puzzle. (He should also be reminded that he is loved and cherished.) Exercising during the day will help with sleep, but exercise should be avoided during the two hours before bedtime.

He should also avoid watching TV or using an electronic tablet or computer during this period. These electronic devices give off blue light, which excites the brain and delays the brain's production of the hormone known as melatonin, which is responsible for making us feel sleepy. It is also a good idea to place your child's clock out of his line of sight from his bed, and to remove his watch before bedtime if he wears one during the day.

Your child's room should be dark. A small nightlight is allowed, however. It should also be quiet, cool, and comfortable. Be sure your child has his security blanket, doll, or stuffed animal waiting for him. In addition, be sure not to let your child go to bed on an empty stomach, which will likely make it hard for him to fall asleep. If he needs a snack before bed, choose from foods high in protein and fiber, such as nuts, sugar-free peanut butter, unsweetened yogurt, hummus, eggs, tofu, berries, and whole grains. Avoid foods with too much sugar or any caffeine.

If your child is a worrier, have a short "worry time" with him before bedtime, in which he can express his worries and agree to let them go until morning. If your child remains awake in bed, tossing and turning, he should get out of bed and do a low-stimulation activity, such as reading, and then return to his bed.

Obstructive Sleep Apnea

Obstructive sleep apnea, or OSA, is a serious sleep disorder in which breathing during sleep repeatedly stops (apnea) for a few seconds or as long as a minute and then restarts. This condition usually starts between the ages of two and eight. Experts report that obstructive sleep apnea affects 1 to 5 percent of children.

During this time when breathing stops, the level of oxygen in the brain decreases, creating what is called *hypoxia,* or low oxygen. Oxygen is crucial for proper brain functioning and helps to send nerve signals throughout the body. When the brain doesn't get enough oxygen, then brain cells start to die.

The most common cause of obstructive sleep apnea in children is enlarged tonsils and adenoids. The tonsils are two round humps of tissue at the back of the throat, while the adenoids sit high in the throat behind the nose and roof of the mouth. If they become enlarged, they can block the breathing tube. Being overweight or obese can also lead to obstructive sleep apnea, as these conditions can cause enlargement of soft tissue around the upper airway, which may result in this airway being closed off at times.

Symptoms of obstructive sleep apnea include snoring, pauses in breathing, restless sleep, mouth breathing, nighttime sweating, bedwetting, and night terrors. A person with obstructive sleep apnea may experience serious daytime symptoms as well, such as daytime sleepiness, poor school performance, inattentiveness, learning problems, behavioral problems, poor weight gain, or hyperactivity.

Your family doctor may make a diagnosis of obstructive sleep apnea, or she may refer you to a pediatric sleep specialist, who has undergone special training to help children with sleep problems. A diagnosis of OSA is typically made by using a sleep study called polysomnography. Painless and noninvasive, this test will measure your child's brain waves, oxygen level, heart rate, breathing, and eye and leg movements.

If testing suggests OSA, your child may be referred to an otolaryngologist, otherwise known as an ear, nose, and throat specialist. After examining your child's tonsils and adenoids, she may recommend that both be removed. The surgery is a safe procedure, done under anesthesia in a hospital or outpatient surgery department. Your child's tongue, mouth, throat, or jaw will be sore from the surgery, and complete recovery may take up to two weeks. If your child is overweight, your doctor may prescribe a change in his dietary habits in order to encourage weight loss and thus improve his OSA.

Allergies, Sleep Problems, and Behavior

Children with allergies are more likely to have a wide range of behavioral or learning issues than are children without allergies. One reason for this fact is that allergies can make falling asleep and staying asleep difficult. For example, if your child has hay fever, his nose will be stuffed up and itchy. Once in bed, he may sniff, snort, sneeze, and cough throughout the night, leading to a lack of sleep. In turn, this lack of sleep may lead to hyperactivity, inattentiveness, and other behavioral problems.

Allergens can also cause the skin condition known as eczema to flare up, making the affected person's life miserable due to feelings of itchiness, to which eczema sufferers often attribute their sleep troubles. In addition, they can trigger asthma symptoms, including coughing and wheezing, which make it very difficult to sleep. A child with poorly controlled allergic asthma may have problems sleeping every night.

If your child has allergies, ask your doctor about treatments that will decrease mucous in his sinuses and help him to breathe better. Having an air purifier in his bedroom may also be beneficial. Prescription creams and medications can relieve symptoms of eczema that have already flared up. If your child's allergies are particularly difficult to manage, a pediatric allergist may also need to be consulted.

Restless Legs Syndrome

Restless legs syndrome, or RLS, sometimes known as *Willis-Ekbom disease,* is a sleep disorder in which uncomfortable leg sensations create an intense, uncontrollable urge to move the legs. It usually occurs at bedtime, but in some children it may occur at other quiet times. It is estimated that 1.5 million children and adolescents in the United States have RLS. It is especially associated with ADHD, ODD, anxiety disorders, and depression, and tends to run in families. Symptoms may even begin in infancy.

Children with RLS often have trouble describing the feelings they have in their legs. They may use terms such as creeping, crawling, tugging, throbbing, or burning. The kicking, tossing, and turning in bed caused by RLS result in trouble falling asleep, restless sleep, and problems staying asleep. The daytime sleepiness that follows can lead to behavioral issues, an inability to complete tasks, and poor academic progress in school.

RLS causes such unusual visible symptoms that it may be an easy consideration for a doctor to make. An overnight sleep study would confirm a diagnosis of RLS and reveal just how many times during sleep your child is affected by restless legs, although a sleep study may not be necessary unless other sleep disorders are suspected.

Iron deficiency may be associated with RLS. Your doctor should order a blood test (serum ferritin) to assess your child's iron level. If it is low, this issue can be easily treated with iron supplementation. Iron is a necessary part of many crucial cellular processes in the body, such as carrying oxygen to brain cells, DNA synthesis, mitochondrial functioning, and making neurotransmitters, which include dopamine and adrenaline. These substances are involved in emotion, attention, reward, movement, and so on. Dopamine dysfunction in particular has been suggested as a contributor to RLS.

Some research suggests that magnesium deficiency can also worsen RLS, perhaps because magnesium blocks calcium in normal body chemistry, helping to relax nerves and muscles. If magnesium is low, nerves and muscles become overactive. Low zinc and vitamin B_{12} levels have also been associated with RLS and poor sleep quality. While supplementation can address these deficiencies, eating a healthy diet may be enough to reverse them.

Medications used to treat RLS in adults have not been thoroughly tested in children, so you will need to try other approaches to remedy your child's sleep troubles. Following good sleep hygiene, using a heating pad on the legs, massaging the legs, and relaxation exercises may alleviate symptoms of RLS.

Sleep Aids

Your child's sleep problems can be treated in a number of ways, all of which you should discuss with your doctor. The following methods of addressing sleep problems are the most common.

Nutrition

As previously mentioned, the nutrients contained in a healthy diet may alleviate sleep problems. Iron-rich foods, including liver, chicken, turkey, lentils, beans, and spinach can be very helpful. Magnesium-rich foods, such as nuts, beans, seeds, tofu, bananas, and whole grains can also benefit people with sleep disorders. Other helpful substances such as zinc and B vitamins can be found in milk products, whole grains, leafy greens, nuts, seeds, beans, oysters, and poultry.

Keep in mind that just a serving of one of these foods before bedtime will not bring restful sleep. Eating a healthy diet over time, however, can build up levels of iron, magnesium, zinc, and other important nutrients, which should encourage good sleep.

Melatonin

Melatonin is a hormone secreted by the pineal gland in the brain to help maintain the natural sleep-wake rhythms of the body. As night arrives with less light, melatonin is secreted by your brain, which helps to induce sleep. In the morning and during the day, however, light stops the release of melatonin. It is nature's way of seeing that you get enough sleep—your own built-in timer.

Melatonin is a widely used sleep aid for children, adolescents, and adults. In the United States, it is available at grocery stores and pharmacies as an over-the-counter oral synthetic supplement. In some countries—England, for example—melatonin is available only by prescription. If you are considering melatonin for your child, check with your child's doctor for her opinion on the matter. If she supports this treatment, ask for a dosage recommendation.

Melatonin should not be used as a stand-alone therapy but may be combined with other sleep treatments for a period of time. This sleep aid should not become a permanent part of your child's sleep routine. It is important for him to learn how to fall asleep and remain asleep overnight without the help of a pill.

L-Theanine

L-theanine is another natural sleep aid. It is an amino acid found in tea and some mushrooms. It has a chemical structure very similar to its relative amino acid *glutamine.* In the brain, glutamine helps to promote sleep. Research has shown that L-theanine supplementation—200 mg in the morning and 200 mg in the afternoon—can improve sleep quality and sleep efficiency (the total time spent in bed minus the total time asleep) in boys with ADHD.

Besides being used to promote relaxation and sleep, L-theanine has been used in the daytime to relieve anxiety, improve memory and thinking skills, increase attention, and decrease depression. A combination of L-theanine and caffeine has been shown to improve sustained attention, inhibitory control, and overall learning performance in children with ADHD.

Physical Sleep Aids

New parents are often told that swaddling their babies makes them feel secure, cry less, and sleep better. Nevertheless, it is important to note that in extremely rare instances unexpected deaths have occurred with swaddled children, so discuss this technique with your doctor. Many experts recommend that infants should be laid on their backs and swaddling be discontinued as soon as an infant can roll over. In terms of helping children who have sleep problems, weighted blankets or sleep sacks may be used to achieve the same effect that swaddling creates for a newborn.

Weighted Blankets. A weighted blanket is heavier than a normal blanket and used for therapeutic purposes, helping to relieve stress and anxiety. The feeling of lying under a weighted blanket has been described as a big, comforting hug. These blankets generally weigh between five and thirty pounds. The weight is added by filling the blanket with plastic pellets or beads. In terms of treating your child's sleep problems with a weighted blanket, it is important to choose one that is the right size and weight for your child.

Studies have evaluated the use of weighted blankets and concluded that they can be a safe and effective treatment for sleep problems in patients with depression, bipolar disorder, anxiety, and ADHD, improving daytime symptoms and hyperactivity.

Sleep Sacks. Sleep sacks are essentially cuddly and soft sleeping bags. They come in forms that kids like and are decorated with cartoon characters, animals, dinosaurs, and other designs that may appeal to a child. They can help to make a child feel secure, calm, and relaxed for sleep.

Ask your doctor what she thinks about these sleep aids. Children with breathing problems such as asthma may not be good candidates for these treatments. These treatments are also not appropriate for very young children, who are weaker than older children and cannot move around in bed as well as they can. Your doctor can tell you if your child is old enough to try a sleep sack or weighted blanket.

When addressing behavioral disorders, sleep is an avenue that must be investigated. Getting enough high-quality sleep is essential not only for good physical health but also for good mental health. A rested brain will bring a child all kinds of benefits. He will feel happy, relaxed, eager to navigate the world, and ready to learn new things.

EXERCISE

Exercise can also have a significant impact on your child's behavior and, of course, overall health. Unfortunately, in today's world, too many children are inactive. They play less, run less, and stay inside watching electronic media rather than getting outside and exercising. About 70 percent of elementary schools, 84 percent of middle schools, and 95 percent of high schools require physical education classes. Only about 4 percent of elementary schools, 8 percent of middle schools, and 2 percent of high schools, however, provide daily physical education.

Benefits of Exercise

Exercise is beneficial for both physical and mental development. Exercise aids in the development of your child's movement skills, also known as physical literacy. It also encourages healthy bones and muscles, and a strong heart and lungs. Of course, it can also lead to weight loss, which is especially relevant now that obesity in children (and adults) has become an epidemic in the United States. Conditions that are associated with obesity, including fatty liver disease, prediabetes, and elevated lipids (fats) in the blood—ailments once limited to adults—are now being diagnosed in younger and younger people. Exercise and diet, thankfully, can help to improve or even reverse these problems.

Questionnaire

The following questionnaire should help you to assess your child's level of physical activity.

Table 9.2. Exercise Questionnaire

Issue	Yes	No
My child is overweight or obese.		
My child plays lots of video games, spends hours online or texting, or watches too much television.		
My child never plays outside.		
My child is driven to school.		
There are no gym classes at my child's school.		
My child does not participate in any group sports.		
My child and his friends engage in sedentary activities.		
In the course of a week, my child does not exercise enough to break a sweat.		

EVALUATING YOUR RESPONSES

The American Academy of Pediatrics states, "Physical activity is a potent 'medicine' in the prevention and treatment of disease and promotion of health and wellness." Your child's behavioral issues would likely improve if his doctor were to write a prescription for physical activity. The Centers for Disease Control and Prevention and the American Heart Association both recommend that children do sixty minutes of moderate to vigorous exercise each day.

Exercise can have a significant impact on your child's brain functioning. Increased blood flow promotes good thinking, planning, and behavior. Exercise also improves blood vessels and brain structure, fostering learning ability and behavioral control. It also increases the volume and compactness of white matter deep in the brain and the myelin that coats these fibers, speeding up the electrical impulses between brain cells and allowing them to transmit information much faster.

Exercise can lead to better hand-eye coordination, problem solving, and attention, all of which can boost school performance. Research has shown that simply spending time playing outside with friends raises test scores and results in better grades on assignments.

Don't forget the benefits your child receives from being outside on a sunny day. The sun strikes your child's exposed face and arms, causing his body to produce vitamin D. Many children in the United States have low vitamin D levels because they always stay inside. Having your child spend at least twenty minutes in the sun will significantly increase his vitamin D level, which, as the next chapter will explain in greater detail, is critical for normal brain functioning. (Although the use of sunscreen may lower the body's production of vitamin D, it is still important to have your child wear sunscreen before he goes outside.)

Exercise can help troubled children in so many ways. Thankfully, it's cheap, easy, and fun to do, and when the whole family gets involved, everyone benefits.

Anxiety

Physical activity causes an anxious child to concentrate on what he is doing physically, distracting him from his anxiety, which is a mental issue. Developing new skills can also give a child a sense of accomplishment, which may reduce anxiety.

Autism Spectrum Disorder (ASD)

Many children with autism spectrum disorder are extremely inactive, especially older children. Moreover, researchers report that vigorous exercise for twenty minutes can have many beneficial effects on children with ASD. These benefits include better focus, improved academic performance, reduced repetitive behaviors, and confidence building. Of course, it's important to choose the right activity for each child with ASD.

Behavioral and Mental Disorders

Research shows that exercise provides many positive effects in children with ADHD and other behavioral disorders, as it changes the brain and its chemistry. In fact, exercise stimulates the same pathways in the brain that stimulant drugs such as Ritalin do, improving symptoms of ADHD just as Ritalin does.

In one study of exercise and behavioral problems, two groups of children with ADHD and other disruptive behaviors were compared, with one group exercising afterschool and the other receiving sedentary attention. After ten weeks, the children in the physically active group displayed much fewer symptoms of hyperactivity and oppositional defiant disorder than those in the sedentary group. Instead of sending misbehaving students to detention, perhaps schools should send them to an afternoon exercise program instead.

Many other controlled studies of exercise and ADHD provide strong evidence that aerobic exercise enhances nerve cell growth and development and improves cognitive and behavioral problems. In a small study of older children with disruptive behaviors, thirty minutes of exercise improved behavior for ninety minutes. Researchers who study exercise and ADHD have concluded that exercise is an unexplored option for managing ADHD symptoms.

Depression

Studies of the effects of exercise on children with depression have also shown benefits. If your child has symptoms of depression or just has a "down" day, exercise will improve his mood and make him more relaxed. When your child exercises, his brain releases feel-good chemicals known as *endorphins*, making his mood better and giving him a sense of wellbeing. The extra oxygen delivered to brain cells during exercise also helps them to perform optimally.

Relationships

If your child is feeling lonely and struggling to make friends, his participation in physical activities with others may give him a sense of belonging and companionship. For example, a child with social anxiety who participates in a team sport may find himself concentrating on the moment rather than on social pressures, which can be relaxing. As he relaxes, he may find friends in the group that lead to friendships.

School Performance

Children who are physically active do better in school than those who are not. They get better grades, attend school more often due to experiencing fewer sick days, pay better attention in class, and behave better in class.

Self-Image

As your child learns that exercise can be fun, he will become more enthusiastic about physical activities—jumping, running, stretching, and playing games. As his body becomes more fit and his mind becomes sharper, he may begin to feel good about himself.

Sleep

Another benefit of exercise is that your child will fall asleep faster than an inactive child would and stay asleep longer. The more vigorous the exercise, the greater the sleep benefits will be. As you learned earlier in this chapter, sufficient sleep can lead to improvements in your child's mood, decision-making ability, and memory.

Getting Your Child to Exercise

Now that you know how important it is for your child to get moving, here are some tips that can make it happen.

- **Become active yourself.** Try to encourage all family members to get moving and be active together as a family. Show your child that exercise benefits not only him but also his family.

- **Make exercise fun.** Encourage your child to try different activities until he finds one or more he enjoys. If he finds an exercise he likes, he will be more likely to stick with it. Some children focus on one activity while others enjoy several different ones.

- **Don't forget to praise and reward his efforts.** In your efforts to encourage physical activity, you could even set up a rewards system—so many tokens for twenty or more minutes of exercise. Then your child could trade them in for something he wants, like a new toy or letting him choose the movie on movie night.

- **Start an exercise program slowly.** Let your child keep track of how much exercise he gets each day. His goal should be to exercise for sixty minutes a day. You don't need to start there, however, but could instead slowly increase the length of time day by day. In addition, keep in mind the sixty minutes could be divided into two or three sessions a day.
- **Never use exercise as a punishment.** Your child should associate exercise with positive feelings, not negative ones.
- **Limit screen time.** Screen time includes watching television, playing video games, and using other electronic devices. Don't use TV as a baby sitter. We know doing so can be very tempting, but it would be doing your child a disservice.
- **Provide opportunities for your child to be active.** Give your child active toys and games, such as a bike, skateboard, scooter, jump rope, or soccer ball, or other equipment for any sport in which he shows an interest. Be sure to get any necessary safety equipment as well, such as a helmet or protective pads, to prevent injuries.
- **Encourage your child to participate in sports or dance.** If he plays baseball or football, make sure he gets plenty of aerobic exercise and doesn't just stand in center field. If he wants to try golf, make sure he walks the course and doesn't ride in a golf cart. If he enjoys dancing, sign him up for a class and let him choose which style of dance to learn.
- **Keep safety in mind.** Let your child walk or bike to places such as school or a friend's house, but go with him the first time to make sure he can do so safely.

CONCLUSION

High-quality sleep and daily exercise are essential elements of good mental and physical health. For a child with a behavioral disorder, they may be life-changing. Adequate sleep may be hard to achieve, however, for a child who has poor sleep hygiene or suffers from obstructive sleep apnea, restless legs syndrome, or allergies. These sleep disorders can keep a child awake at night. Thankfully, there are ways to overcome these problems, including nutritional means, supplements, and physical sleep aids, which should help your child to get a good night's sleep. Once his sleep improves, his behavior and ability to learn should follow suit.

Additionally, exercise is tremendously important for your child's mental health and, when done regularly, has been shown to reduce many of the symptoms associated with the disorders discussed in Part One. By incorporating exercise into your child's life, you will be giving him a lifelong gift that offers benefits far beyond behavioral and learning improvements.

Making a point to address these two lifestyle factors—sleep and exercise—can result in positive changes in your child that you may not have thought possible without medication.

10.

Nutritional Factors

The gastrointestinal tract, or GI tract—also known as the gut—begins at the mouth and includes the esophagus, stomach, small and large intestines, liver, gall bladder, pancreas, and anus. Its main role is to break down food and absorb its nutrients, which may then be distributed throughout the body.

As described in Chapter 7 (see page 141), within the gut, there's a world of bacteria, fungi, and other microorganisms known as the microbiome. The bacteria of the microbiome have proven to be crucial to the body's ability to benefit from good nutrition, as they affect the health of the cells lining the GI tract and therefore impact how food is metabolized and its nutrients absorbed—processes that ultimately affect both health and behavior.

For a child to thrive, he needs to consume the right nutrients in sufficient amounts, not only to fuel his body properly but also to promote a healthy microbiome. (We should also stress the fact that a child's nutrition begins before birth through its mother's diet.) Nutrients are compounds the body must have in order to grow, maintain and repair itself, function properly, and enjoy overall good health. There are six major nutrients—carbohydrates, fat, protein, vitamins, minerals, and water. These substances may be found in different amounts in a variety of foods, including fresh fruits and vegetables, whole grains, legumes, nuts, seeds, lean meats, eggs, and dairy products.

Diet can have a profound effect not only on a child's health but also on his behavior. Improvements in your child's behavior, mood, and learning ability can often be achieved by changing his diet and adding certain supplements to his daily routine.

MACRONUTRIENTS

Carbohydrates, protein, and fat are known as *macronutrients,* as they are the nutrients required by the body in large amounts. Water is also considered a macronutrient, although unlike carbohydrates, protein, and fat, it does not provide the body with energy. *Micronutrients,* on the other hand, are nutrients that are needed by the body only in small quantities. These nutrients include vitamins and minerals. By making sure your child's diet contains healthy amounts of macronutrients and micronutrients, you will be making him better able to handle any challenges he might face, and possibly reducing the symptoms associated with certain behavioral disorders.

Carbohydrates

Often referred to as "carbs," *carbohydrates* are composed of carbon, hydrogen, and oxygen. There are three main forms of carbohydrates: *sugar, starch,* and *fiber*. Most carbohydrates are converted by enzymes into the simple sugar known as *glucose* in the digestive tract. Glucose is the major source of energy for the entire body, including the brain. In other words, it is the "fuel" of the body.

When it comes to feeding your child, you need to make sure he is able to fill his "tank" with the best "fuel" possible. A healthy diet will allow him to maintain a relatively stable level of blood glucose—one without high peaks and low valleys. In doing so, he will keep himself on an even keel and avoid stark ups and downs in his behavior.

Sugar

The most basic form of sugar is called a *monosaccharide,* also known as a simple sugar. Monosaccharides contain one sugar molecule and include *glucose, fructose,* and *galactose.* When two monosaccharides bond, they create a *disaccharide,* such as *sucrose* (glucose and fructose), *maltose* (two molecules of glucose), or *lactose* (glucose and galactose), which is the sugar found in dairy products.

Glucose is the main energy source for brain cells, and too little or too much glucose affects levels of neurotransmitters (chemical messengers in the brain). Your blood glucose level is measured by a simple blood test and, along with other tests, helps your doctor to recognize the presence of low blood sugar (*hypoglycemia*) or high blood sugar (*hyperglycemia*), the latter of which may indicate diabetes.

Fructose, or fruit sugar, is found plentifully in fruits and some vegetables. Unlike glucose, which is metabolized throughout the body, fructose is primarily metabolized by the liver, which converts it into glucose, lactate, and glycogen. This glucose and lactate are then used as fuel for the body. When a person consumes too much fructose, however, the liver becomes overloaded and turns this sugar into fat.

Galactose, also known as "brain sugar," is used to make special chemicals called *glycolipids*, which insulate nerves and nerve cells. Glycolipids also help to maintain the stability of the cell membrane.

Although sugar is the brain's main source of energy, excess sugar intake can be harmful to the body and the brain. While it is difficult to consume too much sugar from fruits and vegetables, the added sugars used to sweeten processed foods make it quite easy to overconsume this carbohydrate. For example, high-fructose corn syrup and table sugar (sucrose) are eaten to great excess in the Western diet thanks to our love of junk food and sugary beverages, resulting in obesity, tooth decay, and even behavioral and learning problems.

Starch

Another form of carbs is starch. Starches are made up of multiple glucose molecules that have been linked together in a chain. Most starches are considered complex carbohydrates, as they take longer to be metabolized and used as fuel by the body. As such, complex carbohydrates do not cause a person's blood sugar level to spike, allowing blood sugars levels to remain stable. They also promote a more prolonged feeling of fullness, which discourages overeating. Starch can be found in high amounts in plant foods such as legumes, certain vegetables, and whole grains. Good sources of starch include kidney beans, garbanzo beans, lentils, quinoa, potatoes, brown rice, and oatmeal.

Fiber

Fiber is a type of carbohydrate that cannot be broken down into sugar molecules, passing through the body largely undigested. Some fiber, however, is fermented in the large intestine and used for food by the microorganisms in the gut. Amazingly, these gut microorganisms interact chemically with the brain and may be related to autism, anxiety, depression, and other mental disorders.

In addition to its critical role in normal bowel functioning, fiber also helps to regulate the body's use of sugar, which it does by slowing down sugar absorption. This ability is important for a healthy brain. Fiber also provides bulk, making the body feel full and satisfied while keeping blood sugar in check. Examples of fiber-rich foods are legumes, fruit, vegetables, and whole grains.

Protein

Protein is made up of chemical building blocks called *amino acids*. There are nine essential amino acids. They are deemed "essential" because they must be consumed in the diet or as supplements, as the body cannot make them itself. Think of these nine amino acids as cars on a train, each linked together in a particular sequence. These cars can be uncoupled and then reassembled into a completely different sequence. Proteins are divided by digestion into their individual amino acids, and then these amino acids can form other proteins needed by the body.

The brain is composed mostly of water, with protein coming in second. Proteins and their amino acids make the machinery and enzymes in brain cells function. They play important roles in brain development and growth in infants, young children, and older children, too. They repair damaged nerve cells. They help make connective tissue in the brain, which binds brain cells to each other and supports them. They can also act as cellular receptors that help to initiate biochemical responses. For example, proper blood glucose regulation depends on proteins known as G-protein-coupled receptors.

Proteins and their amino acids are also used to make neurotransmitters. For example, *tryptophan*, an essential amino acid, is used to make the neurotransmitter serotonin. Without enough serotonin, you would feel depressed and more aggressive. As you know from Part One, various neurotransmitters in the brain are associated with behavioral issues. As you also know from Part One, the bacteria of the microbiome make most of the body's serotonin and therefore play a huge role in mood and GI activity.

Fat

Fat is a compound of fatty acids that is found in animals and plants. Solid fat, commonly found in animals, is composed of fatty acids that remain solid at room temperature. Oil, found in many plants and fish, consists of fatty acids that are liquid at room temperature. The diet must contain fat to ensure good health, but there are both "good" and "bad" types of fat, so it is important to learn a little more about them before you decide what to put on your child's plate.

Some fats found in oils are good and can dramatically affect behavior. These good fats are called omega-3 fatty acids and omega-6 fatty acids. Two of these fatty acids, *alpha-linolenic acid* (ALA)—an omega-3 fatty acid—and *linoleic acid* (LA)—an omega-6 fatty acid—are termed *essential fatty acids,* as they cannot be made by the human body and therefore must be consumed in the diet or through supplementation.

Omega-3s and omega-6s are a major component of cell membranes, which separate each cell from other cells, and are critical to the brain's ability to do its work properly. These fatty acids have "kinks" (double bonds) in their carbon chains, so they are not straight or packed tightly together. As such, they make cell membranes more fluid, resulting in positive effects on what enters and exits the cell. In addition to their role in cell membrane formation, these fatty acids act as raw material in the creation of hormone-like compounds that have multiple functions in the body and brain.

Alpha-linolenic acid may be found in oils such as soy, canola, walnut, and flaxseed. Linoleic acid may be found in oils such as safflower, sunflower, grape seed, hemp, and corn. Although the body is able to manufacture the fatty acids known as *eicosapentaenoic acid* (EPA) and *docosahexaenoic acid* (DHA) from ALA, the conversion of ALA is inefficient, and therefore these fatty acids, which play crucial roles in brain health, should also be consumed in the diet or as supplements. EPA and DHA may be found in abundance in fish and other seafood. It is also important to achieve a proper balance between omega-3s and omega-6s in our bodies. A healthy ratio of omega-6s to omega-3s seems to be somewhere between 1:1 and 4:1. Most Americans consume too many foods that contain omega-6s and too few foods that contain omega-3s, at a ratio of approximately 15:1.

Antioxidants and Free Radicals

In order to have a full understanding of the importance of nutrients, it's necessary to learn about antioxidants, free radicals, and oxidative stress. A free radical is a molecule with an uneven number of electrons, which can borrow an electron from another molecule, causing that molecule to become a free radical and do the same. Think of a free radical as a highly reactive molecule that acts like a "spark," causing other molecules to become "sparks," which lead to other "sparks" in a chain reaction. Free radicals can be beneficial or harmful.

When the body goes through the normal metabolic process of using oxygen to generate energy, it actually produces the most potent free radicals, which are known as *reactive oxygen species,* or *ROS.* When the production of reactive oxygen species in cells overwhelms the body's ability to neutralize these free radicals, a phenomenon known as oxidative stress occurs, which can be very damaging to the body.

High levels of oxygen in the brain can lead to greater levels of free radicals in this organ than in others. Free radicals may also be generated by toxic chemicals outside the body, such as those found in polluted water or air, and by ultraviolet light. Free radicals must be neutralized by antioxidants, which are mainly found in plant foods and include nutrients such as vitamin C, vitamin E, beta-carotene, selenium, and manganese—yet another reason to eat a healthy diet.

Omega-3 and omega-6 fatty acids may play a significant part in a number of behavioral disorders. Research has shown that omega-3 and omega-6 fatty acid levels are lower in children with behavioral problems than they are in those without. It has also shown an association between learning problems and low levels of omega-3s. Low blood levels of certain fatty acids have also been linked to violent behavior.

Signs of low fatty acid levels in your child may include excessive thirst, frequent urination, dry skin, dry hair, dandruff, broken nails, and tiny hard bumps on the backs of the arms and thighs. (If your child has excessive thirst and frequent urination, however, he should first be checked for diabetes, as these symptoms can signal this condition.) One way to see if an increase in your child's intake of omega-3s and omega-6s is actually raising his blood levels of these fatty acids would be to notice improvements in these symptoms, which may occur before any improvements in behavior appear.

While it is possible to acquire omega-3s and omega-6s in the diet, mainly through eating fish and seafood, sometimes supplementation may be warranted. Studies have shown an association between supplementation with EPA and DHA—sometimes including *gamma-linolenic acid* (GLA) and other nutrients—in children and improvements in several types of behavioral problems and learning problems. Keep in mind, however, that these types of supplements do not work overnight but may take a couple of months to show results. Finally, always talk to your child's doctor about any supplements you may be considering for your child before beginning any regimen.

MICRONUTRIENTS

Although micronutrients are needed by the body in much smaller amounts than are macronutrients, they are just as vital. Vitamins and minerals are micronutrients that are necessary for good health. Other micronutrients, such as phytochemicals, are not essential but have healthy effects in the body. When children don't get enough micronutrients in their diets it can be devastating, as this micronutrient deficiencies have been associated with lower IQ score, poor memory, learning disabilities, depression, and ADHD. These issues occur because micronutrients are needed for several cellular functions, including the synthesis of neurotransmitters, which, as you know, are the body's chemical messengers.

Vitamins

Vitamins contribute to good health by regulating metabolism, which refers to the chemical reactions that occur to maintain life. Thirteen vitamins are generally recognized as being essential, meaning they are needed for the body to function: vitamins A, C, D, E, and K, and all eight B vitamins. The vitamins that are especially needed by the brain to function optimally are vitamins A, C, D, and the B vitamins. Making sure your child gets enough of these essential nutrients can be an effective way to address several types of behavioral problems.

Vitamin A

Vitamin A is derived from animal sources as well as certain fruits and vegetables. Plant sources of vitamin A, however, contain only *provitamin A carotenoids,* which include *beta-carotene.* While provitamin A carotenoids have almost no actual vitamin activity, the body can convert them into the active form of vitamin A known as *retinol.*

Vitamin A plays a major role in brain development and functioning, memory, normal behavior, and learning. It also supports healthy eyesight and immune system functioning. Excellent food sources of vitamin A or beta-carotene include sweet potatoes, spinach, carrots, cheese, herring, milk with added vitamins A and D, fortified breakfast cereals, and eggs.

Vitamin A deficiency is very rare in the United States. Keep in mind that too much vitamin A is toxic. The vitamin A found in multivitamins is fine, but don't give a vitamin A supplement to your child unless your doctor orders one.

Vitamin B

There are eight B vitamins—*vitamin B_1 (thiamine), vitamin B_2 (riboflavin), vitamin B_3 (niacin), vitamin B_5 (pantothenic acid), vitamin B_6 (pyridoxine), vitamin B_7 (biotin), vitamin B_9 (folate),* and *vitamin B_{12} (cobalamin).* These vitamins are collectively known as the B complex vitamins, which often work together in the body and are found together in the same foods.

In particular, vitamins B_1, B_6, B_9, and B_{12} are important in many different pathways in the brain. They are needed only in small amounts but play vital roles in maintaining good health and wellbeing. These B vitamins impact metabolism in each cell and boost energy levels and brain functioning. B vitamins are cofactors in the synthesis of the neurotransmitters dopamine and serotonin, which affect mood, emotions, and sleep, and have been found to impact children's mental growth and behavior significantly.

B vitamin deficiencies are rare in children in the United States. B vitamins can be obtained from fish, poultry, meat, liver, eggs, and dairy. Plant sources include leafy green vegetables, beans, and peas. Foods often fortified with B vitamins include flour, breads, and cereals.

Vitamin C

Vitamin C (ascorbic acid) is necessary for your body to build blood vessels and muscle. It acts as an antioxidant, neutralizing harmful free radicals, which damage cells. Vitamin C plays a significant role in neurotransmitter synthesis in the brain. It also helps to protect the insulating layer around nerves known as the *myelin sheath,* making it essential for normal learning, and supports the immune system.

The association between vitamin C deficiency and adverse psychiatric effects has been known for centuries. While vitamin C deficiency, also known as scurvy, is extremely rare in the United States, if your child is a picky eater and doesn't consume enough fruits and vegetables, his vitamin C intake may be low. Children who don't get enough vitamin C may be moody, anxious, fatigued, or depressed, and may have problems learning.

Encourage your child to eat foods rich in vitamin C, such as citrus fruits (oranges, grapefruit, tangerines, etc.), peppers, strawberries, blackcurrants, broccoli, and tomatoes. If he absolutely refuses to eat these foods, he may need a vitamin C supplement.

Vitamin D

Vitamin D is probably familiar to you because of its role in building strong bones and teeth. What you may not know is that vitamin D plays important roles in the brain. For example, vitamin D helps to regulate many genes important for brain functioning. It protects nerve cells by reducing inflammation and oxidative stress. Children who have vitamin D deficiency during their elementary school years appear to be more affected by behavioral problems than other children when they reach adolescence.

Vitamin D is called the "sunshine" vitamin because your body can make it when your skin is exposed to the sun. In addition, certain foods contain significant amounts of vitamin D, such as salmon, herring, sardines, cod liver oil, egg yolks, and mushrooms. Several foods have vitamin D added to them, including various kinds of milk, some orange juices, and some cereals.

Unfortunately, approximately 42 percent of Americans are deficient in vitamin D, as are almost 97 percent of African Americans. When it comes to your child, his doctor can easily take a reading of his vitamin

D level by using a 25-hydroxy vitamin D test. If the reading is low (less than 30 ng/ml), she may prescribe vitamin D_3 supplements, as this form of vitamin D is more efficient than the other form of vitamin D supplement available, vitamin D_2.

Depression is the most likely observable behavioral condition that may be seen with vitamin D_3 deficiency. A blood level of 40 to 80 ng/ml is ideal, but at a minimum it should be greater than 30 ng/ml. (If your child's vitamin D level is particularly low, your doctor may prescribe supplements at a higher dosage than recommended in Table 10.1. Vitamins—Dietary Reference Intakes, Ages 1–13 on page 198. She will be able to explain the dosage and why it is recommended.)

Minerals

Although all minerals are micronutrients, some are needed in larger amounts than others, including magnesium, calcium, sulfur, sodium, and potassium. Minerals required in smaller amounts are known as trace minerals and include iron, chromium, selenium,

All minerals are essential for good health and normal brain functioning, but the following minerals are especially important in terms of behavior and mental health.

Copper

Copper is an essential mineral that plays a key role in the production of neurotransmitters in the brain, namely dopamine and norepinephrine. Copper plays a role in ADHD because, along with zinc, it helps to neutralize free radicals. Too much copper, however, can cause aggression, hyperactivity, insomnia, and anxiety. Too much copper can also cause a zinc deficiency. We do not recommend copper-only supplements, but the amount of this micronutrient that is typically found in multinutrient children's supplements should be fine. Discuss the issue with your child's doctor if you are considering such supplementation.

Iron

Iron deficiency is the most common nutrient deficiency worldwide and affects 2.4 million US children. Determining whether or not your child has enough iron is very important for his physical and mental health. If he is iron deficient, he may develop *iron deficiency anemia* (IDA), in which there are too few red blood cells in the body. Red blood cells carry oxygen to all cells in the body. Without sufficient oxygen, cells cannot do their jobs. IDA is associated with behavioral and learning delays. A child with IDA may have pale skin and display irritability, fussiness, or fatigue.

Even if your child does not have IDA, low levels of serum ferritin, a storage form of iron, are associated with psychiatric disorders such as sleep disorders, anxiety disorders, depression, tic disorders, autism, and ADHD. In one study, 84 percent of children with ADHD had low serum ferritin compared with 18 percent of healthy control subjects. In another study, researchers reported that iron supplements (80 mg ferrous sulfate) improved symptoms of ADHD in children with low serum ferritin.

Besides its connection with red blood cells, iron has many other roles that impact the brain. In the womb and during early life, iron helps the brain grow and develop. Later on it continues to participate in the making of the myelin sheath, which allows electrical impulses to transmit quickly and efficiently along nerve cells. Iron is also needed to synthesize neurotransmitters such as dopamine and serotonin, and affects how they function.

If your child is low in iron, the first step would be to give him iron-rich foods in his diet, such as red meat, seafood, fortified breakfast cereal, peanut butter, eggs, beans, or nuts. Never give your child iron supplements without the guidance of your child's doctor, as getting too much iron is dangerous.

Magnesium

Magnesium is another mineral that plays a crucial role in more than 300 chemical reactions in the body. Magnesium is important for the production of neurotransmitters such as serotonin and dopamine. It is also involved in the metabolism of essential fatty acids and glucose. In other words, having enough magnesium is essential for normal brain functioning and behavior.

Approximately 68 percent of Americans consume less than the recommended levels of dietary magnesium. One reason for this deficiency is the depletion of soil, meaning foods grown now contain less magnesium than they did in earlier times. In addition, processing methods of certain foods can also deplete them of magnesium.

Magnesium deficiency has been associated with headaches, muscle cramps, constipation, anxiety, high blood pressure, chronic fatigue, muscle weakness, heart rhythm irregularities, depression, and irritability. A magnesium-deficient diet is associated with depression, and magnesium supplementation has been shown to be as effective as antidepressant medicines. Magnesium also relieves anxiety.

There is an inverse relationship between blood levels of magnesium and ADHD symptoms. In other words, as levels of magnesium decrease in an ADHD child, symptoms of ADHD increase. In a study of twenty-five patients with ADHD, aged six to sixteen, 72 percent of the children were deficient in magnesium. The magnesium-deficient children received 200 mg of magnesium each day for eight weeks. By the end of the trial, hyperactivity, impulsivity, inattentiveness, and opposition had improved. In a different study of children with ADHD, B vitamins and magnesium were given, which resulted in higher plasma levels of magnesium and led to improved hyperactivity and inattentiveness scores. Finally, supplements of vitamin D_3 and magnesium were given to a group of children with ADHD. After eight weeks, their conduct problems, social problems, and anxiety had improved.

Choosing a magnesium supplement is not easy, as they come in many different forms. Some forms contain a large amount of magnesium, such as magnesium oxide, which helps relieve constipation but may not be absorbed as well as magnesium in other forms. Magnesium threonate is a form that is well tolerated and known to increases levels of magnesium in the brain. It may diminish symptoms of hyperactivity, depression, anxiety, and other brain-related disorders.

Zinc

Zinc is involved in the actions of over 300 enzymes that are necessary for the production of chemicals needed in all parts of the body. Zinc is required for normal growth and development. It is also important for normal immune function. In the brain, zinc is necessary in the maintenance of neurotransmitter activity. It also stimulates the thymus gland, which improves the functioning of the immune system.

Studies have reported that zinc levels are lower in children with ADHD. Furthermore, the lower the zinc level, the greater the symptoms of inattentiveness, hyperactivity, impulsivity, and conduct problems. One study reported that of 118 children with ADHD, those with the lowest blood levels of zinc had the most severe conduct problems, anxiety, and hyperactivity.

Zinc supplementation has been shown to improve symptoms of not only ADHD but also oppositional behavior disorder, conduct disorder, anxiety, and depression. Finally, if your child is taking stimulant medication, zinc appears to enhance the effects of this type of medication.

Phytochemicals

Found in plants, *phytochemicals* are substances that are thought to provide many health benefits to humans. Unlike the vitamins and minerals we have discussed in this chapter, phytochemicals are not known to be essential, but they nevertheless seem to keep us healthy. They give plants their specific colors, odors, and flavors. Plants depend upon them for growth, defense against plant diseases, and prevention against predators. Very few phytochemicals are actual vitamins. One exception is the yellow, orange, or reddish pigment known as beta-carotene, which, as you know, can be converted into vitamin A by the body.

Phytochemicals help to neutralize free radicals, improve the thinking process by increasing connections between brain cells, and improve blood flow, which helps other vital nutrients to reach brain cells. In other words, they can improve the brain's abilities to do all its various tasks.

So, how can be sure your child gets sufficient phytochemicals in his diet? Think of the rainbow of colors found in fruits and vegetables. Different colors offer different phytochemicals and benefits. Consider red foods—red apples, strawberries, raspberries, red beets, radishes, and so on. Different red foods have different red pigments. Next, consider yellow or orange foods—peaches, apricots, nectarines, carrots, squash, and sweet potatoes. Next, consider blue or purple foods—blueberries, blackberries, purple grapes, purple cabbage, purple potatoes, etc. Don't forget green foods—green grapes, green apples, green cabbage, kiwis, green leafy vegetables, asparagus, broccoli, and green beans. There are even white foods to add to the menu—onions, scallions, and garlic. Choose several differently colored fruits and vegetables each day to make sure your child gets a variety of phytochemicals needed for good health. Phytochemicals are helpful for your child's brain to function and can easily be added to his diet.

Table 10.1. Vitamins—Dietary Reference Intakes, Ages 1–13

VITAMINS													
Ages	A ug/d	C mg/d	D ug/d	E mg/d	K ug/d	B_1 mg/d	B_2 mg/d	B_3 mg/d	B_5 mg/d	B_6 mg/d	B_7 ug/d	B_9 ug/d	B_{12} ug/d
1–3	300	15	15	6	30	0.5	0.5	6	2	0.5	8	150	0.9
4–8	400	25	15	7	55	0.6	0.6	8	3	0.6	12	200	1.2
9–13	600	45	15	11	60	0.9	0.9	12	4	1	20	300	1.8

Table 10.2. Minerals—Dietary Reference Intakes, Ages 1–13

MINERALS												
Ages	Calcium mg	Iron mg/d	Copper ug/d	Magnesium mg/d	Zinc mg/d	Iodine ug/d	Manganese mg/d	Potassium mg/d	Phosphorous mg/d	Selenium ug/d	Chromium ug/d	Molybdenum ug/d
1–3	700	7	340	80	3	90	1.2	2,000	460	20	11	17
4–8	1,000	10	440	130	5	90	1.5	2,300	50	30	15	22
9–13	1,300	8	700	240	8	120	1.9 (males), 1.6 (females)	2,500 (males), 2,300 (females)	1,250	40	25 (males), 21 (females)	34

MICRONUTRIENT SUPPLEMENTS

You may be thinking, "Why does my child need supplements if he eats a healthy diet?" For one, crops grown today have fewer nutrients than those found in the same foods during the last century. This change is partly due to genetic manipulation of crops to provide bigger, more beautiful, but not necessarily as nutritious, produce. In addition, produce can be depleted of many nutrients because of overuse of the soil. Of course, some children—especially ones with behavioral problems—are picky eaters and simply do not eat a healthy diet, which inevitably leads to low levels of important vitamins and minerals in the body.

Fortunately, there are supplements containing a broad spectrum of the nutrients we've discussed. Micronutrient supplements typically contain multiple vitamins—A, B complex, C, D and E—and multiple minerals—iron, copper, magnesium, zinc, and a few others. Some contain fatty acids such as EPA or DHA. When considering supplementation for your child, be sure to choose a product that has nutrients in amounts that are appropriate for him, and talk to his doctor to verify the safety of these nutrient levels.

Supplements such as Efalex and Equazen contain DHA, EPA, and GLA, and come in various forms, including capsule and liquid. In a study of children with motor skill problems and ADHD-type symptoms, participants received Equazen supplements. After three months, the children showed no improvement in motor skills but reading, spelling, and behavior had each improved. Another study of ADHD children with conduct disorder showed improvement in CD after a few months of supplementation.

Smartfish is juice drink that contains omega-3 fatty acids. Research on the use of Smartfish has reported a 42 percent reduction in problem behavior in children aged eight to sixteen who were aggressive, showed antisocial behavior, got into fights, and told lies. It has also shown a 62 percent reduction of symptoms of depression, anxiety, and withdrawal in children who used Smartfish. In another study, researchers used Smartfish Recharge, which contains vitamin D and antioxidants in addition to fatty acids from fish oil. They reported that the supplement reduced antisocial behavior and aggression.

In a study of children aged five to twelve with ADHD, scientists used the supplement Esprico, which contains DHA, EPA, zinc, and magnesium. They reported beneficial effects on ADHD symptoms, behavior, sleep, and emotional problems.

When choosing a supplement, be sure to select one that does not contain sugar, artificial colors, or artificial flavors. To help you choose the right supplement, consult the tables on page 198, which list the Dietary Reference Intakes (DRIs) recommended by the Food and Nutrition Board of Institute of Medicine, National Academy of Sciences, for children aged one through thirteen.

Broad-spectrum micronutrients have been used with success as a form of treatment for psychiatric symptoms, including:

- aggression
- anxiety
- autism symptoms
- conduct problems
- hyperactivity
- impulsivity
- inattentiveness
- irritability
- mood difficulties
- poor academic performance
- poor self-regulation
- poor social behavior

As you can see, these symptoms are involved in many of the disorders discussed in Part One. Not only did these behaviors improve with micronutrient supplementation, the supplements were well tolerated, with few or no side effects.

A HEALTHY DIET

Feeding your child an optimal diet is important in his journey to overcome his behavioral or learning problems. An optimal diet is one that meets all your child's nutritional needs and decreases or eliminates unhealthy foods. Unfortunately, few children in the United States eat a healthy diet, which includes fruit, vegetables, whole grains, and other nutrient-dense foods.

Fruit

Fruit provides many healthy nutrients, including potassium, vitamin C, vitamin A, and vitamin B_9 (folate). It also contains a substantial amount of fiber. Aim to give your child two to three servings of fruit a day. If you choose a variety of colors you will be providing your child with many different phytochemicals as well. When it comes to consuming fruit, eating whole fruit is better than drinking fruit juice, as the pith and skin of fruit contains many beneficial nutrients. One group of phytochemicals known as *flavonoids* is found plentifully in the pith of citrus fruit, for example. In fact, by eating a whole orange, you get five times as many flavonoids as you would by drinking eight ounces of orange juice. Moreover, the fiber in a whole orange slows down the absorption of the fruit's sugar, while the absence of fiber in fruit juice can lead to a spike in your blood sugar level.

Serving your child fruit can be a sane way to satisfy his sweet tooth, but avoid sweetened fruit, including canned fruit in sugary syrup and applesauce with added sugar.

Vegetables

Like fruit, vegetables provide a wide variety of nutrients, including potassium, folate, vitamin A in the form of beta-carotene, vitamin C, and vitamin K. And like fruit, vegetables contain dietary fiber and phytochemicals. Aim to give your child two to four servings of vegetables each day. Try different colors and types. For example, try yellow squash, sweet potatoes, or carrots. For your green choices, go for green leafy vegetables or broccoli. Throw in beets for your red color, and try purple cabbage for your purple color.

Keep in mind that some children are not going to go overnight from barely eating vegetables to consuming multiple servings a day. Keep presenting vegetables to your child, but don't turn mealtime into a battle. A helpful tip is to keep cut-up carrots and celery in the refrigerator for snacks. In addition, as you are making dinner and your kids are telling you they are starving, put out a plate of vegetables (cherry tomatoes, carrots, celery, radishes, and broccoli florets) and a tasty dip. They will gobble them up because they are hungry.

Whole Grains

Examples of whole grains include amaranth, barley, buckwheat, millet, bulgur, wild rice, and rye berries. When a food states it is "whole grain," it means it contains or is made from the whole seed of the grain, which includes all three parts of the kernel. Refined grains have had the outside layer (bran) removed, leaving little dietary fiber or nutrients. Foods made from refined grains include white flour, white rice, quick oats, and refined corn meal. Aim to give your child six to ten servings of whole grains each day.

Whole grains provide nutrients such as B vitamins, iron, folate, selenium, and potassium. They are also very high in fiber. Whole grains are digested more slowly than refined grains due to their fiber content. This fiber content benefits blood sugar levels. When your child has healthy blood sugar levels, his behavior may be more stable. Whole grains also benefit the good bacteria in your child's gut, allowing these bacteria to produce chemicals that interact in a positive way with your child's brain.

Meat and Other Proteins

Meat and other sources of protein provide essential amino acids for your child's brain, but how much protein does your child need? Children who are aged four through eight need about 19 grams each day, while those who are aged nine through thirteen need about 34 grams. In short, aim to give your child about one to two servings each day.

In the United States, the most commonly consumed proteins often come from animal sources—red meat, eggs, fish, and poultry—which contain all nine essential amino acids, making them complete proteins. Milk and yogurt can also be good sources of protein. In addition, some plant foods are complete proteins, including soybeans, quinoa, and buckwheat. Other plant foods such as beans other than soy, whole grains, nuts, and seeds have several but not all nine amino acids. If you combine a couple of these foods in a day, however, your child will consume all nine amino acids for normal brain functioning.

Some children with behavioral disorders do better with more protein in their diets. If your child seems to fit into this category, try to give him a serving of protein at each meal and snack. Eggs, yogurt, nut butter on whole-wheat bread, three-bean salad, and a handful of nuts and seeds are all relatively easy to incorporate into a meal or snack. If you opt for red meat, look for a leaner cut and remove any visible fat before you cook it. Chicken and turkey contain less saturated fat than red meat. Fish is another great source of protein, but it should be baked or broiled, not fried. Cold-water fish are also rich in omega-3 fatty acids. Finally, don't be shy to a vegetarian dish such as chili, which gets its protein from beans. You can serve your chili with whole-grain bread to make a complete protein.

Dairy

As mentioned in the previous section, dairy products such as milk and yogurt are good sources of protein, but dairy can also add calcium, magnesium, potassium, phosphorous, riboflavin, vitamin D, vitamin A, and vitamin B_{12} to your child's diet—nutrients that feed your child's brain. When shopping for dairy products, look for items that do not have any added sugar. If something needs to be sweetened, you can use fresh fruit to do so. Aim to give your child two to three servings of dairy each day.

Some children are dairy intolerant or allergic to dairy, or perhaps you would prefer not to use animal products for other reasons. When looking for a substitute for dairy milk, keep in mind that soy milk is the only one with nutrients similar to cow's milk. Almond, rice, or coconut milk may be used to replace cow's milk in the diet and in recipes, but not all these options contain the nutrients found in cow's milk unless these nutrients have been added, so read labels. Some of these milks contain added sugar as well, which should be avoided.

Nuts, Seeds, and Oils

As you know, essential fatty acids play a vital role in the health of your child's brain. Dietary sources of omega-3 fatty acids include flaxseeds and walnuts, as well as flaxseed, soy, canola, and walnut oils. Some children behave better if they take one to three teaspoons of flaxseed oil orally each day. The oil should be kept refrigerated after opening to prevent spoilage of the delicate fatty acids.

FOODS TO AVOID

As you may have suspected, most items to avoid in the diet are found in processed foods. If you give your child a diet that consists of real foods that you prepare yourself, then you can skip this section. It is a rare feat to eliminate all forms of processed foods, however, so the following ingredients are what you should look to avoid when buying something that comes in a package.

The Indirect Effect of Too Much Salt

Although there is far too much salt in the average American diet, there is no evidence that salt contributes to behavioral problems. Nevertheless, salt is found in many unhealthy foods, such as French fries, hamburgers, pizza, and snack foods. The high levels of salt in these unhealthy foods may contribute indirectly to behavioral problems by making children reach for sugary sodas or other sweetened items to counteract the intense saltiness. Eating overly salty foods and sugary beverages or foods on a regular basis promotes childhood obesity, which, as you know, has been linked to behavioral problems.

Artificial Colors

British studies have confirmed that artificial colors can cause inattentiveness in children—even those without ADHD. In 2010, these studies led European scientists to require warning labels on all foods containing dyes, stating that these products "may have an adverse effect on activity and attention in children." This warning, however, was rejected in the United States, likely due to pressure from food manufacturers. Nevertheless, if present, artificial dyes must be listed in the ingredients of a food product. You may see such ingredients as red dye #40 and yellow #5 on a label. These additives may be abundantly found in soft drinks, fruit drinks, puddings, ice cream, snacks, and candies. They are used to make the food item attractive, and sometimes to make you think there is real fruit in a product. For example, there are strawberry milks that are dyed with red dye #3 or #40 and contain artificial strawberry flavoring, but which have no actual strawberries in them.

Preservatives

Preservatives keep foods from spoiling and in this sense play an important role in food safety. For example, sodium nitrite and sodium nitrate protect meats from botulism, a very serious food-borne disease. Nevertheless, research shows that nitrites may cause mania in some people, and altered behavior in rats. Research also suggests that nitrites may trigger migraine headaches. On an ingredients label, the preservatives you'll typically find include:

- BHT and BHA
- TBHQ
- sodium benzoate
- sodium bisulfite
- calcium propionate
- MSG (monosodium glutamate)

Some food manufacturers use vitamin C or vitamin E to preserve their products. These preservations are fine to eat. Nevertheless, you can often find similar foods that don't use preservatives. For example, certain loaves of bread contain preservatives while others do not.

Bad Fat

While we've discussed the importance of fat in the diet, some types of fat are actually bad for the body. These fats include *saturated fat, hydrogenated fat*, and *partially hydrogenated fat*. Saturated fats are long, straight chains of carbon that easily pack together, making cell membranes stiff. Stiff membranes affect which nutrients can enter and exit each cell. Saturated fat is found plentifully in fatty meats, sausage, bacon, and luncheon meats. Hydrogenated and partially hydrogenated fats are fats to which hydrogen has been added, making them higher in saturated fat content. Manufacturers like these fats because they increase the shelf lives of many different products. They also produce different feelings on the tongue, which manufactures believe consumers like. You can avoid these fats by cutting down on vegetable shortening, baked foods, fried foods, and other processed foods in the diet. The amounts of these fats must be listed on a food product's ingredient label.

Sugar

The average American child consumes 19 teaspoons (76 grams) of added sugar daily. That's nearly half a cup each day. When your child eats something sugary, his blood sugar rises, increasing the level of dopamine in his brain. This increased amount of dopamine creates a feeling of happiness. As his blood sugar drops, so does his dopamine level, making him tired and irritable, so he reaches for more sugar. Sugar has become an addiction. In addition, a child who is hooked on sugar gets lots of calories but no healthy nutrients to allow his brain to function normally. This lack of nutrients may cause him to act out.

When reading ingredient labels, look not only for sugar but also for ingredients that are sugar under another name, such as dextrose, cane juice, corn syrup, maltose, agave, and many others. How much sugar is okay for your child to eat? In an ideal world the amount would be zero, but that is a truly difficult goal to achieve in today's world. For children, the American Heart Association recommends no more than 6 teaspoons, or 24 grams, of added sugars a day. Some children, however, may not tolerate that much sugar and will do better with as little sugar as possible.

Artificial Sweeteners

You may be thinking that you'll just replace sugar with artificial sweeteners. Like added sugar, however, artificial sweeteners are almost never found in healthy foods. They include substances such as saccharin, aspartame, and sucralose. In general, there is a lack of studies on the effects of artificial sweeteners on children. They are definitely not recommended during the first twelve months of life, however. At the moment, the main problem with artificial sweeteners would seem to be that they negatively affect the good bacteria in the gut. As you know, gut bacteria may play a major role in your child's behavior.

Artificial sweeteners have has been associated with obesity in humans, too. You would think that the decrease in calories afforded by these sweeteners would lead to weight loss, but instead these sweeteners stimulate hunger, encouraging more food to be consumed.

Natural Alternatives to Sugar

There are certain natural sweeteners that may act as a safe alternative to sugar, including monk fruit (made from a melon grown in China) and stevia (made from the plant *Stevia rebaudiana*). Neither of these options increases insulin or blood sugar levels, but each has its own particular taste that is slightly different from sugar and may not be liked. Sugar alcohols, such as sorbitol, xylitol, and mannitol, do not affect insulin or blood sugar levels, but they are metabolized by the bacteria in the gut and may cause stomach upset.

DETECTING FOOD SENSITIVITIES

Unfortunately, it is not just unhealthy foods that can cause a child to react poorly, affecting his brain and behavior. Food intolerance or sensitivity can cause some healthy foods to result in such problems as well.

If you haven't started a diet record for your child, buy a notebook and keep track of the foods and beverages your child consumes, describing his behavior before and after he consumes these foods and beverages. If you can't see a change in mood or behavior associated with a particular food or drink, then try an elimination diet, which removes common foods from your child's diet and then reintroduces them one at a time. You may be able to see which foods change his behavior when you add them back to the menu. If you find the idea of placing your child on an elimination diet overwhelming, you may find it easier to have him follow a "few foods" diet, which restricts what he eats to a few foods in particular. The information you may learn from using one of these diets can be very helpful.

Elimination Diet

The most common foods assoiated with food intolerance or sensitivity are:

- chocolate
- citrus fruit (orange, grapefruit, etc.)
- corn
- eggs
- legumes (kidney beans, chickpeas, etc.)
- milk and milk products
- wheat, rye, and barley

Carefully plan a diet without these common foods. You will need to read all ingredient labels on packaged foods, looking carefully for these items. If you don't recognize the name of an ingredient, look it up. It may be related to one of the recently listed common foods. The fact is that almost all packaged products will contain one or more of these substances.

Have your child follow this elimination diet for seven to ten days. If his behavior is better during this period, you are on the right track. Then add each food back to his diet, one at a time, starting with ones you least suspect. Give your child a small portion and if no reaction occurs, let him eat more of the food later on in the day. If your child shows an obvious reaction after eating a food, don't give him any more of this food. Wait until the reaction subsides (usually twenty-four to forty-eight hours) before you add another food back to his diet.

"Few Foods" Diet

Some doctors refer to this type of diet as the caveman diet due to its lack of modern processed foods. "Few foods" diets have been studied in children with ADHD, migraine, bedwetting, and seizures. Researchers have reported that a "few foods" diet can be helpful in identifying foods that adversely affect a child.

One of the first successful research trials of a "few foods" diet included 78 children with ADHD symptoms who used a "few foods" diet for three to four weeks. In addition to hyperactivity, parents reported that many of the children studied also had asthma, hay fever, eczema, skin rashes, headaches, gastrointestinal symptoms, and even seizures. Their prescribed diet consisted of two meats (often lamb and turkey), two carbohydrates (rice and potato), two fruits (often banana and pear), various root and green vegetables, bottled water, safflower oil, and milk-free margarine. If any one of these foods was suspected of causing problems, it was replaced by another food. Approximately three-fourths of the children showed improvements in behavior. Similar studies have reported improvements in migraines, bedwetting, depression, and seizures.

To create a "few foods" diet, make a list of all the foods your child eats less than once a month and then choose two foods from each type of food (fruit, vegetables, meat, grains, oils, etc.). Once your child has started the diet, keep a careful record of everything he eats and drinks, as well as how he acts and what physical symptoms he might experience (migraines, bedwetting, etc.) At the end of three to four weeks, reintroduce one food to his diet each day and make note of any behavioral changes. Start with the foods you least suspect of causing problems. If he reacts to a food, remove it from his diet again. Once the reaction has worn off, you can try another food.

CONCLUSION

What you feed your child is extremely important in terms of both his health and his behavior. In order for their brains to develop and function well, children require the necessary macronutrients and micronutrients, which can be acquired from a healthy diet. It may not be easy to change your child's diet from an unhealthy one to one that meets his nutritional requirements fully, but in doing so you will be giving him the best chance at avoiding behavioral issues, as well as the lifelong gift of knowing how to feed himself wisely. Micronutrient supplements can be beneficial, of course, and may be necessary for some, but they should never be considered a substitute for eating optimally.

You may notice that your child feels better, behaves better, and learns more easily when he avoids certain foods. Tracking down food sensitivities and intolerances can be a difficult task, though, and you may need to put your child on an elimination diet or a "few foods" diet as you play detective.

Needless to say, nutritional factors can have a tremendous impact on behavioral disorders and should always be considered in your efforts to help your child to overcome his difficulties.

11. Environmental Factors

Our planet is polluted. Exposure to toxins in the environment that may cause behavioral or health problems is a huge problem in the United States and around the world. Your child's environment consists of everything he comes in contact with at school, home, and elsewhere—not to mention all the things to which he is exposed in the womb. Although harmful substances in the environment can affect adults and children alike, young children are especially vulnerable to them because their bodies are still developing.

The Environmental Protection Agency (EPA) has estimated that there are 85,000 different chemicals in the United States. Of this number, the EPA is able to test about 200 chemicals per year. Research has revealed that blood taken from the umbilical cord of ten mothers contained 287 different chemicals, including pesticides, ingredients from consumer products, and waste products from the burning of gasoline, coal, and garbage. Moreover, research on children has associated these chemical exposures with disorders such as ADHD and ODD.

A person's exposure to environmental toxins begins in the womb, where they are passed from a mother's blood to her fetus's blood via the placenta. Once born, an infant may be exposed to heavy metals and chemicals from contaminated air, water, or even food. As the child gets older, he may continue to be exposed to heavy metals such as lead, mercury, cadmium, and aluminum, often causing permanent damage to his brain, immune system, etc. He may also be exposed to other toxic substances such as tobacco smoke, air pollution, and certain problematic chemicals found in plastics.

Your child may also react to so-called "safe" chemicals in his environment. Most children and people do not react to them, but about 10 percent of the people react with behavioral, mental, or physical symptoms. These substances vary from person to person, but may include chemicals found in carpeting, perfumes, scents, personal care products, and cleaning products.

Finally, in addition to the impact of chemical pollutants in the environment on a child, natural allergens such as pollen, dust, and mold can affect children profoundly as well and have been associated with a number of the disorders described in this book.

HEAVY METALS

A heavy metal is a metallic chemical element that has a high density and is toxic or poisonous in very small concentrations. Arsenic, cadmium, lead, and mercury are prime examples of heavy metals in the environment that can affect a child's ability to learn and function properly. They interfere with many chemical and biological components of cellular functioning.

Arsenic

Unlike the other substances in this section, arsenic isn't technically a metal. It is considered a metalloid, which refers to a chemical element that exhibits some properties of metals and some of nonmetals. Nevertheless, it is even more dangerous than the metals that follow. Arsenic toxicity can occur in two ways—acute (quickly) and chronic (over time). In terms of the subject matter of this book, chronic arsenic toxicity is of paramount concern, as it may begin in the womb, contributing to abnormal growth of neurons. Continued arsenic exposure will, in this way, negatively impact behavioral development over time.

Arsenic may be found in food, water, or air, and is mainly absorbed by mouth and through the skin. It is also a known carcinogen.

Cadmium

A study measured cadmium levels in the urine of children aged six to fifteen years old who participated in a national survey. It found that children with higher levels of cadmium in their urine were at increased risk of having a learning disability or requiring special education.

In the United States, cadmium is found in areas where zinc, lead, and copper are mined, which may pollute the surrounding plants, fish, or other animals. It is also found in batteries, pigments, metal coatings, plastics, fertilizers, and cigarettes. If you work in a factory that uses cadmium, it is highly recommended that you change your clothes and shoes before you leave your workplace in order to avoid bringing traces of cadmium home.)

Lead

Lead is one of the most commonly discussed heavy metals in the environment. Exposure to lead can cause severe mental, behavioral, learning, and health problems, especially in infants, toddlers, and children. Once this causal relationship had been identified, Congress took action to ban lead from all paints in 1978. By 1996, the Clean Air Act had banned the use of lead in gasoline.

If your house or school was built before 1978, it likely contains lead paint. Problems with lead-based paint start when it chips off the walls and small children have opportunities to put these chips in their mouths. Moreover, during renovations of old schools or homes, paint is scraped or sanded, releasing lead into the air. Before starting a renovation project in your home, ask your local health department to test your paint. If they find lead, you will need to hire experts who know how to remove the paint safely. This is definitely not a do-it-your-self project.

Certain states test children for lead at age one and again at age two according to law. The amount of lead considered toxic has decreased dramatically over the years. Now researchers have declared that blood levels should ideally be zero. In other words, no amount of lead is safe. If your doctor measures your child's lead level and finds it worrisome, she will report this to the health department to investigate the source of lead exposure.

In order to reduce your child's lead exposure, eliminate all sources of lead from his environment. Although lead-based paint has been banned, foreign-made toys and jewelry may still contain lead. When a toddler puts one of these toys or items of jewelry in his mouth, he is also ingesting lead. Your child may be exposed to lead because a family member works in a factory or laboratory that uses lead and may bring lead dust home on his clothes and shoes. Living near a lead processing factory, a chemical dump, or abandoned housing can also increase lead exposure. A simple way for you to prevent your child from ingesting lead is to make sure he washes his hands thoroughly before eating.

Moreover, a diet rich in calcium, iron, and vitamin C can protect against lead poisoning.

Symptoms of lead poisoning include severe headaches, stomachaches, and vomiting. Behavioral issues include fatigue, inattentiveness, impulsiveness, and hyperactivity. A high lead level is also associated with low IQ, although even low levels can negatively and irreversibly impact IQ.

Mercury

Like lead, mercury is toxic to brain cells. Exposure to high levels of mercury has been linked to mental retardation, ADHD, and inattentiveness. Dietary intake of fish is the most significant source of mercury exposure. Fish that may be contaminated with high levels of mercury include white albacore tuna, mackerel, and swordfish.

Dental fillings known as amalgams have come under scrutiny for mercury exposure, as they are composed of silver, zinc, copper, and mercury. There is some research that showed children with amalgam fillings displayed slightly worse behavior than the average child, but it also showed that children with composite fillings (white fillings) displayed slightly worse behavior as well. This finding may simply suggest that kids with behavioral problems are less likely to brush their teeth sufficiently, leading to cavities and fillings. Another study showed that children who had at least six amalgam fillings had a 20 percent increased risk of having ADHD, but again, if a child has a behavioral disorder such as ADHD, he may do a poor job of brushing his teeth. If you have concerns about fillings, talk to your child's dentist.

AIR POLLUTION

Some areas of the United States have high levels of air pollution or smog for many days of the year, such as Los Angeles and many other large cities with heavy traffic or a large number of factories emitting toxic fumes. The air we breathe may contain many different pollutants. For example, fossil fuels (coal, gas, and natural gas) that are burned for energy add many harmful particles to the air. These particles can lead to a number of illnesses, including lung disease and cancer. They also contribute to climate change.

Air pollution is especially harmful to children. Unfortunately, air pollution tends to affect children of color in particular, who often live in neighborhoods near factories or high-traffic areas. Not surprisingly air pollution can cause respiratory diseases, such as asthma. It is also associated with many of the behavioral disorders discussed in Part One, as well as a number of cognitive disorders, including memory problems, low IQ, inattentiveness, and decreased learning ability. It can lead to premature delivery and low birth weight in infants, which have been linked to various problems that can appear later in a child's life.

CHLORINE

Chlorine in large amounts is toxic to all of us, but in small amounts it is useful for killing germs in our drinking water and swimming pools, and as an active ingredient in cleaning products. Both the CDC and the American Society of Pediatrics, however, have reported that even small amounts of chlorine can cause a reaction in sensitive children.

If your child is fine and then jumps into a chlorinated pool, starts sneezing, wheezing, or itching, he may be allergic to chlorine. He may also react with sudden behavioral changes—crying, aggression, hyperactivity, etc. Nevertheless, these reactions don't mean your child should not learn how to swim properly, but the joy of swimming recreationally and the enriching social experiences that can accompany swimming must be weighed against any reaction he has to chlorine. If you are fortunate, your community might have a pool that is purified by some other system. Of course, natural bodies of water are also good options for swimming if you happen to live near one.

Chlorine is normally added to the community water supply for purification purposes. If your child is sensitive to chlorine, he may benefit from the use of a water filter that removes chlorine and other chemicals from the tap water in your house. Additionally, you should avoid the use of chlorinated cleaning products, such as Clorox.

FOOD CONTAMINANTS

There are many toxic contaminants that can find their way into the food supply, including PCBs, lead, dioxins, and pesticides. During their growing and processing phases, certain foods may be contaminated with small amounts of toxic chemicals, such as pesticide residues from treated crops; industrial contaminants, which can form as a result of cooking or heating foods; or chemicals in food packaging, which can leach into the foods. Even the chemicals used to clean the machinery used in processing often are not washed away completely and enter the next batch of food being processed.

A 2021 report by the Subcommittee on Economic and Consumer Policy of the House Committee on Oversight and Reform revealed testing that proved that many commercial baby foods, including organic brands, contained high levels of heavy metals, including arsenic, lead, cadmium, and mercury. These findings are particularly disturbing in light of the fact that even small amounts of heavy metals in the diet can lead to health, behavioral, or learning problems in children.

While contaminants in food are harmful to children and adults, they are especially damaging to young infants and toddlers. When in doubt, make your own baby food from organic produce. It is a time-consuming process, but it is also well worth the effort. In addition, avoid rice-based products for infants and toddlers, as most rice grown in the United States is known to contain high levels of heavy metals. If you are planning on becoming pregnant, it is also important that you remain vigilant about the foods you eat, as food contaminants can seriously impact a fetus as well.

PETROCHEMICALS

Petrochemicals are toxic chemicals derived from petroleum and natural gas. The most obvious petrochemical product is gasoline, but petrochemicals are used to manufacture all sorts of common substances, including plastics, foams, synthetic fibers, synthetic rubbers, paints, dyes, adhesives, resins, and detergents. These substances are then used to make furniture, electronics, clothing, packaging, building materials, pharmaceuticals, personal care products, and countless other products. In short, petrochemicals are everywhere.

Research of residents living near petrochemical factories showed that children born from pregnant women who were exposed to petrochemicals while pregnant had an increased risk of ADHD, as did babies who were exposed to these chemicals in early life.

TOBACCO SMOKE

More than 7,000 chemicals have been identified in tobacco smoke, and at least 250 are known to be harmful. Research suggests that secondhand smoke is a risk factor for almost all the problems discussed in Part One. For example, childhood asthma, obesity, and intelligence are related to maternal smoking. If you smoke, you should avoid smoking in your car or home. Nevertheless, even if you smoke outdoors, smoke particles can still cling to your clothes and be brought indoors as a result.

PESTICIDES AND HERBICIDES

Pesticides and herbicides are chemicals that are used to kill unwanted pests, such as insects, or unwanted plants, such as weeds. This ability to kill living matter can make them harmful to humans—especially to children. Whether you live in a farming community, where pesticides and herbicides are commonly used, or a suburb, where pesticides are often used to treat yards, gardens, golf courses, and parks, these chemicals are hard to avoid. If you live in the country, the air may contain herbicides and pesticides as a result of planes spraying them on the crops. Of course, the food produced by these crops will also be contaminated by these substances. The fact is that pesticides and herbicides may be found in the air we breathe, the food we eat, and the water we drink.

Exposure to pesticides or herbicides can cause birth defects, premature births, and a variety of mental or behavioral problems. While the use of some of these substances has been restricted or banned, these kinds of chemicals tend to linger in the environment, unfortunately, and are even stored in our fat tissue. For example, we are still finding toxic breakdown products of DDT in the environment, despite the fact that this chemical has been outlawed since the 1970s.

PLASTICS

Our homes, schools, parks, garbage dumps, and even oceans are overflowing with plastics. This problem stems from the fact that plastics, which are used to make countless products in the world, don't truly biodegrade. They may be broken down into smaller pieces, or microplastics, by photodegradation (degradation from exposure to sunlight), but even this process can take hundreds and hundreds of years, and ultimately, the molecular structures remain. When interviewed on CNN, one expert researcher on plastics and their toxicity said, "We have enough evidence right now to be concerned about the impact of these chemicals on a child's risk of attention, learning, and behavioral disorders."

The chemicals in plastics find their way into the food supply when they are ingested by the animals we eat, or when they leach out of plastic food packaging. Moreover, the heating of foods in plastic wrap, on plastic dishes, or in plastic containers increases the amount of chemical components leached from these sources of plastic into the foods being heated. Two particular chemical components of plastics—*bisphenol A* (BPA) and *phthalates*—are known to disrupt hormones that play important roles in a developing child.

In addition to hormone disruption, BPA has been associated with hyperactivity, aggression, and learning problems. BPA may be found in personal care products and plastic products—e.g., liners of canned goods, plastic containers, plastic wrap, plastic water bottles, etc. So, when you buy what you think is pure water in plastic bottles, that water may contain BPA. Even breast milk can contain BPA if the mother has been exposed to this chemical.

Research done on volunteers who drank soy milk stored in plastic-lined cans showed that the amount of BPA in their urine rose about 1,600 percent compared with when they drank soy milk stored in glass containers. The lesson here is that you should store as many foods and beverages in glass rather than plastic (although these days that is not an easy task). And although the use of BPA in packaging for infant formula, baby bottles, and sippy cups was banned in the United States in 2013, it remains a component of many other products.

Phthalates are chemicals added to plastics to make them more flexible. They are found in a large number of products we use in our daily lives, including the coating of certain medications, gelling agents, lubricants, adhesives, glue, vinyl flooring, paints, inks, food packaging, and even clothing. These chemicals can be released into the air from the products that contain them in a process known as "off-gassing."

Most people in the United States have low levels of phthalates in their urine. Infants and toddlers are most vulnerable to ingesting phthalates because they tend to suck on plastic items that contain these chemicals. Researchers in several studies have reported that children who were exposed to phthalates prenatally were more likely to be diagnosed with ADHD or conduct disorder. They also reported that the more severe the case of ADHD in a child, the greater the amount of phthalates in that child's urine.

VOLATILE ORGANIC COMPOUNDS

Volatile organic compounds, or VOCs, are found in many products used to build and maintain our homes. VOCs include benzene, ethylene glycol, formaldehyde, methylene chloride, tetrachloroethylene, toluene, xylene, and 1,3-butadiene. These chemicals may be found in products such as petroleum fuels, hydraulic fluids, and paint thinners.

VOCs may be present in the air and often pollute groundwater. When you bring home clothes from the dry cleaner, the smell of your clean clothes contains VOCs. The well-known "new car" smell contains VOCs. If you purchase a new car, keep the windows rolled down as much as possible when you bring it home so these VOCs dissipate into the air. (This is especially important in hot weather, as heat increases the release of VOC fumes, so a car sitting in the sun will release more VOCs.)

Particle-board shelves, new carpeting, and furniture often contain formaldehyde, a VOC, although formaldehyde-free and low-formaldehyde options are becoming more available. When choosing paint for your child's room, opt for a low-VOC or VOC-free brand. Once you've finished painting, have him sleep in a different room until the paint smell has gone. It can take up to fifteen years for products such as carpets or furniture to off-gas their VOCs completely. Therefore, children may be breathing in these chemicals for a long time.

NATURAL ALLERGENS

Allergic reactions to natural substances occur when the immune system overreacts to their presence with symptoms, which typically include sneezing and a runny nose. The reaction could also manifest itself as wheezing, coughing, hives, or a rash. What may surprise you is that natural allergies can affect your child's behavior, learning ability, mood, and attention span, even without causing the well-known respiratory or skin reactions.

Animal Dander

If your child has a pet, he may be sensitive to its dander. Typical pets with dander include dogs, cats, rabbits, and gerbils. Animal dander comes from the animal's saliva, urine, and skin cells. To see if your child is having a reaction to his pet, ask a close friend or relative to keep the animal for a week and see if your child's behavior improves. If he is too attached to his pet, find ways to reduce his exposure, such as keeping it out of his bedroom, making his bedroom a safe haven.

Dust

Dust is an extremely common cause of allergic reactions, and even the best-kept houses have dust. Along with dust come dust mites, which are microscopic pests that live on dead skin cells, of which household dust is partly composed. Dust mites can also cause allergic reactions.

According to experts, children with ADHD frequently react to dust by exhibiting changes in mood or sleeping excessively during the day. In addition, children who react to dust are more susceptible to infections.

To reduce your child's exposure to dust, start with his bedroom. If possible, remove his bedroom rug, as it can harbor both dust and mold. Cover your child's mattress and pillow with hypoallergenic coverings, and wash all bedding regularly in hot water. Buying an air purifier with a HEPA filter for your child's bedroom might be helpful, and having your air ducts cleaned by a professional might also be worthwhile.

Mold

Mold is a type of a fungus that can grow both indoors and outdoors, and can travel through the air in the form of microscopic spores. When a person is exposed to mold, a neurotransmitter known as *histamine* is released by the immune system, causing sneezing, coughing, and itchy skin or eyes—a typical allergy attack. Mold exposure can also affect the central nervous system. Histamine is also associated with other neurotransmitters and genes that play a role in ADHD and other behavioral disorders.

Mold can also affect learning ability. In a Polish study, children were assessed from birth until the age of six. Mold levels in their houses were also assessed. At age six, the children exposed to mold had weaker cognitive abilities than the children whose homes had no evidence of mold.

Signs of possible mold in your home include dampness in the house and a musty smell when you first step into your home or a particular room. Mold may also be identified by presence of black, green, or brown spots on walls or other surfaces. Mold loves dark, warm, wet areas to grow and thrive. You may need to pull up the edge of carpets or look behind cardboard boxes to find mold. Look around areas that have once been wet due to leaks.

If your house has mold problems, you should first make sure you don't have any leaks of any kind, as moisture is required for mold growth. There are many sources online that suggest ways to kill mold with natural methods, such as spraying the mold with a solution of baking soda or vinegar, but you may need to bring in an expert to identify the type of mold and treat it professionally.

Outdoor mold can also be a problem. Typically, when the weather is rainy and damp, mold spores increase in number. Your child should avoid activities that increase exposure, such as gardening, composting, mowing the lawn, or playing with or raking leaves. If he must do any of these activities, wearing a mask may provide some benefit.

Pollen

Pollen refers to the yellow particles in the center of flowers, which are required for the pollination and reproduction of a plant. If there is a seasonal aspect to your child's behavioral problems, he may be affected by pollen. Depending upon where you live, your pollen seasons will vary with the months, although climate change has made pollen season last longer and longer. Generally, tree pollens are present in the spring and summer months, grass pollens in the summer, and weed pollens, such as ragweed, in the summer and fall. You can check online for pollen season information in your area.

In research that studied pollen exposure as a cause of brain dysfunction in children with ADHD and ASD, parents completed questionnaires about their children's behavior for two weeks during winter, and then for two weeks during pollen season. More than half the children with either ASD or ADHD demonstrated a deterioration of their behavioral problems during pollen season. In another study performed by the same scientists, children with ASD or ADHD were challenged by a mix of pollens sprayed into their noses. After receiving the spray, more than half the children showed increased behavioral symptoms. Moreover, these symptoms were not associated with respiratory or other physical reactions of any kind. In other words, the behavioral symptoms that occurred seemingly in response to pollen exposure were not related to typical allergic reactions.

To reduce your child's pollen exposure, keep him inside when pollen levels are high in your area. In general, pollen counts are lowest just after sunrise and highest at midday, remaining elevated throughout the afternoon. To ensure that pollen does not enter your home, keep your windows closed during the day and at night, and use air conditioning if it is too hot inside. Don't use a fan placed in an open window, as doing so will bring pollen in from outside.

TREATING ALLERGENS

Complete avoidance of allergens is the best way to treat typical respiratory, skin, or behavioral reactions, but in daily life this may not be a possibility for your child. Other solutions include using an over-the-counter or prescription antihistamine that does not cause side effects such as sleepiness. Discuss this option with your child's doctor before giving your child an antihistamine. She also may recommend a decongestant. (Medications should ideally be free of dyes.)

If your doctor refers you to a pediatric allergist, the allergist will take a complete medical history and thorough physical exam of your child to look for signs of allergies. She may then test your child to see which allergens might affect him. She may order a blood test known as a *radioallergosorbent test*, or *RAST*, or perform a skin prick or scratch test in her attempt to determine the source of the allergy.

She may recommend he be treated with allergy shots once or twice a week, possibly for months. This regimen can be time consuming and expensive, and many children will be fearful of the needle.

Sublingual immunotherapy, or *SLIT*, is a form of immunotherapy that involves putting a tablet or drops of allergen extracts under the tongue. Many people refer to this process as "allergy drops," and it is an alternative treatment to allergy shots. This form of immunotherapy has been used for years in Europe and has recently attracted increased interest in the United States. Children appear to tolerate it well if they are allergic to grass or dust mites, although children with severe asthma may need special monitoring. If your child has multiple allergies, it may not be appropriate.

The FDA has approved three SLIT tablet products in the United States: Grastek (grass allergy), Oralair (grass allergy), and Ragwitek (ragweed allergy). Non-FDA-approved drops are legal and may be available through your doctor, but they are usually not covered by health insurance.

CONCLUSION

By now you have learned that environmental pollutants such as heavy metals and manmade chemicals can contaminate your child's world and cause him to experience both physical and behavioral symptoms. Your child may even be sensitive to certain chemicals in his environment that don't bother most people. He may also react to the natural allergens to which he is exposed. It may sound like a difficult and confusing task to uncover your child's allergens, but if you take it one step at a time, you will be able to manage it. Your child's behavior and health may dramatically improve thanks to your efforts, making all the work worthwhile.

One way to identify an environmental element to your child's behavior is to observe if his behavior is affected by a change of environment. For example, if you note that your child acts out only at home but is better outside the home, this observation may be a clue. If you suspect an environmental cause, start keeping a log of your child's behavioral changes relative to location. If you are able to determine which toxic element is playing a role in his condition, the key to improvement would then become avoidance of this substance.

12.

Helpful Programs and Devices

This chapter looks at other ways to help your child in addition to all you may currently be doing. First, it discusses summer camps. For the right child, going to summer camp may be just what he and his parents need: a break away from each other and time for him to expand his horizons. Here you will find guidance on how to find the right summer camp for your child. This chapter also discusses helpful video games, neurofeedback, and even vision therapy as methods that may help with your child's attention problems or emotional outbursts.

SUMMER CAMPS

A summer camp experience might offer all types of benefits for your child, including the development of lifelong skills such as knowing how to swim, horseback ride, sail, camp in the woods, etc. He will experience hours of fun activities and play. He will learn about problem solving, which will help him in school and in life. He will learn how to get along with other children and improve his social skills. He will learn how to function as part of a team. He will make friends and look forward to seeing them the next year. After summer camp, he will likely feel more independent and confident.

Children today spend way too much time looking at screens. One advantage of a summer camp is that there are no screen activities, which gives kids a break from TV, video games, and social media. Living without these things will give your child a chance to learn how to avoid turning into a couch potato. He will be free to breathe fresh air, run, skip, jump, climb, and laugh. He will exercise every day, improve his coordination, and build up his physical strength. He may play games or sports that are new to him or learn how to do arts and crafts. He may learn new skills and discover that he excels at some of them. He will no doubt learn camp songs and perhaps even dances. He will also learn the joys of connecting with nature, which may be a new experience for him if he lives in a big city. Nature will allow your child to experience the wonder of the world.

Finding the right camp for your child will take some work on your part. You will need to consider his unique personality, what he likes to do, and where he will feel welcomed. Your choice of camp could be a day camp that meets each day for a week or longer, or it could be an overnight camp that lasts a week, two weeks, or even a whole summer. Of course, affordability and your child's ability to adapt will be major factors in your decision.

You will want to investigate camps in your community or your state. You can do an online search for camps in your area. You can also ask your friends, your child's therapist, or your child's teacher for recommendations. One organization that has a lot of experience with making fun and affordable camps is the YMCA, or the "Y." The YMCA offers a number of fun activities for kids, including day camps and sleepover camps.

There are also specialty camps where children who are computer savvy can increase their computer skills. If your child is interested in music, he might enjoy a music camp. There are also camps for budding artists.

There are also special camps designed for children with particular disorders or special needs, including camps for children with ADHD, ODD, learning disabilities, autism, depression, or conduct disorder. You can search online for these camps using the search terms "registry of camps for special needs children." You will want to verify ahead of time the type of activities that are offered at a camp and the exact ways in which children are taught to behave when they act out, which should never include physical punishment or cruelty of any kind. And be sure that whichever camp you choose does not use sugary treats as rewards. You don't want your child to return home with behavioral problems that are worse than they were before he left. If possible, ask a parent who has sent her child to the camp you are considering for a review of his experience.

Safety Tips

Of course, above all, you will want to make sure your child's experience at camp is a safe one. In order to give yourself some peace of mind regarding your child's stay at a camp, you may wish to check on a few relevant matters before signing him up.

- **Accreditation and Licensing.** Make sure the camp you're considering is accredited and licensed. Accreditation means the camp meets certain standards of quality in terms of its activities and facilities, and in relation to the care and safety of your child. For example, the American Camp Association (ACA) requires over 300 different health and safety tests for accreditation.

- **Background Checks.** Each camp employee should have undergone a background check. Employees should also know how to recognize the signs of sexual or physical abuse and how to report it.

- **Certification.** Do all camp employees have the appropriate certifications? Each should have Red Cross CPR/AED/O2 certifications.

- **Communication.** Make sure there is a means of communication between you and the camp. The camp should be able to reach you when needed, and vice versa.

- **Diet.** Ask about the food served at the camp you are considering. Do meals and treats emphasize fruits and vegetables, avoid too much added sugar, and contain no artificial food dyes? If your child must avoid certain foods, ask if accommodations can be made.

- **Policies on Abuse.** The camp should have clear policies to prevent abuse of any kind. A child should never be left alone with a counselor and there should never be any inappropriate touching of the children. Feel free to ask pointed questions on this subject before signing up your child.

- **References.** Ask for references, which may be available online. Ask other parents whether their child had positive, safe experiences in the past at the camp. (Camps should be willing to refer you to other parents.)

Summer camps can vary greatly in price depending upon their lengths and locations. The American Camp Association (www.acacamps.org) believes that there should be a camp for every child who wants one. It even sponsors camp scholarships indirectly through the Ultra Camp Foundation (https://foundation.ultracamp.com). Please check out both websites.

A summer camp experience may help both you and your child. You will get a break, which will give you time to pursue other interests, relax, and unwind. You will have more time to spend with other family members and friends. For your child, the experience may help him in all the ways previously mentioned while giving him happy memories that will last a lifetime.

VIDEO GAMES

In today's world of widespread technology, you may not be surprised to learn that the treatment of certain behavioral disorders may include interactive video games. While using video games in behavioral treatment may seem counterintuitive in light of their potential connection to addictive behavior (see the inset titled "Video Game Addiction" on page 86), specially designed video games can actually play an important part in your child's improvement.

EndeavorRx

EndeavorRx (www.endeavorrx.com) is a video game designed to help children aged eight to twelve years old with inattentiveness problems associated with ADHD. The U.S. Food and Drug Administration (FDA), which oversees all prescription medications, actually approved this video game as the first "virtual prescription."

The game targets and activates systems in the brain through the presentation of sensory stimuli and motor challenges in order to improve cognitive functioning and focus. It was developed and tested by researchers at Duke University as well as other universities. EndeavorRx has been studied in more than 600 children with ADHD and evaluated in children across five clinical studies. Side effects were mild and included frustration and headache. The game requires a prescription to purchase it.

A child plays the video game for about twenty-five minutes each day, five days a week, for four weeks. According to research, a second four-week regimen leads to increased benefits. EndeavorRx is drug-free and is associated with few side effects.

EndeavorRx can be added to your child's current ADHD treatment. Although only children with ADHD have been studied in connection with this video game, children with other disorders that include problems with attention might also benefit from using it. Ask your child's doctor or therapist what she thinks about it.

Mightier

If your child has trouble controlling his temper, a video game called "Mightier" may help him. Mightier was developed and tested at Boston Children's Hospital and Harvard Medical School. In trials, researchers reported that Mightier helped children to have fewer outbursts, less oppositional behavior, and less aggression.

Using biofeedback, Mightier can teach your child how to calm his reactions to stressors presented by the game. Over time, with continuous practice, he can re-train his brain to respond to stressors in a better way. The game can help him with problem solving and pattern recognition, and will even provide him with a sense of adventure.

Mightier is meant to be used three times a week for fifteen to twenty minutes at a time over ninety days. The child wears a heart monitor on his wrist like a watch and can hear his heartbeat. When he faces challenges in the game, he will hear his heart speed up. He is taught to pause and take a deep breath. The goal is to make his heart rate go down. If he accomplishes this goal, he is rewarded by the game. Over time he will be able to use this new ability at home, in school, and with friends.

Mightier is available in most app stores. You can choose to purchase the game along with an electronic tablet on which to play it, or you can download the game to your own device. It is a great tool for your child to use between therapy sessions, as it allows him to practice the skills he has learned.

Nutrition Games

There are several video games that can help your child to learn more about nutrition while having fun. For example, the Smithsonian has a free game called "Pick Your Plate!" (https://ssec.si.edu/pick-your-plate), which teaches children about the nutritious foods they can choose when building their meals. It also allows children to learn about healthy foods from all over the world.

Another helpful free game comes from the United States Department of Agriculture (USDA) in the form of an activity sheet called "MyPlate Maze" (www.myplate.gov/life-stages/kids). On this activity sheet, a child traces his way through a maze, choosing foods that should go on his plate.

The USDA also offers virtual flashcards in its collection of activity sheets that can help children to learn about fruits and vegetables. It's called "Fruit and Vegetable Flash Cards" (www.myplate.gov/life-stages/kids). Finally, the Diary Council of California has an interactive game called "MyPlate Match Game" (www.healthyeating.org) available in its "Products + Activities" section. This game teaches children about food groups and the amount of physical activity kids should get each day.

NEUROFEEDBACK

What is neurofeedback, and is it right for your child? When a child uses neurofeedback, it is like he is playing a video game, but instead of using his hands to manipulate the controls, he uses only his brain. The brain generates electricity. Neurofeedback uses sensors that record brain waves to monitor and ultimately control alertness. It is noninvasive and painless. This electricity may be recorded by gluing sensors on specific areas of the head, or a neurofeedback therapist may use caps containing sensors that come in different sizes, which are pulled over the head. These sensors send the electricity to an *electroencephalogram*, or *EEG*, machine, which transforms the electricity into patterns of waves.

There are several kinds of brain waves produced by the brain, each with a different height and frequency. Using this information, your child can determine if his concentration is wavering and adjust it accordingly. Ultimately, he will learn to make these adjustments without neurofeedback monitoring.

For example, delta waves are produced during sleep. Theta waves are generated during moments of relaxation. Alpha waves occur during the act of daydreaming. Beta waves are produced during the act of thinking. The *sensorimotor rhythm,* or *SMR,* refers to a brain wave that occurs when someone remains quietly alert without fidgeting. Your child will experience all these waves throughout an entire day and night. In order to pay attention, he will want to produce more of some waves and fewer of others. In a learning situation, he will want to produce more beta waves and fewer alpha waves. Neurofeedback can teach him how to optimize his brain waves for better learning and behavior.

In neurofeedback, a computer is used to convert the brain waves registered on the EEG into pictures on a screen. The picture might be of a fish attempting to swim through a maze. If your child pays attention, he can learn to guide the fish in the correct direction and get a virtual reward for doing so. The picture might be of someone playing basketball. If your child is concentrating and not daydreaming, he will score a basket. If he is not attentive, however, his opponent will score. Now you see how using neurofeedback is similar to playing video games. Neurofeedback can improve attention, concentration, memory, eye-hand coordination, math skills, and problem solving.

You could tell your child that neurofeedback is like going to the gym. In a gym, the goal is to strengthen your muscles, while neurofeedback strengthens brain circuits, helping him to pay attention and learn.

Researchers who study neurofeedback in children with ADHD have reported that thirty to forty sessions of neurofeedback are as effective as medication in reducing inattentiveness and hyperactivity symptoms. They have also reported that children do better academically after treatment. In a study that combined results from fifteen studies, researchers concluded that neurofeedback in children with ADHD can have significantly positive effects on impulsivity and inattentiveness and result in modest improvement of hyperactive behavior.

One of the advantages of neurofeedback is that it does not involve the use of medication, so it has no side effects. Moreover, the beneficial effects of neurofeedback tend to last after the neurofeedback sessions have ended—more often than not for the rest of the user's life.

One disadvantage of neurofeedback is that the cost of this form of therapy is substantial. Treatment can be anywhere from two thousand dollars to five or six thousand dollars for approximately thirty sessions. Each session lasts about forty minutes. There may also be the added cost of an initial evaluation. Your health insurance may cover neurofeedback, so be sure to get in touch with the company and find out.

Ask your child's doctor or therapist what she thinks of neurofeedback and if she has had patients who used this therapy. She may even have a local neurofeedback provider in mind to recommend to you.

As always, before you add neurofeedback to your child's treatment, consider how he may respond to it. Will he be cooperative? After all, the cost of this therapy is rather high and requires repeated sessions, so it may not be appropriate for your child, your wallet, or your schedule. On the other hand, if neurofeedback seems like a possibility, its benefits will likely last a lifetime.

VISION THERAPY

We usually think of a vision problem as an inability to see up close (farsightedness) or at a distance (nearsightedness) that is easily corrected by eyeglasses or contact lenses. There are other vision problems, however, that can affect your child and lead to his having difficulty reading, one of which is *convergence insufficiency*, or *CI*. In CI, a child has trouble with both eyes working together to focus. CI effects one in eight children, or 13 percent of all school-aged children. Those affected are three times more likely to be diagnosed with ADHD than are children without the disorder.

You have probably never heard of CI. It is a very common and treatable vision problem that affects near vision and coordination of the eye muscles. Convergence of the eyes occurs when the image from one eye comes together with the image from the other eye, these images merge, and this merged image is then sent to the brain. Without this ability, it is very difficult to read, work on a computer, or even dial a phone. Most of us merge these images easily, but if your child cannot do so, his ability to read will be severely hindered.

Of course, good reading skills are necessary for success in almost every school subject—math, writing, social studies, science, etc. CI will also interfere with a child's ability to pay attention, so he may act as though he has ADHD. He may also seem clumsy at sports because his hand-eye coordination is poor. If terms such as lazy, spacy, clumsy, or anxious have been used to describe your child, or if he has been diagnosed with ADHD, dyslexia, or even autism, he may have convergence insufficiency.

According to the Mayo Clinic, symptoms of CI may include:

- eyestrain (tired, sore, or uncomfortable eyes)
- frequent headaches
- difficulty reading
- avoidance of reading and trouble completing schoolwork
- double vision
- difficulty concentrating
- squinting, rubbing the eyes, or closing one eye

If your child has any of these problems, he must be frustrated. Can you imagine trying to read and seeing the words float across the page, or seeing two of some words? School might feel impossible to manage. You might wonder why reading is so hard for you and so easy for everyone else.

Thankfully, CI can be treated by an optometrist using eye exercises. An optometrist is an eye doctor who cares for people's eyes after having spent four years earning a doctor of optometry degree, or OD. An optometrists is different from an ophthalmologist, who has a medical degree, or MD, and can do major eye surgery. In general, ophthalmologists do not do eye exercises (vision training), nor does every optometrist. The cost of treatment will vary depending upon the provider. Some vision insurance plans cover vision therapy, so check with your insurance company before you start treatment for your child. Treatment involves eye exercises done in an optometrist's office about once a week.

Feel free to ask your child's optometrist how many treatment sessions are typically needed before CI improves, and how many are typically needed to normalize vision. Finally, ask if there are exercises your child can do at home to quicken his improvement and reduce the number of his office visits.

To find a vision therapist near you, simple do an online search for "vision therapy near me." When you call an optometrist's office, be sure the vision therapy it offers is for convergence insufficiency.

Reading by the Colors

Another technique for helping children who struggle to read is called "reading by the colors." This method involves placing differently colored clear plastic sheets over a page one at a time to see if letters and words appear more readable. Sometimes the most helpful color is added to eyeglass lenses or even contact lenses. This therapy has been shown to help some children who are slow readers, read some words incorrectly, or have poor comprehension of what they have read. This overlay technique is also known as the Irlen method, named after its creator, Helen Irlen.

Colored overlays are commonly used in schools. Some occupational therapists and optometrists use them to help children with reading problems. Some studies have reported high success rates from their use, while others have reported very few benefits. The nice thing about this technique is that it is relatively cheap to try. Simply do an online search for "Irlen colored overlays" and you should have no trouble finding them for purchase. When they arrive, try each color one at a time, laying it over the same printed material. Let your child read this material aloud and see if he reads better with one colored overlay in particular. Not every child will be helped by these colored overlays, but they may be useful to your child.

CONCLUSION

This chapter has presented you with several ways to help your child. Summer camp may be just what you and your child need—a break for you and an opportunity for your child to expand his world, learn valuable lessons, and have fun.

Special "video games" may also be helpful. The Mightier app can decrease his emotional outbursts, while EndeaveorRx may boost his attention. Neurofeedback can also be effective in improving his attention.

Finally, vision therapy using special eye exercises or reading by the colors can help a slow reader to improve his reading skills. Choosing one or more of these options can help your child's behavior and learning problems, and each may be combined with other therapies discussed in this book.

Conclusion

In the Introduction, we lamented the fact that newborn babies don't come with instruction manuals that teach parents how to raise a happy, healthy children who will do well in school and at home. Parents simply struggle as best they can to bring their kids up "right." Some children are easy to parent, while others are much more challenging. You know this fact all too well. If you have noticed behavioral issues in your child that seem beyond reasonable, we hope this book has helped you to understand why he acts the way he does, and how you can assist him to overcome this problematic behavior.

Perhaps the most important thing for you to know right now is this: Behavioral disorders are nothing to be ashamed of. They can occur in any family and are no one's fault. Do not hesitate to seek help because of what you fear other people might think. Instead, start by talking to your family doctor. If specialized care is needed, you may then consult the recommended healthcare professional, who has likely helped hundreds of children just like your own.

When it comes to the diagnosis and treatment of your child, remember that you are his greatest advocate and you know him best. The expertise of the healthcare professionals you see during this process is vitally important, but at the end of the day, the ultimate decisions regarding your child's welfare will be yours. This idea is especially important to consider if your child comes from a background that has suffered cultural or racial disparities, which may hinder the system's ability to make an accurate diagnosis. In other words, don't be shy to question the advice being offered if something doesn't feel right.

So many factors can play a role in behavioral disorders, including genetics, gut health, nutritional deficiencies, sleep patterns, and so on. Thankfully, there are lots of things that can be done to improve your child's condition. Therapy can result in substantial positive changes in a child's behavior. For a young child, therapy is usually preferable to medication, but some children won't see the same benefits from this treatment as others, and medication may be warranted. There are many different medications used to treat behavioral disorders, and your child's doctor will work with you to find the best one for him. Medication can be very helpful and actually allow a child's behavioral therapy to work more effectively.

You can also try to improve your child's condition through the use of complementary interventions that are supported by medical research, which include dietary changes, environmental changes, sleep training, physical activity, and even specially designed video games. Being aware of what works and what doesn't work for your child can give you a sense of control and hope for a better future. Some of these interventions are relatively easy to make, while others are harder to accomplish successfully but still extremely important. Whether an adjustment to your child's routine takes a little effort or a lot, the results can be immensely rewarding to acknowledge as you witness your child change for the better. In fact, you may see all members of your family acting and feeling better.

We wish you well as you use this book to give your child the life every child deserves.

Resources

Once you've found the right healthcare professionals to diagnose and treat your child's behavioral disorder, these qualified experts are sure to give you lots of advice and recommendations on how to improve it. While this expertise is necessary and should be much appreciated, don't forget to remain an active participant in your child's healthcare journey. The following resources can help you in this role.

BEHAVIORAL DISORDERS

ADDitude
www.additudemag.com
ADDitude *is a magazine that is published five times a year. It is available in digital and print versions and contains a wealth of information for parents of children with ADHD. Adults with ADHD will also find it helpful.*

American Academy of Child & Adolescent Psychiatry
www.aacap.org
This website contains material written by experts on the disorders discussed in Part One of this book. On it you can also find information about sleep, obesity, and exercise.

Centers for Disease Control and Prevention (CDC)
www.cdc.gov
This government agency has lots of helpful information about the disorders discussed in Part One of this book.

Child/Mind Institute
https://childmind.org
The Child Mind Institute seeks to improve the lives of children and families struggling with mental health and learning disorders. This organization provides scientific information, educational material for teachers, and guidance for parents of children with specific needs.

Children and Adults with Attention-Deficit/Hyperactivity Disorder (CHADD)

https://chadd.org

CHADD was founded in 1987 to offer parents of children with ADHD emotional support and information. Every year, CHADD holds an international conference for parents, teachers, and other professionals who work with children affected by ADHD.

Cleveland Clinic

https://my.clevelandclinic.org

By using the search engine found on the website of the Cleveland Clinic, you will be able to acquire basic facts on your child's disorder, including its causes, symptoms, diagnosis, treatment, management, prevention, and outlook.

Mayo Clinic

www.mayoclinic.org

The Mayo Clinic has its own search engine that can help you to find more information on children's mental health issues.

Verywell Mind

www.verywellmind.com

This website offers compassionate, up-to-date resources and research on mental health. It includes discussions and information on all the disorders discussed in this book.

WebMD

https://webmd.com

WebMD has its own search engine that you can use to find more information on practically any diagnosis you might like to explore.

NUTRITION

Center for Science in the Public Interest (CSPI)

www.cspinet.org

The Center for Science in the Public Interest is dedicated to the promotion of healthy foods for all Americans. Its website has all kinds of helpful information on healthy living. It also offers a magazine called Nutrition Action, *which contains stories on various health-related issues.*

Fed Up

www.youtube.com/watch?v=ceRFvhlcsiY

If you have a child who is overweight or obese, gather your family and watch Fed Up, *a documentary film on the American diet. Your child will identify with the children interviewed, and you with their parents. The message is clear: Sugar and junk food are responsible for the epidemic of obesity in the United States.*

The Feingold Association of the United States

www.feingold.org

The Feingold Association of the United States is a nonprofit organization dedicated to helping parents track down hidden food sensitivities in their child's diet. The dietary solutions outlined on this website were originally proposed by Dr. Ben Feingold, a California allergist who published his theories in the 1970s.

United States Department of Agriculture (USDA)

The USDA has information on the foods that healthy children should consume, as well as information on serving sizes, recommended sugar amounts, foods with added sugars, healthy snacks, and more.

University of Wisconsin School of Medicine and Public Health

https://fammed.wisc.edu

If you would like to put your child on an elimination diet, you will find this website from the University of Wisconsin Medical School very helpful. It has clear instructions on how to carry out a simple elimination diet and also provides directions for a "few foods" diet.

SUPPLEMENTS

ConsumerLab

www.consumerlab.com

If you are considering a vitamin, mineral, or herbal supplement, this website can be of help to you. ConsumerLab performs independent tests of many different supplements, giving ratings, costs, and reviews.

Efalex Brain Formula Capsules

www.efamol.com

This fish oil supplement contains the omega-3 fatty acids EPA and DHA, as well as the omega-6 fatty acid GLA.

EMpower Plus Advanced

www.truehope.com

This micronutrient supplement contains vitamins, minerals, and amino acids that are essential to proper brain functioning in dosages that have been proven successful in studies. It is also free of dyes and sugar.

Equazen

www.equazen.com

This fish oil supplement comes in capsules that provide the omega-3 fatty acids EPA and DHA, as well as the omega-6 fatty acid GLA.

Smartfish Recharge Omega 3

www.smartfishnutrition.com

This fruit-based liquid supplement contains EPA and DHA, as well as a small amount of vitamin D. It does not contain added sugar, artificial flavors, or artificial colors.

References

The information and recommendations presented in this book are based on numerous scientific studies, academic papers, and books. If the references for all these sources were to be printed here, they would add considerable bulk to the book and make it more expensive. For this reason, we have decided to present this book's complete list of references, categorized by chapter, on the publisher's website. This format has the added advantage of enabling the publisher to make the reader aware of further relevant research as it becomes available. You can find the references under the listing of this book at www.squareonepublishers.com.

About the Authors

Laura J. Stevens, MSci, received her master's degree in nutrition science from Purdue University in West Lafayette, Indiana. Since graduation, she has worked at Purdue as a researcher, investigating the relationship between diet and health disorders. Apart from her work at Purdue, Laura is the author of eight books on diet, behavior, and allergies. Laura lives with her amazing cats, Bentley and Seis, in Lafayette, Indiana.

Richard W. Walker, Jr., MD, MBA, received his medical degree from the Albert Einstein College of Medicine in New York and completed his residency at the University of Michigan. He earned his MBA from the Jack Welch Management Institute. He has served on the faculty of the University of Texas Medical Center, and is the founder and CEO of Walker Health Care Holdings and TVP-Care, Houston-based national healthcare companies. In addition to being a published writer, Dr. Walker is a highly sought-after speaker.

Index

OTHER SQUAREONE TITLES OF INTEREST

Creative Therapy for Children with Autism, ADD, and Asperger's

Using Artistic Creativity to Reach, Teach, and Touch Our Children

Janet Tubbs

It is no easy task to find a teaching technique that can truly change the course of a child with special needs. Thirty years ago, when Janet Tubbs began working with children who had low self-esteem and behavioral problems, she developed a successful program using art, music, and movement. Believing that unconventional children required unconventional therapies, she then took her program one step further—she applied it to children with autism, ADD/ADHD, and Asperger's Syndrome. Her innovative methods and strategies not only worked, but they actually defied the experts. In this new book, Janet Tubbs has put together a powerful teaching tool to help parents, therapists, and teachers work with their children.

The book is divided into two parts. Part One provides an overview of Autism Spectrum Disorders and introduces and explains Janet's novel approach to teaching. Her goal is to balance the child's body, mind, and spirit through proven techniques. Part Two provides a wide variety of exercises, activities, and games that are both fun and effective. Each is designed to reduce hyperactivity, increase and prolong focus, decrease anger, develop fine motor skills, or improve social and verbal skills. All are part of a program created to help these children relate to their environment without fear, anxiety, or discomfort.

A child may appear stubborn and difficult, but that doesn't mean that the child isn't intelligent, curious, or creative. With the right treatment, such a child can be reached, taught, and set on the road to improvement. The lessons provided in this book may be just what you and your child have been waiting for.

A.D.D.

The Natural Approach

Nina Anderson and Howard Peiper, ND

In their new book, *ADD: The Natural Approach*, authors Nina Anderson and Dr. Howard Peiper provide a creative and nutritional solution for treating ADD and ADHD. Divided into two parts, the book first explains how ADD is actually triggered by an imbalance within the body's central nervous system. Part two includes a wide variety of natural treatments for ADD and ADHD, including a simple lesson in proper nutrition. The authors explain how certain supplements, minerals, and herbs can effectively treat a child's ADD without any of the risky side effects associated with drug therapies. Also included is a chapter on natural remedies for those common ailments associated with ADD like fatigue, depression, and more.

$7.95 US • 50 pages • 5.5 x 8.5-inch paperback • ISBN 978-0-7570-0383-7

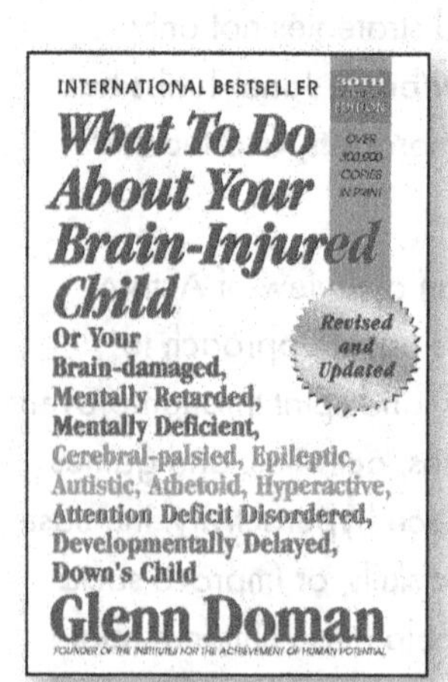

What To Do About Your Brain Injured Child

Glenn Doman

In this updated classic, Glenn Doman—founder of The Institutes for the Achievement of Human Potential and pioneer in the treatment of the brain-injured children—brings real hope to thousands of children who have been sentenced to a life of institutional confinement. He shares the staff's lifesaving techniques and the tools used to measure (and ultimately improve) visual, auditory, tactile, mobile, and manual development. Doman explains the unique methods of treatment that are constantly being improved and expanded, and then describes the program with which parents are able to treat their own children at home in a familiar and loving environment. Included throughout are case histories, drawings, and helpful charts and diagrams.

$18.95 • 336 pages • 6 x 9-inch quality paperback • ISBN 978-0-7570-0186-4
$24.95 • 336 pages • 6 x 9-inch hardback • ISBN 978-0-7570-0187-1

The A.D.D. & A.D.H.D. Diet!

Rachel Bell and Howard Peiper, ND

Authors Rachel Bell and Dr. Howard Peiper take a uniquely nutritional approach to treating ADD and ADHD. The authors first address the root causes of the disorders, from poor nutrition and food allergies to environmental contaminants. They discuss which foods your child can eat and which foods he should avoid. To make changing your child's diet easier, the authors also offer you their very own healthy and delicious recipes. Final chapters examine the importance of detoxifying the body, supplementing diet with vitamins and nutrients, and exercising regularly in order to achieve good health.

$10.95 • 112 pages • 6 x 9-inch quality paperback • ISBN 978-1-884820-29-8

ADHD & the Focused Mind

A Guide to Giving Your ADHD Child Focus, Discipline & Self-Confidence

Sarah Cheyette, MD, Peter Johnson, and Ben Cheyette, MD, PhD

Written by three experts in their fields—a pediatric neurologist, a psychiatrist, and a martial arts instructor—*ADHD & the Focused Mind* provides a complete program for instilling the ability to focus in both children and adults with Attention Deficit Hyperactivity Disorder. The book begins by explaining the common signs of ADHD. It then looks at the brain and discusses what researchers have discovered about Attention Deficit Hyperactivity Disorder. The remaining chapters detail the components of the program, including its principles, its goals, and the practical ways in which these goals can be achieved. The authors recognize that all children are different, so the program has the flexibility to work within a child's comfort level while still attaining the necessary level of discipline. The text concludes with a discussion of medications and ADHD, and what's right for your child.

$17.95 US • 256 pages • 6 x 9-inch paperback • ISBN 978-0-7570-0414-8

Breaking Through

Using Educational Technology for Children with Special Needs

Barbara Albers Hill

The introduction of new and easy-to-use technological devices has created a quiet revolution in the field of special education. When the iPad—a portable interactive Internet device—was introduced, Apple's marketing people correctly predicted the iPad's popularity, but they did not expect how uniquely appealing this device would be to children with autism, attention issues, physical challenges, and a host of other learning disabilities. Today, numerous programs can break through the barriers caused by psychological and physical challenges. Here is a book to help you understand how you can optimize the use of these devices and select the best programs available.

$16.95 US • 160 pages • 6 x 9-inch quality paperback • ISBN 978-0-7570-0395-0

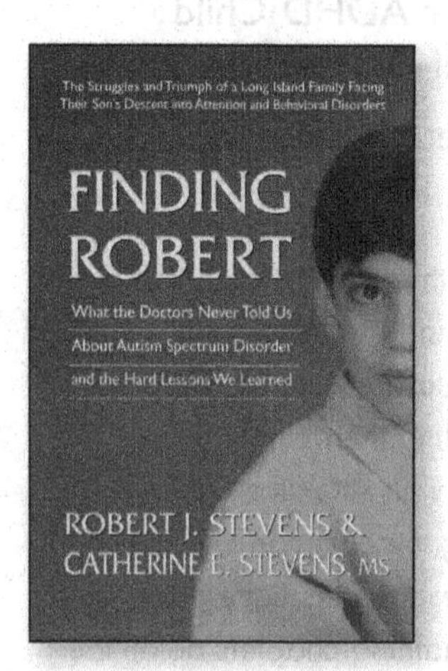

Finding Robert

What the Doctors Never Told Us About Autism Spectrum Disorder

Robert J. Stevens and Catherine E. Stevens, MS

Robert's parents saw they were losing him to his many behavioral disorders. Witnesses to Robert's drastic mood swings and anxious displays, they did not know whether they were seeing their son or the results of the medications he was taking. While initially helpful, his special education class began to create its own world of problems, with Robert taking a step backwards for each step forward. Desperate, the Stevens family turned to holistic therapies. Using nontraditional approaches, Robert was found. By third grade, he was off all medications, attending a mainstream school, making friends, and simply being himself. *Finding Robert* chronicles one family's journey through the world of developmental disorders.

$16.95 US • 256 pages • 6 x 9-inch quality paperback • ISBN 978-0-7570-0402-5

Does Your Baby Have Autism?

Detecting the Earliest Signs of Autism

Osnat Teitelbaum and Philip Teitelbaum, PhD

Although experts agree that early intervention is key to the effective treatment of autism, most believe that the telltale signs of this disorder don't reveal themselves until the age of two or three. Does Your Baby Have Autism? focuses on detecting signs of potential autism or Asperger's syndrome through early motor development. The book first provides general information about the Ladder of Motor Development. Then each chapter examines one motor milestone—righting, sitting, crawling, or walking—making it easy to recognize unusual patterns of movement. Detecting signs of autism early in a child's life, when therapy can do the most good holds the key to a brighter future for children and their families.

$17.95 • 176 pages • 7.5 x 9-inch quality paperback • 2-Color • Fully illustrated • ISBN 978-0-7570-0240-3

Reversing Dyslexia

Improving Learning & Behavior without Drugs

Dr. Phyllis Books

Dyslexia is often accompanied by social, emotional, and even physical issues that can make everyday tasks unmanageable. Unfortunately, mainstream treatment often focuses on compensatory techniques that leave dyslexics feeling hopeless. Reversing Dyslexia offers a new approach that can actually reverse dyslexia in a wide number of cases. The author begins by defining dyslexia and associated conditions, and then explains how an improperly functioning brain can be "rewired" through therapy. Finally, she discusses the steps you can take to enjoy significant improvements not only in reading, but also in general learning ability and psychological well-being.

$16.95 US • 160 pages • 6 x 9-inch quality paperback • ISBN 978-0-7570-0378-3

The Irlen Revolution

A Guide to Changing Your Perception and Your Life

Helen Irlen

After decades of revolutionizing the treatment of dyslexia through the use of colored lenses, Helen Irlen has turned her attention to children and adults who suffer from light sensitivity, headaches, attention deficit disorder, and other visual perception-related conditions and learning disabilities. The book begins with an overview of learning disabilities and a look at standard treatments. The book then examines the Irlen Method and explores the scientific basis of the program. Finally, the author discusses the individual disorders—what they are, and how the Irlen approach may be used to treat them successfully. An extensive resource section provides additional guidance for readers who want to learn more about the program.

$17.95 • 224 pages • 6 x 9-inch quality paperback • ISBN 978-0-7570-0236-6

The Word Gobblers

A Handbook for Parents Working with Children Struggling to Read

Catherine Matthias

Is your child reading below grade level? Does he or she miss words while reading? Read choppily? Does your child avoid reading? Millions of children and adults throughout the world cope with reading, writing, and depth perception problems, such as dyslexia. For one in every six, this problem is the result of a condition called Irlen Syndrome—the inability of the brain to process certain light waves or colors. As a result, visual information is not interpreted correctly. *The Word Gobblers* is a beautifully illustrated handbook for any parent whose child is struggling to read. It provides reading exercises to help determine if he or she may have this condition. Most important, it offers easy-to-implement modifications to help overcome the problem.

$15.95 US • 96 pages • 7.5 x 9.25-inch quality paperback • ISBN 978-0-7570-0502-2